Future Cities Laboratory
Indicia 01

Stephen Cairns
Devisari Tunas (ed.)

ETH Zürich /
Singapore – ETH Centre

Lars Müller Publishers

Future Cities Laboratory

Indicia 01

Indicia 01

A   37

High-Density Mixed-Use Cities

B   91

Responsive Cities

C   157

Archipelago Cities

Foreword

Future Cities Laboratory (FCL) is an interdisciplinary research programme of the Singapore-ETH Centre, organized within the framework of Singapore's Campus for Research Excellence and Technological Enterprise (CREATE).

First launched in 2010, FCL has the ambitious goal of providing the knowledge and ideas needed to make cities more sustainable. The original programme—the brainchild of a group of architects from ETH Zürich—was built around the concept of 'urban metabolism' and focused especially upon the stocks and flows of resources such as energy, water, capital, people and information. Since then, the understanding of cities as complex systems has advanced enormously, and FCL is now at the cutting edge of a rapidly developing field, the 'new urban science', which brings together the traditionally separate fields of science, engineering, information technology and design. However, the purpose of our research is not merely to understand how cities work, but to improve the quality and sustainability of urban life by translating this understanding into practical solutions. To achieve this, FCL researchers work closely with stakeholders in government, industry and society, and have developed many simulation tools to help practitioners visualise the social, environmental or economic consequences of particular planning decisions.

This volume illustrates the richness and diversity of research at FCL, and describes the new methods and types of data that are being used both to understand and improve cities. At a time when our planetary life-support systems are increasingly threatened, many argue that academic institutions should do more to help societies move towards sustainability. These critical voices point out that science has often been late or ineffective in preventing or mitigating emerging risks, so that even well-known environmental problems such as biodiversity loss and climate change remain unsolved. The new approaches pioneered by FCL and its partners offer one important way that this gap between knowledge production and action is being bridged, with the aim of ensuring the sustainability of future cities.

Peter Edwards
Director of the Singapore-ETH Centre

Future Cities Laboratory
Indicia

This book series aims to foreground the process, rather than the polished outcomes, of the research efforts of the Future Cities Laboratory. It reports on preliminary findings and speculative propositions, as well as drawing out the challenges of research when it is directed to complicated, multifaceted phenomena such as cities. In this respect the series is a hybrid publication, combining the forms of the scholarly paper, the laboratory notebook and the annual report.

There are risks in making a book on the process rather than the outcomes of an endeavor. The most obvious being that we commit thoughts and reflections to print prematurely.

Yet there are also benefits, we think, in breaking with a more conventional academic production schedule and committing to print early. The research challenges of future cities are complex and must be tackled from multiple disciplinary perspectives, and attuned to various stakeholders. Provisional reporting and openness to feedback are crucial to robust outcomes. This is nowhere more so than in the initial stage of research reported upon here in the first issue of our planned book series. At this point our research hypotheses are still fluid, research questions are being refined, appropriate literatures are being identified and mastered, and methods are being trialed. But we also anticipate that later research stages will benefit from circulation for the purposes of reporting on process and progress as much as certain findings.

The series subtitle 'Indicia' registers the provisional status of the research reports presented. 'Indicia', from the Latin *indicare*, meaning 'to point out', has a fairly banal association with the alphabetical list of themes and names normally found in the back of a book. As the title to our work in progress series, 'indicia' flags forwards to more formal publications to follow. But it is more suggestive than that for it carries with something particularly useful when thinking about large, complex entities like cities, which are necessarily experienced, planned and managed through myriad component parts. The noise of city traffic, the air quality measure, the stain on the curtain wall of a high-rise tower, the lonely senior citizen, are clues to larger urban processes to be augmented or revised. Indicia, in fact, has multiple meanings which resonate with our wider project of establishing and executing research agendas that can speak to better urban futures:

Disclosure	Information	Pointer
Discovery	Informer	Sign
Evidence	Inscription	Title
Forefinger	Key	
Indicator	Notice	

Our aspiration to report on our research on-the-go is buoyed by two innovative publishing projects: a book series titled *Forerunners*, a 'thought-in-process' series; and a book, *Thought in the Act: Passages in the Ecology of Experience*, by Erin Manning and Brian Massumi (2014). Both book and book series (products of same publishing house: University of Minnesota Press), offer crisp recognition of the value of documenting the processes of thinking as much as outcomes.

This first volume in the series comes at the beginning of the Future Cities Laboratory (FCL) in its second phase (2015–2020). It focusses on the challenges that future cities pose for city makers, be they researchers, policy experts, business people, civil society or city residents. Future editions in the series will focus on methods, tools and data for future cities research.

Stephen Cairns
8 November 2016

Stephen Cairns

Future Cities, Plural?

Multiply, Diversify, Converge

Future cities, plural. To underscore the plurality of cities sounds like common sense. Cities are many and diverse. Singapore is different from Zürich, is different from New York, is different from Los Angeles, is different from Seoul, is different from Dhaka. Cities are, after all, incubators of difference, attractors of unique talents, disruptors of norms, wellsprings of culture, and platforms for individual and collective self-expression.

This common sense would lead us to imagine that future cities will continue to differentiate and diversify. Demographers forecast that an additional 2.5 billion people will be living in cities by 2050 (UN 2014). Some will be living in brand new cities, most will be living in rapidly growing existing cities, while others might find themselves in shrinking cities left behind by changing fortunes. If their forecast is correct, then future cities will require both visionary rethinking and sensitive retrofitting. Cities new and old, we might reasonably assume, will diversify, with their populations realising their varied social, cultural, and economic aspirations within their respective environmental and political contexts. This diversity of future city types is likely to have many names: primate cities, polycentric cities, megacities, edge cities, port cities, frontier cities, arrival cities, sin cities, border cities, cul-de-sac cities, heritage cities, pop-up cities, cyber-cities, garden cities, horizontal cities, vertical cities, sub-urbs, ex-urbs, con-urbs, tourist meccas, motowns, shrinking cities, boom towns and ghost towns.

By emphasising the plurality of future cities there is a risk of missing structural and infrastructural commonalities. While city types multiply and city lives diversify, there is at the same time a notable convergence of technologies, knowledges and institutional arrangements that shape cities. This is because cities are also connected by global networks of relations which create comparative development aspirations, benchmarked standards, and world markets for technical 'urban solutions'.

The fortunes of cities have always been shaped by non-local exchanges involving trade, culture and conflict, and we can see that in the historical importance of riverine, maritime, and terrestrial transportation networks in early city development. Later, processes of imperialism, industrialisation, and modernisation drew vast regions of the earth into complex, and usually unequal, interdependent relationships. These relations were preconditions for globalisation, wherein the ease of world travel and the arrival of the digitised information age integrated old and new networks. Market-based economic principles—monetisation, commodification, consumer-choice, efficiency—are the normative logic of exchange that governs these networks.

Today rapidly developing accounting technologies—from micro sensing devices, such as cameras, gyroscopes, accelerometers, pressure gauges, light meters, biosensors, to satellite-based remote sensing technology, through to new forms of data mining of human behavior—have further empowered information technology. With the assistance of a new generation of cyber-physical platforms for storage and coordination of information, we have entered a new era of 'big' data. It is within this pervasively panoptic, polysensing, neosentient, 'smart' or responsive medium that future cities will take shape.

So, the future city emerges in an age that has been theorised as global, be that the tight interdependence of Emmanuel Wallerstein's 'world system' (1974) or the loose connectivity of Manfred Steger's 'global imaginary' (2008). Governing any locality, including urbanised ones, is no longer simply a municipal or national responsibility. City governance must often comply with laws that were set nationally and globally (Nye and Donahue 2000). The ecological imperatives of our time—most notably global warming and climate change—give further impetus to such global thinking and action. Canonical texts such as *The Limits to Growth* (Meadows et al 1972), *The Quest* for *Gaia* (Lovelock and Epton 1975), *Our Common Future* (1987), and *Our Ecological Footprint* (Wackernagel and Rees, 1996) all stress the planetary resonance of ecological systems. Researchers at the International Geosphere-Biosphere Programme (IGBP) gathered the data and coined the term 'the great acceleration' to underline the anthropogenic character of current and future ecological systems (Steffen et al. 2004). And the various attempts at global climate change agreements emphasise a new understanding of the collective responsibility that humankind has to steward such systems (e.g. Sustainable Development Goals, *New Urban Agenda*; see below). We are now in an era where there is an acceptance that at least part of the work of futures thinking must be at the planetary scale (see Steffen 2004 et al.; Brenner and Schmid 2011; see also *Urbanisation Indicators* this volume). At the same time, much action happens at the scale of the regional or the local, including at the scale of the city and through the medium of urbanised lives and environments.

For all their differences, cities today and in the future will have many things in common. Shahjalal airport (Dhaka) for all its quirks, is structured by precisely the same functional, technological and economic systems as Changi (Singapore) and Kloten airports (Zürich). Likewise, malls like Singapore's Vivo City, Zürich's Einkaufszentrum Glatt and Dhaka's Jamuna Future Park ('South Asia's largest mall') share a common planning template. As *Trip Advisor* reports, one of the world's best Bengali restaurants is in Dhaka, but also has branches in Singapore, Sydney, London and Dubai. While cities are wellsprings of innovation, those innovations nowadays can fast become generic templates of development. While cities incubate difference, those differences are nowadays readily incorporated into flattening global circuits of consumption.

Through Science, by Design,
in Place

Grasping the challenges posed by future cities involves acknowledging this formative tension between the potential for innovation and the logics of convergence. To ignore this tension trivialises the complex dynamics that have shaped cities historically. In other more philosophical words, it would 'undermine' the claims of everyday experience of cities in the name of a deeper, structural reality, and 'overmine' the structural reality by insisting that only the everyday experiential effects of cities count (Harman 2011, 8; 10) (see Tim Morton, this volume, on the ramifications of this line of thinking for megacities).

The Future Cities Laboratory (FCL) necessarily has such tensions at the heart of its work. Taking seriously the tension between difference and convergence has direct consequences for how we frame research questions, develop methods, and seek to positively impact future city policy, plans, designs and visions. In many respects, we are an example of their positive productive force. Take for example our institutional arrangement. The Singapore-ETH Centre's Future Cities Laboratory is a Swiss higher education institution internationalising its research efforts in and through an opportunity hosted by Singapore's National Research Foundation, which itself has sought to enhance the knowledge economy of Singapore by establishing CREATE, the Campus for Research Excellence in Technology and Enterprise, which hosts a range of such internationalised research centres. So, our research effort is in a place, Singapore, but is by no means parochial, being the product of globally circulating personnel, knowledge and technologies, thought about in relation to a wide array of case studies and located applications.

More centrally, the scholarly work that goes on in FCL brings together a unique amalgam of science, engineering, social science and design expertise. Our stated mission, 'sustainable cities: through science, by design, in place' gives expression to this. Our mission acknowledges the complexity of how urban environments are produced. The development of cities proceeds through an amalgam of science, technology and design realised in the messy social contingency of place, which includes citizen efforts to make urban places, as well as all the unevenness of imperfectly realised plans. This generates new challenges and possibilities. Our scientific scholarship rightly aspires to universal truths and applications, although it also knows that in the context of application many localised adjustments will occur. Our social science offers important framing knowledges for our efforts, as well as essential expertise for how science and design best manifest on-the-ground. Our urban design research examines how to tune into local specificity, but operates also in a register of replicable typologies and globally circulating 'solutions'. At FCL scientists, engineers, social scientists and designers alike work in a milieu that seeks to understand and respond to the tension between divergence and convergence.

We have a particular interest in the role of the design project for its capacities to function as a medium for multi-disciplinary work, as a kind of grounded or physical thinking that allows us to negotiate, in an interdisciplinary way, historical circumstances, current parameters and future possibilities. In what follows, I indicate some of the ways in which the issue of divergence and convergence in cities is addressed in different disciplinary lenses, before concluding with some reflections on formats for thinking future cities.

Science and Technology

The recent proliferation of data sources, the sheer quantity (or 'bigness') of data that can be amassed, and the computing power to make sense of them, has triggered a 'new science of cities' (Batty 2013; Solecki, Seto and Marcotullio 2013). Of course, the idea that there is a science of cities is not entirely new, and to make such a claim tends to overlook the necessary relationship between urban development and science. The interlinked processes of mechanisation, industrialisation and urbanisation, first in Europe in the early nineteenth century (Sutcliffe 1981; Hohenberg and Lees 1995), and then America (Boyer 1983) in the twentieth century would not have been possible without science. Science is central to the calculative logic that enabled modern cities to take shape and be managed, dividing complex urban phenomena into self-consistent parts, and allowed them to be measured according to the abstract criteria of space, time, mass, motion, quantity (Mumford 1934, 48; see also Paulinyi 1986; Gideon 1948). Furthermore, the city became the geographical nexus for the institutions, human capital and infrastructure (the universities, laboratories, and hospitals) that housed the production of scientific knowledge (Dierig, Lachmund and Mendelsohn 2003, 5; Taylor, Hoyler and Evans 2010, 40). The development of infrastructural systems such as railways, dams, mechanical mills, sewers, plumbing, lighting and heating was propelled by science. Finally, as rapid urbanisation drove the demographics of cities beyond their physical capacities, it was scientific methods of social survey and mapping, often in conjunction with engineering solutions that addressed negative outcomes such as poverty, ill-health, congestion and pollution.

This is not the first time where there has been a self-conscious call for a 'science of the city'. Previous examples have not always turned out well. One that is of specific relevance to FCL, because of its vision of linking design, technology and science, was offered by Congrès International de l'Architecture Moderne (CIAM). After a 1933 meeting on the theme of the Functional City, Le Corbusier assembled and published the proceedings as the *Athens Charter* (Le Corbusier 1973 [1943]). This document blended science, quasi-science, reforming zeal and utopian thinking. It became an international rallying point for architecture and urban planning, an optimistic vision for future cities, and a practical guide for the reconstruction of cities in Europe and construction of new cities around the world in the postwar period (Mumford 2000, 76). But the optimism captured by the *Athens Charter* was punctured by the failure of many urban development projects inspired by its principles. Those principles, wielded by centralised planning bureaucracies and private sector actors alike, and allied to newly industrialised construction systems, shaped cities with mono-functional land-use zoning, mass highrise housing, and car dominated transport systems. For many cities, this proved to be a destructive combination, wreaking havoc on their physical and social fabrics. These failures tarnished the legacy of the *Athens Charter* in many parts of the world, particularly Europe and North America, and with it, scientific approaches to city development (Turner 1977; Sutcliffe 1981, 202; Boyer 1983; Rowe 1993; Mumford 2000, 271–73).

The 'new science of cities' emerges in the wake of those previous, technocratically diminished legacies. What is novel about the current science turn is that there is not only an abundance of new data but also novel capacities to integrate that data, which encourages research efforts to cross disciplinary boundaries and broach new transdisciplinary possibilities. We appear to be on the brink of novel possibilities with respect to understanding what some commentators have dubbed the 'DNA' of cities, meaning seeing into the hitherto ungraspable structures of urbanisation processes. Cities are now, as Michael Batty puts it, 'yielding up their secrets' (2013, xix). Scholars from disciplines as diverse as ecology (Forman 2014), geography (Seto and Solecki 2016), economics (Thisse 2014), waste studies (Bacinni, 2012), theoretical physics (Bettencourt and West 2010) concur. The hope is to 'unpick [the] physical form [of cities] to reveal the networks that enable them to function' (Batty 2013, 8). Rather than doggedly viewing cities as 'sets of spaces, places, locations', advocates of the new science of cities urge us to regard them as 'sets of *actions*, *interactions*, and *transactions*' (Batty 2013, 9).

The science turn in the study of cities and urbanisation is, in itself, an example of the convergence discussed above—using comparable, quantitative approaches to discern like patterns and logics. As West pointedly observes: 'every city is unique, [...] but focusing on those differences misses the point' (cited in Lehrer 2010). The 'diversity and plurality' of cities are, in Batty's terms, reflections of deeper 'comprehensive structures', and it is these structures that should underpin efforts to analyse, model, plan and even design future cities (2013, 14).

Social Science

In many respects what we recognise today as the science of the social came into being in response to the massive social changes resulting from rapid urbanisation in Europe and North America in the eighteenth to the early twentieth centuries. The novel social and psychic intensities of cities, the unprecedented proximity of poverty and wealth, and the new racial and ethnic settlement geographies, all demanded explanation. There are many notable examples of social scientific responses to urbanisation—from Charles Booth's mapping of poverty and wealth in London, through to the Chicago School's sociologies of the city.

Empirically grounded social scientific efforts to understand urbanism and urban ways of life sit alongside a complex terrain of social theory, not all of which endorse the methodological assumptions of science. One contentious aspect of the social science of cities has been linked to the role of space and place, an issue crystallised in the thinking of Henri Lefebvre in his mediation on the social 'production of space'. Was urban space merely the universal 'container' for the lives and activities of people who 'filled' it? Moreover, had a science-informed city building of the kind promoted by the *Athens Charter*, and realised in mainstream urban planning in the postwar period, misapprehended urban space as 'homogenous', 'pure', 'innocent' and 'neutral'? Social theoretical perspectives such as these resisted the calculated and abstracted conception of space bequeathed by science, and instead foregrounded both the phenomenological, 'concrete life-world' of human experience as well as the relationships of power that govern them (Lefebvre 2009 [1970], 168).

Lefebvre's theorisation of space as social turned upon understanding its three-fold nature: something that is perceived (sensed and made sense of), something that is conceived (shaped by ideas and visions), and lived (enacted and acted in). This reformulation of space necessarily reshapes parameters and possibilities by which the science of (urban) space operates:

> The science of space, therefore, must be assessed at several levels. It can be taken as a science of formal space, that is to say, close to mathematics; a science that employs such concepts as sets, networks, branches, lattices. However the science cannot be situated at this level; it cannot remain formal. Critical analysis defines how and according to what strategy a given space has been produced; finally, there is the study and science of the contents, that is, of the contents which may resist the form or the strategy: namely, the users (Lefebvre 2009 [1970], 171).

Lefebvre reminds us that a narrowly 'formal' science of the city is insufficient, or insufficient in and of itself. City development proceeds by way of political and lived realities, with which such science must interact. Urban science is inevitably placed, which generates particular responsibilities with respect to understanding its 'localization [...] on the terrain' (Lefebvre 2009 [1970], 171).

The latter part of the twentieth century saw such theoretical concepts reshape the processes and practices of urban planning and design. The belief in universally applicable, science-linked, technocratic solutions gave way to grassroots approaches to city building, which foregrounded participatory approaches. In this context, social science methods were repurposed as techniques that could serve to thicken the relationship between the institutions of city building and the communities served, creating better understandings of preferences, needs and levels of satisfaction (Healey 1997). As planning theorist Patsy Healey notes, the social sciences offer 'more subtle and interactive ways of grasping the relations between structuring forces and human agency' (2003, 105). Furthermore, any new 'formal' science of the city proceeds in a planning context that increasingly deems some variant of citizen participation and consultation, mediated by social science methods, as a desirable norm.

Design
Architectural and urban design approaches to the city have also been articulated through the tension between divergence and convergence: should design in cities embrace generic and replicable styles, or is the responsibility of the designer one of expressing difference or extracting and giving form to some authentic local identity? This tension between a generic aesthetics of urban built form and what might be thought of as a more authentic architecture of place has been a long and contentious issue among urban designers. Architects have even gone so far as to argue that generic urban forms are the true, authentic architecture of cities. For example, architects Robert Venturi and Denise Scott-Brown believed that the 'authentic' urbanism of twentieth century America belonged not to the city square or street of the traditional downtown, but the car-dominated suburbs. 'Americans feel uncomfortable sitting in a square', Venturi famously quipped, 'they should be working at the office or home with the family looking at television' (1966, 131). They called for a new aesthetics of the generic, in which everyday things—cars, television, washing machines, advertising—were celebrated.

As architectural critics William Mitchell (1995) and Martin Pawley (1996) have noted, the idea of architectural design as place-oriented continues to be challenged by convergent technologies such as digital information networks, which herald, what they describe as a 'city of bits' composed of 'terminal architecture'. Rem Koolhaas in a similar vein argued that we are in the era of the 'generic city', which is made out of 'what is left after large sections of urban life cross over to cyberspace' (1995, 1250). From the perspective of these architects, the traditional city is but a residue, and the dominant architectural logic of cities comprises genericised and flattened aesthetics that is evident not only in hotels, airports and offices, but also even in our homes. The generic city involves a process of 'convergence' that 'is possible only at the price of shedding identity' (1995, 1248), Koolhaas concludes.

Other threads in urban design practice and criticism regarded such celebrations of the effects of convergence to be an undue capitulation to the homogenising tendencies of contemporary urbanism. In the US, for example, architectural critic Kenneth Frampton regarded Venturi and Scott-Brown's position as 'manipulative', serving only to emphasise 'the impotence of an urbanized populace which has paradoxically lost the object of its urbanization' (Frampton 1983, 25). Instead, Frampton garnered the generic advances offered in building technology by science to an architectural practice dedicated to creating new 'bounded place-form' (1983, 24). In Europe, critics and architects (such as Aldo Rossi, Vittorio Gregotti and Manfredo Tafuri) began to analyse urban morphologies to reveal obdurate traditional logics, underscoring their relative permanence and resilience to the generic forms of globalisation. Such persistent patterns of urbanism, they argued, remained in place despite the fluctuations of use and even the vagaries of building styles. They pointed to the ways in which a locally distinct urbanism could remain locked over time into the accreted imprint of a city on the ground.

This rich intellectual tradition has more recently given rise to approaches that emphasise the interpenetration and coexistence of differentiating and converging dimensions of the city. Urban scholars, such as Grahame Shane (2005), found value in the work of Michel Foucault, and his idea of 'heterotopology' of space as a means of understanding how certain kinds of space—hospitals, prisons, asylums—resisted incorporation into the generic fabric of the city and functioned as 'counter-sites', or 'heterotopias', in the city (Foucault 1984, 22). For Shane, this reinforced his view of the city as a set of urban figures—districts, units, quarters—which could be combined and recombined around scaffolds or armatures.

Architecture and urban design is then increasingly an art of curating difference within a generic condition. This is evident in the idea of the 'open city' (Sigler, Rieneits and Christiaanse 2009). Here the physical fabric of the city—block sizes, pavement widths, and street network configuration—is designed to support social interaction. Building on an intellectual thread linking Christopher Alexander, Leslie Martin, Jane Jacobs and Albert Pope, Kees Christiaanse describes the open city as an 'operating system' supporting 'communication, exchange, and mobility among people, ideas, and goods' (2009, 34). Unlike the *Athens Charter*, the open city is not a rigid doctrine for making cities, but a set of 'active intervention strategies' that resist 'large-scale monofunctionality' and 'uniformly populated enclaves' (Christiaanse 2009, 35).

At a different scale, the city-focused research in architecture and urban design of ETH Studio Basel forthrightly resists the idea of the generic city in its publication, *The Inevitable Specificity of Cities* (ETH Studio Basel 2015). As Jacques Herzog notes in his introduction to the book, the implementation of ideal structures, be they utopian city plans or global branding schemes, stimulate the emergence of differences in everyday life. He concludes that registering these differences takes a special kind of attentiveness and way of seeing. Sociologist Christian Schmid, writing in the final chapter of the book, reflects explicitly on the relationship between difference and convergence. He agrees that cities are inevitably specific, but does not give up on the idea that there are generic forms and structures that replicate from city to city and tie one city to another. Instead he reminds us that such replicating structures are so because they are locality specific. To call structure 'specific' may sound contradictory, but it reminds us that networks, systems and structures are not merely abstract topological configurations, nor solely large scale engineered infrastructures. They can be specific and small, depending on how they are connected to situations, circumstances and uses. As Schmid concludes, urban territories result from the 'interplay of specific structures' (2015, 305).

Future Cities Consensus?

Interestingly, while the challenges posed by future cities require researchers with different disciplinary perspectives, there appears to be an emerging consensus in contemporary urban development agendas, as expressed in a host of recent reports. The convergence is well articulated in three important frameworks recently facilitated by the United Nations across 2015 and 2016, these being the:

1   Sustainable Development Goals (SDGs)
2   Paris Agreement (United Nations Convention on Climate Change)
3   *New Urban Agenda* (Habitat III)

Each of these frameworks set planning and funding priorities for government agencies (at all scales), multilateral development banks, civil society groups and industry. Although separate initiatives, the frameworks cross-reference each other and use

mutually recognisable vocabularies to articulate complementary and overlapping agendas that draw on shared forms of evidence relating to demographic, economic and environmental change. For example, all draw on influential state of the world reports such as *Urbanization and Development: Emerging Futures* (UN Habitat 2016) from the UN's World Cities Report series, and *Human Settlements, Infrastructure, and Spatial Planning* (Seto et al. 2014) from the Intergovernmental Panel on Climate Change (IPCC). Significantly, all three frameworks foreground urbanisation as the defining development logic of our time, and each foresees new levels of responsibility for city institutions and policy makers.

The SDGs, published under the title *Transforming Our World: The 2030 Agenda for Sustainable Development*, consist of 17 goals and 169 targets, and are designed to refocus and expand upon the (eight) Millennium Development Goals (MDGs), which guided macro-policy from 2000 to 2015. The SDGs are conceived as a 'universal agenda' for sustainable development, which is conceived as 'integrated' with and 'indivisible' from economic development, social inclusion and environmental sustainability. The challenges facing future cities are explicitly addressed in Goal 11, but urban processes are implicated throughout the whole document—such as Goal 6 on access to clean water and sanitation, Goal 7 on energy, Goal 9 on infrastructure, and Goal 15 on terrestrial ecosystems. In the explicitly urban focused Goal 11 the aim is to 'make cities and human settlements inclusive, safe, resilient and sustainable'. There are 10 targets listed under this goal:

- adequate housing
- sustainable transport
- participatory planning processes
- safeguarding cultural and natural heritage
- disaster preparedness
- air quality and waste management
- public space and universal access
- strengthening urban-rural links
- climate change adaptation
- financial and technical assistance for developing countries.

The Paris Climate Agreement, negotiated and announced at the United Nations Framework Convention on Climate Change (UNFCCC) at the 21st Conference of the Parties (COP21), also aims to be a 'universal', legally binding climate agreement for the 195 countries that adopted it. The focus of the agreement is to restrict global warming to below 2°C, and will come into force in 2020. Signatory parties agreed to a set of six key elements which include reducing emissions, tracking progress towards set emission reduction goals, supporting developing countries in adapting to climate change, focusing on the role of cities and regions in mitigating climate change, and mobilising financial support for climate action. Each element is supported by a much more detailed action agenda. The one on the role of cities is set out in the Chapter 12 of the IPCC report (Seto et al. 2014). Here concrete guidance is offered on:

- population density
- land-use mix
- connectivity
- accessibility.

Given the resonance with the past and current work of FCL it is useful to outline this guidance in more detail. With respect to density, the IPCC report argues that high-density, medium-rise built forms perform better than high-rise or single storey freestanding ones for GHG emissions (Seto et al. 2014, 955). With respect to land-use mix, the report promotes a diverse land-use mix which reduces travel distances and supports active mobility such as walking and cycling, which in turn helps reduce motorised mobility and so GHG emissions. In contrast, the report speaks against monofunctional zones, which promote private vehicle travel over longer distances. Mixed-use zones also have social and economic sustainability benefits, supporting a mixture of work, leisure and residential activities, creating vitality and vibrancy (Seto et al. 2014, 955–56). With respect to connectivity, the IPCC report emphasises the importance of the design of streets and how they are configured into a finely-meshed network. Finally, with respect to accessibility, the report defines this in terms of 'access to jobs, housing, services, shopping and to other people and places in cities'. Accessibility as an urban attribute combines proximity and travel time. Access to jobs, the report notes, is the best way of reducing GHG emissions from motorised transport because it lowers commuting distances and times. The combination of these factors make for a compelling alternative urban future.

The most directly relevant of these recent frameworks is the *New Urban Agenda*. It was adopted at the United Nations Conference on Housing and Sustainable Urban Development (Habitat III) in Quito, Ecuador in October 2016. One of its aims is to contribute to 'the implementation and localization of the 2030 Agenda for Sustainable Development in an integrated manner, and to the achievement of the Sustainable Development Goals (SDGs) and targets, including SDG 11 of making cities and human settlements inclusive, safe, resilient, and sustainable'. The *New Urban Agenda* embraces the universalism of the SGDs, affirming that in the variety of city and settlement types, 'the *New Urban Agenda* is universal in scope'.

The development assumptions underlying these three United Nations' frameworks have generally been welcomed, but they have not gone without some dissenting voices. Critics have pointed, for example, to the contradiction of SDGs relying on economic growth mechanisms and the private sector to secure environmental goals (Scheyvens, Banks and Hughes 2016). Related is the critique of the implicit assumption that economic growth will reduce poverty (Hickel 2015) or tackle specific challenges like food security (Battersby 2016). Others point out the difficulties in measuring goal attainment and compliance and so limiting the capacity to assess progress (Sachs 2015; Hák, Janoušková and Moldan 2016). While others argue that the SDGs are 'sprawling and misconceived' and 'unfeasibly expensive' (Economist 2015). There is certainly a bold ambition in these most recent frameworks, as indicated by Juan Clos' characterisation of Habitat III's *New Urban Agenda* as a current day 'Charter of Athens'. I have already reflected upon the misguided aspects of that earlier moment of urban visioning by the CIAM group, a failure Clos acknowledges. Nonetheless he also admires and subscribes to its universal aspirations, which he says were as 'transformative' as they were 'disruptive' (cited in Scruggs 2016).

Ways of Working

There is then an emerging consensus on future city development and governance which is remarkably consistent. Each of the frameworks detailed in the previous section places particular emphasis on the role of urban planning and design in

Future Cities, Plural?

addressing the challenges future cities face as entities in themselves and as generators of externalities impacting on the planet. All three frameworks for action underline the need to monitor and measure 'means of implementation' (SDGs). They also emphasise filling the 'policy value chain' by linking cutting edge research with policy formulation and action on the ground.

The research that is underway at FCL is necessarily in conversation with these influential frameworks and the agendas for research, policy and action they set. Some of the research we do is directly in line with articulated in the frameworks. Some of it forges new agendas which relate, for example, to the integrative role of urban ecosystems, the planetary extent of urbanisation, the metabolism of cities, and the importance of understanding urban-rural systems. We order the research efforts of FCL under three main headings:

1   *High-Density, Mixed-Use Cities* aims to develop new integrated planning paradigms, research methodologies and implementation processes to support higher population densities, higher standards of environmental sustainability, and enhanced liveability

2   *Responsive Cities* harnesses the power of information technology to support an integrated, transdisciplinary planning approach that engages the large scale and complexity of future city systems

3   *Archipelago Cities* proposes viable pathways to sustainable urbanisation in developing regions, to ameliorate the threat of uncontrolled urbanisation, and deliver resilient forms of development.

In conducting our research into these topical areas, we draw on the differing epistemic and methodological traditions discussed in the opening sections of this essay. Each offers conceptual insights, analytical tools, and attitudes relevant to future cities. Aligning them to the kinds of challenges outlined by the UN frameworks requires new ways of working. A unit such as FCL, must dare to fashion novel alliances between a multi-disciplinary group of scholars, new technologies, and urban and engineer designers. We must offer not only cutting edge findings, but credible transformational projects that will inspire city builders of the future.

As we have seen, such a challenge must draw on the insights that the burgeoning science of cities promises. These afford a new kind of generalisable, macro-view—often expressed as revelatory 'laws' (Bettencourt and West 2010), 'hidden universality' (Schlaepfer, Szell, Ratti and West 2016), 'nature' (Townsend 2015)—of cities and urban systems. They could well offer urban planning the 'firm scientific footing' that the precursor science of modernism promised but did not deliver (Townsend 2015, 201). The science of cities is already changing the way traffic is planned, pollution monitored, land-uses distributed, and security realised. But the most powerful case for a new scientific approach to cities relates to sustainability debates. As cities are the primary drivers of global warming—generating the majority of greenhouse gases—better mechanisms for measuring their effects as well as their compliance to mitigation regulations 'help urban areas become the meaningful catalysts for sustainability solutions' (Solecki, Seto and Marcotullio 2013).

Approaching future cities from such a data-fuelled perspective raises the question of accessibility and quality of data. The pervasiveness of information technology and the ability to generate extensive and harmonised data sets are important preconditions for big-data science. If either the quantity or quality of data is compromised, then the capacity for scientific insight is diminished. For example, even in data-rich regions, data is not always available for scientific research purposes. Perhaps data has been generated commercially and has commercial value, or perhaps access creates security risks, or compromises privacy norms. And, of course, there are data-poor regions and areas of society, which are the result of the lack of capacity for data collection or the absence of resilient systems of quality assurance. There are ingenious ways around such problems, ranging from analysing multi-spectral satellite imagery, to crowdsourcing social media data, to agent-based modelling. Yet, it remains true that those parts of the world where the current patterns of urbanisation are most intense, Asia and Africa, are also where data may be absent, quality uncertain or tightly guarded. Special vision and leadership will be required to bring the promise of the new urban science to the regions where it is needed the most.

A similar point might be made about the complex array of institutions and agencies involved in making future cities. Accountable and integrated systems of governance are usually necessary to develop, implement and manage credible urban plans.

But as the bitter experience of *Athens Charter* legacy has shown, and as social science and urban planning practice insists, this is not enough. The many hands and many minds of individuals, community groups, companies, government agencies, inter-governmental agencies make cities thrive. This means understanding how data is gathered, curated and wielded in the name of sustainable, resilient and liveable cities of the future.

Forging the relationships between scientists, social scientists, engineers, designers, the many hands and minds of city makers, the technologies and places necessary for viable future cities, involves paying close attention to the medium in which that work might take place (see Hirsch Hadorn et al. 2008; Lawrence and Després 2004). Here design is valuable as a discipline in its own right, combining analytical techniques, imaginative strategies and transdisciplinary knowledge to generate new ideas and bring them to fruition. Design skills bring, often conflicting, technical, economic, social and cultural demands (such as environmental sustainability, profit, comfort, convenience, identity, security, satisfaction and desire) into innovative relationships. In this respect, recent work on improving the evidentiary base of design can only be welcomed. But design can also serve as a medium for futures thinking. It does this by inducing hybrid, heuristic and non-linear forms of thinking, that often short circuit more scientific formats for knowledge production. Rather than offering 'solutions' to predefined 'problems', design can help us rethink the problem. Design, in this particular sense, can set the stage for a different kind of inclusive thinking that allows possible rapports, empathies, and alliances between material, social and aesthetic worlds to come into view. In doing so it broaches new relationships between what we know and what might be.

Finally, the challenges of future cities must be sensitive to where we are—in Singapore, a city located in one of the most rapidly urbanising regions in the world. Urbanisation today has its geographical focus in Asia and Africa and will substantially shape the fortunes of these regions in the coming decades (see *Urban Indicators*, this volume). Of the 6.5 billion people, or two-thirds of the total human population predicted to be living in cities by 2050, some 52 per cent will be in Asian cities and some 21 per cent in African cities. In contrast, only modest population growth is predicted in the Americas and shrinking cities are predicted for Europe. The manner by which these Asian and African future cities take shape will have significant consequences for sustainability at a planetary scale. If they were to develop in the same resource-intensive manner as western cities did during the twentieth century, humankind would exceed the biophysical capacity of the planet several times over.

While the event of urban growth has now shifted to Asia and Africa, it is the historical experience of urbanisation in Europe and the Americas that underpins most of what is called 'urban theory' today. Will our existing bodies of theory, policy precedents and practices of city building be sufficient for challenges of an 'urban age' that is located primarily in Asia and Africa? Will they be adequate to an urbanisation process that, as Brenner and Schmid (2011) argue, is already planetary in reach? If a tension between divergence and convergence shaped the development of cities historically, will this tension intensify for future cities, and how should it be addressed? Given the rich disciplinary mix within the research community at FCL, how should it be oriented towards action in those localities?

We ourselves are learning how to speak across epistemological and methodological divides, working to negotiate the finely drawn distinctions between multi-, inter- and trans-disciplinary work (see Balsiger 2004). As we have seen, research of this kind will likely involve hybrid knowledge formations, scientific and non-linear modes of working, theoretical and context-specific work, with an orientation towards action, frequently with a real-world character.

Organisation of the Volume

This first volume of our planned *Indicia* series follows the structure of the FCL research programme, with three primary sections on: high-density, mixed-use cities; responsive cities; and archipelago cities, respectively. Each of these sections contains four chapters, authored by members of the respective research teams. A total of 12 research groups are represented, spanning architecture, urban design and planning, engineering, ecology, computer science, social sciences, arts and humanities.

In addition to these 12 contributions on research challenges, we have included a number of other indicia from our research partners and fellow travellers. These include the work of two photographers, Caleb Ming and Carlos Cazalis. Caleb is a

Future Cities, Plural?

Singaporean whose work focusses on various forms of public space in cities throughout Asia. We showcase some of his recent work from Tokyo, Hong Kong and Singapore as these cities begin to address emerging demographic, economic, technological challenges associated with what Scott calls 'cities and regions of advanced cognitive-cultural capitalism' (2014). By contrast, Cazalis, a well-travelled Mexican born documentary photographer, offers insights on the city of Dhaka. As one of the world's fastest growing cities, Dhaka simultaneously confounds the norms of what constitutes a city.

We also include the record of two interviews conducted by FCL researchers, Aurel von Richthofen and Naomi Hanakata. The first, with Richard Hassell, Founding Director of Singapore-based architectural firm, WOHA, looks at future city research with a focus on tropical urban design principles. The second, with Werner Sobek, Founding Director of the Stuttgart University Institute for Lightweight Structures and Conceptual Design, on engineering innovation in future cities research.

FCL researchers work closely with the team at our Collaborative Interactive Visualisation and Analysis Laboratory (CIVAL). The CIVAL team supports FCL research through the development of cutting-edge visualisation and interaction techniques. Their contribution in this volume, by Simon Schubiger, Stefan Mueller Arisona, Chen Zhong, Zeng Wei and Remo Burkhard, addresses advances in digital technologies for urban design.

Finally, we are delighted to feature a chapter by philosopher Timothy Morton, titled 'Where are all the megacities'. As we have seen, the FCL research community is committed to developing the remarkable consensus that has emerged around documents like the '2030 Agenda for Sustainable Development' (SDGs). And the chapters that follow set out our progress towards addressing many of the goals and targets of that agenda. However, as good academics, scientists, designers and researchers, we have a duty to pause and reflect on the presuppositions and foundations of such a consensus and reshape it where necessary. Timothy Morton's chapter in this volume is such an occasion.

Bibliography

Balsiger, Philip (2004). 'Supradisciplinary research: History, objectives and rationale', Futures 36 (4): 407–21.

Battersby, Jane (2016). 'MDGs to SDGs—new goals, same gaps: The continued absence of urban food security in the post-2015 global development agenda', African Geographical Review 18 August: 1–15.

Batty, Michael (2013). The New Science of Cities. Cambridge, Massachusetts: MIT Press.

Bettencourt, Luis and Geoffrey West (2010). 'A unified theory of urban living', Nature 467 912–13.

Boyer, Christine (1983). Dreaming the Rational City: The Myth of American City Planning. Cambridge, Massachusetts: MIT Press.

Brenner, Neil and Christian Schmid (2011). 'Planetary urbanization', in Urban Constellations: An Overview of Contemporary Urban Discourse, ed. Mathew Gandy, 10–13. Berlin: Jovis Verlag.

Christiaanse, Kees (2009). 'The open city and its enemies', in Open City: Designing coexistence, ed. Jennifer Sigler, Tim Rieniets and Kees Christaanse, 25–36. Amsterdam: SUN Press.

Dierig, Sven, Jens Lachmund and Andrew Mendelsohn (2003). 'Introduction: Toward and urban history of science', Science and the City, Osiris 18: 1–19.

Economist Group (2015). 'The 169 commandments', Economist 28 March 2015.

Forman, Richard T T (2014). Urban Ecology: Science of Cities. Cambridge: Cambridge University Press.

Foucault, Michel (1986). 'Of other spaces: Utopias and heterotopias', Diacritics 16 (1): 22–7.

Frampton, Kenneth (1985). 'Towards a critical regionalism: Six points for an architecture of resistance', in The Anti-Aesthetic: Essays in Postmodern Culture, ed. Hal Foster, 16–30. Seattle: Bay Press.

Gideon, Siegfried (1948). Mechanization Takes Command: A Contribution to Anonymous History. New York: Oxford University Press.

Hák, Tomáš, Svatava Janoušková and Bedřich Moldan (2016). 'Sustainable Development Goals: A need for relevant indicators', Ecological Indicators 60: 565–73.

Healey, Patsy (1997). Collaborative Planning: Shaping Places in Fragmented societies. Vancouver: UBC Press.

Healey, Patsy (2003). 'Collaborative planning in perspective', Planning Theory 2 (2): 101–29.

Herzog, Jacques and Pierre de Meuron (2015). 'How do cities differ'? The Inevitable Specificity of Cities, ed. ETH Studio Basel, 15–19. Zürich: Lars Müller Publishers.

Hickel, Jason (2015). 'The problem with saving the world', Jacobin, 8 August. Available from <https://www.jacobinmag.com/2015/08/global-poverty-climate-change-sdgs/> Accessed on 2 November 2016.

Hirsch Hadorn, Gertrude, Holger Hoffmann-Riem, Susette Biber-Klemm, Walter Grossenbacher-Mansuy, Dominique Joye, Christian Pohl, Urs Wiesmann, Elisabeth Zemp (eds) (2008). Handbook of Transdisciplinary Research. Dordrecht: Springer.

Hohenberg, Paul M and Lynn Hollen Lees (1995). The Making of Urban Europe, 1000–1994. Cambridge: Harvard University Press.

Keil, Roger and Sara Macdonald (2015). 'Rethinking urban political ecology from the outside in: Greenbelts and boundaries in the post-suburban city', *Local Environment: The International Journal of Justice and Sustainability*, 21 (12): 1516–33.

Lawrence, Roderick and Carol Després (2004). 'Introduction: Futures of transdisciplinarity', *Futures* 36 (4): 397–405.

Le Corbusier (1973). *The Athens Charter*. New York: Grossman Publishers.

Lefebvre, Henri (2009 [1970]). 'Reflections on the politics of space', in *State, Space, World: Selected Writings*, Henri Lefebvre, ed. Neil Brenner and Stuart Elden, 167–84. Minneapolis: University of Minnesota Press.

Lehrer, Jonah (2010). 'A physicist solves the city', *New York Times Magazine*. 17 December. Available from <http://www.nytimes.com/2010/12/19/magazine/19Urban_West-t.html> Accessed on 2 July 2013.

Lovelock, James and Sidney Epton (1975). 'The quest for Gaia', *New Scientist*. 65 (935): 304–06.

Meadows, Donella, Randers, Jorgen, Meadows Dennis and Behrens William (1972). *The Limits to Growth; A Report for the Club of Rome's Project on the Predicament of Mankind*. New York: Universe Books.

Mumford, Eric (2000). *The CIAM Discourse on Urbanism, 1928–1960*. Cambridge, Massachusetts: MIT Press.

Mumford, Lewis (1934). *Technics and Civilization*. Chicago: Chicago University Press.

Nye, Joseph S, and John D Donahue (eds) (2000). *Governance in a Globalizing World*. Washington DC: Brookings Institution Press.

OMA, Rem Koolhaas and Bruce Mau (1995). 'Generic city', *S, M, L, XL* ed. Jennifer Sigler, 1238–64. Rotterdam: 010 Press.

Paulinyi, Akos (1986). 'Revolution and technology', in *Revolution in History*, ed. Roy Porter and Mikulás Teich, 261–89. Cambridge: Cambridge University Press.

Rieniets, Tim, Jennifer Sigler and Kees Christiaanse (eds) (2009). *Open City: Designing Coexistence*. Amsterdam: SUN Press.

Rowe, Peter G (1993). *Modernity and Housing*. Cambridge, Massachusetts: MIT Press.

Sachs, Jeffrey D (2015). 'Goal-based development and the SDGs: Implications for development finance' *Oxford Review of Economic Policy* 31 (3–4): 268–78.

Scott, Allen J (2014). 'Beyond the creative city: Cognitive-cultural capitalism and the new urbanism, *Regional Studies* 48 (4): 565–78.

Scheyvens, Glen Banks and Emma Hughes (2016). 'The private sector and the SDGs: The need to move beyond 'business as usual', *Sustainable Development*

Schlaepfer, Markus, Markus Szell, Carlo Ratti and Geoffrey West (2016). 'The hidden universality of movement in cities', *Conference on Complex Systems (CCS)*, Amsterdam, 19–22 September.

Schmid, Christian (2015). 'Specificity and urbanisation: A theoretical outlook', in *The Inevitable Specificity of Cities*, ed. ETH Studio Basel, 287–305. Zürich: Lars Müller Publishers. Scruggs, Gregory (2016). 'A Clos-up view on urbanization', *Cityscope*, October 10. Available from <http://citiscope.org/story/2016/clos-view-urbanization> Accessed on 12 October 2016.

Seto K C, S Dhakal, A Bigio, H Blanco, G C Delgado, D Dewar, L Huang, A Inaba, A Kansal, S Lwasa, J E McMahon, D B Müller, J Murakami, H Nagendra, and A Ramaswami (2014). 'Human settlements, infrastructure and spatial planning', in *Climate Change 2014: Mitigation of Climate Change. Contribution of Working Group III to the Fifth Assessment Report of the Intergovernmental Panel on Climate Change*, ed. Edenhofer, O, R Pichs-Madruga, Y Sokona, E Farahani, S Kadner, K Seyboth, A Adler, I Baum, S Brunner, P Eickemeier, B Kriemann, J Savolainen, S Schlömer, C von Stechow, T Zwickel and J C Minx. Cambridge and New York: Cambridge University Press.

Seto, Karen and William D Solecki (2016). 'The road ahead for urbanization and sustainability research', in *The Routledge Handbook of Urbanization and Global Environmental change*, ed. Karen C Seto, William D Solecki, Corrie A Griffith, 561–75. London: Routledge.

Shane, Grahame (2005). *Recombinant Urbanism: Conceptual Modeling in Architecture, Urban Design and City Theory*. London: Wiley.

Silva, Elisabete A (2004) 'The DNA of our regions: Artificial Intelligence in regional planning', *Futures* 36 (10): 1077–94.

Solecki, William, Karen C Seto and Peter J Marcotullio (2013). 'It's time for an urbanization science', *Environment Magazine*. January-February. Available from <http://www.environmentmagazine.org/Archives/Back%20issues/2013/January-February%202013/urbanization-full.html> Accessed on 22 November 2016.

Steffen, Will, Regina Angelina Sanderson, Peter D Tyson, Jill Jäger, Pamela A Matson, Berrien

Moore III, Frank Oldfield, Katherine Richardson, Hans Joachim Schellnhuber, Billie L Turner, Robert J Wasson (2004). *Global Change and the Earth System: A Planet under Pressure*. Berlin: Springer.

Steger, Manfred B (2008). *The Rise of the Global Imaginary: Political Ideologies from the French Revolution to the Global War on Terror*. Oxford: Oxford University Press.

Sutcliffe, Anthony (1981). *Towards the Planned City, Germany, Britain, the United States and France, 1780–1914*. Oxford: Basil Blackwell.

Taylor, Peter J, Michael Hoyler and David M Evans (2010). 'A geohistorical study of "the rise of modern science": Mapping scientific practice through urban networks, 1500–1900', in *Geographies of Science*, ed. Peter Meusburger, David N Livingstone and Heike Jöns, 37–56. Dordrecht: Springer.

Thisse, Jacques-François (2014). '*The New Science of Cities* by Michael Batty: The opinion of an economist', *Journal of Economic Literature* 52(3): 805–19.

Townsend, Anthony (2015). 'Cities of data: Examining the new urban science', *Public Culture* 27 (2): 201–12.

Venturi, Robert (1966). *Complexity and Contradiction in Architecture*. New York: Museum of Modern Art.

Wackernagel, Mathis. and William Rees (1996). *Our Ecological Footprint: Reducing Human Impact on the Earth*. Gabriola Island, BC: New Society Publishers. Wallerstein, Immanuel (1974). *The Modern World-System: Capitalist Agriculture and the Origins of the European World-Economy in the Sixteenth Century*. New York: Academic Press.

Future Cities, Plural?

Stephen Cairns, Maria Papadopoulou,
Devisari Tunas

Urbanisation Indicators

This short report compiles a set of statistics concerning urbanisation. They do not represent an integrated quantification of urbanisation effects, but function rather as indicators on demographics, economic growth and income inequality, CO_2 emissions and what has been described as 'decoupling' economic growth from emissions.

It begins with a set of graphs (Figures 1–2) showing the macro-trends in socio-economic and earth systems since 1750. The graphs show a sharp upturn across a range of indicators—demographics, energy use, GDP, greenhouse gasses, and temperature—from around that time. Scientists have dubbed this phenomenon 'the great acceleration' (Steffen et al. 2004).

The great acceleration graphs demonstrate a powerful worldwide transformation. Yet, as data is aggregated at a global level, it is difficult to appreciate the regional differences in the trend. As Steffen et al. (2015) note, without differentiating the data geographically, 'strong equity issues are masked'. For example, 'most of the population growth since 1950 has been in the non-OECD world but the world's economy (GDP), and hence consumption, is still strongly dominated by the OECD world' (Steffen et al. 2015). The most recent graphs are reproduced here followed by the authors' own indicative regional disaggregation.

Demographics

The UN Department of Economic and Social Affairs (DESA) has long tracked the growth of urban populations as a percentage of the world population in its *Urbanization Prospects* series. In the 2008 edition, it reported that the world population had reached a tipping point, in which the total population, having been mostly rural for all of human history, had shifted to being mostly urban for the first time (Figure 3). It also predicted that the gap between rural and urban populations would continue to diverge (UN DESA 2008). This report suggested that while the urban population accounted for less than one-third (30 per cent) of the total world population in 1950, the ratio would grow to two-thirds (66 per cent) by 2050 (UN DESA 2014).

The UN demographics report relies on many assumptions, not least regarding the definition of 'rural' and 'urban' populations, and data gathering and processing methods. That said, the 2008 edition articulated an important headline that triggered mainstream interest in the topic of urbanisation around the world.

Although it had significant impact in the mainstream media, the world rural-to-urban tipping point headline disguised a number of important issues that have a bearing on how the challenges of urbanisation might be addressed. First, are the differences in that ratio between world regions. Urban populations in Europe, Latin America, the Caribbean and Northern America account for well over 70 per cent of their total respective population totals. This figure remains below 50 per cent in Africa and Asia (Figure 4).

Second, these ratios do not capture the quantum differences in populations by region. With Asia's population at 4.4 billion, it accounts for close to two-thirds of the world's population (7.4 billion) in 2015 (UN DESA 2015). Third, the rate of urbanisation differs from region to region: while Europe, North America, Latin America and the Caribbean will see more modest growth of urban populations, Asia and Africa are in the midst of the steepest points in their respective urbanisation curves (UN DESA 2014).

Asia's relatively low rural-to-urban ratio, its rapid rate of urbanisation and its large (two-thirds) proportion of the world's population all together indicate that urbanisation is, on the whole, a historical phenomenon in Europe and the Americas, and that it is a current and future one for Asia. These factors will likely apply to Africa too in the coming century. If we broaden the scope of the key terms, 'urban' and 'rural' to incorporate concepts like 'ecological footprint' (Wackernage and Rees 1996), and 'planetary urbanisation' (Brenner and Schmid 2011), then the manner in which Asia urbanises will have worldwide consequences.

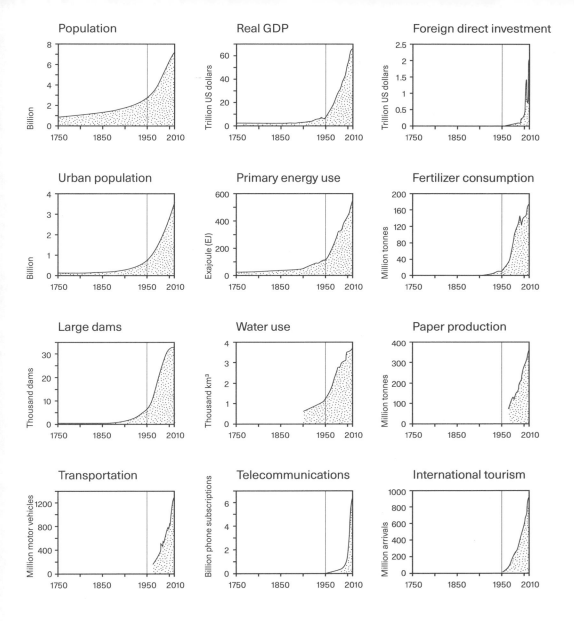

Fig. 1   Trends from 1750 to 2010 in globally aggregated indicators for socio-economic development.

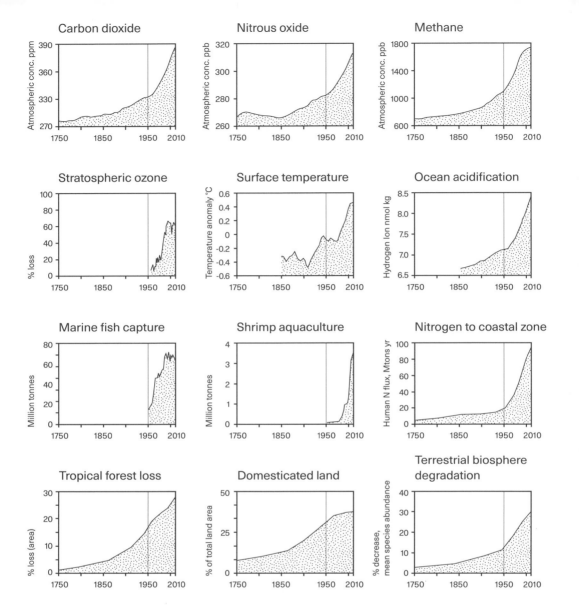

Carbon dioxide

Nitrous oxide

Methane

Stratospheric ozone

Surface temperature

Ocean acidification

Marine fish capture

Shrimp aquaculture

Nitrogen to coastal zone

Tropical forest loss

Domesticated land

Terrestrial biosphere degradation

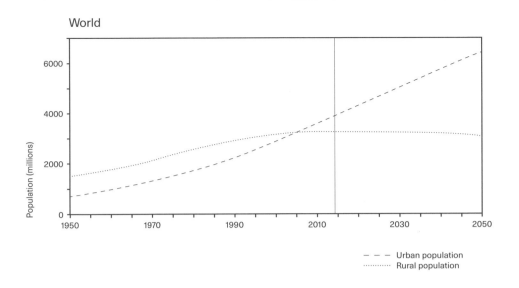

World

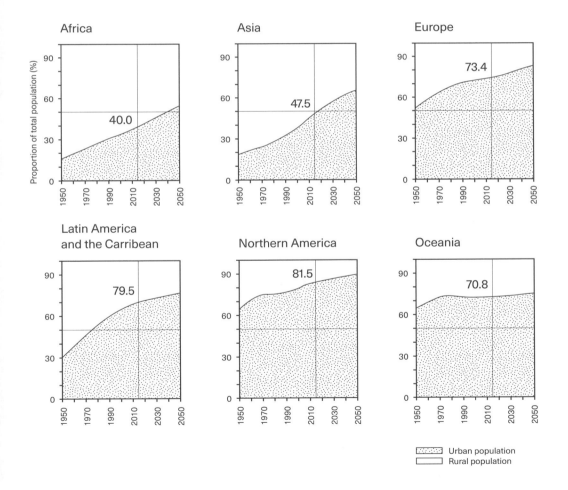

Africa

40.0

Asia

47.5

Europe

73.4

Latin America and the Carribean

79.5

Northern America

81.5

Oceania

70.8

Urban population
Rural population

Fig. 2	(Left page) Trends from 1750 to 2010 in indicators for the structure and functioning of the Earth System.
Fig. 3	(Top) Urban and rural population of the world, 1950–2050.
Fig. 4	(Bottom) Urban and rural population as proportion of total population, by major region, 1950–2050.

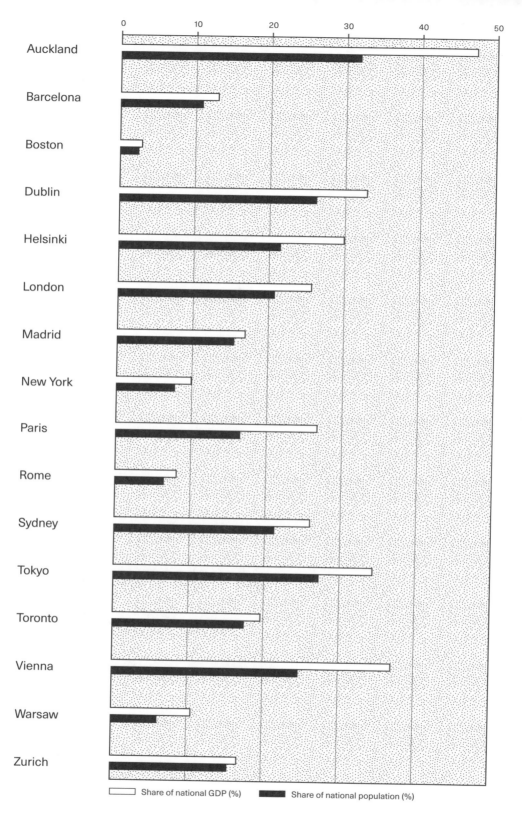

	0	10	20	30	40	50

Auckland

Barcelona

Boston

Dublin

Helsinki

London

Madrid

New York

Paris

Rome

Sydney

Tokyo

Toronto

Vienna

Warsaw

Zurich

☐ Share of national GDP (%) ■ Share of national population (%)

Urbanisation Indicators

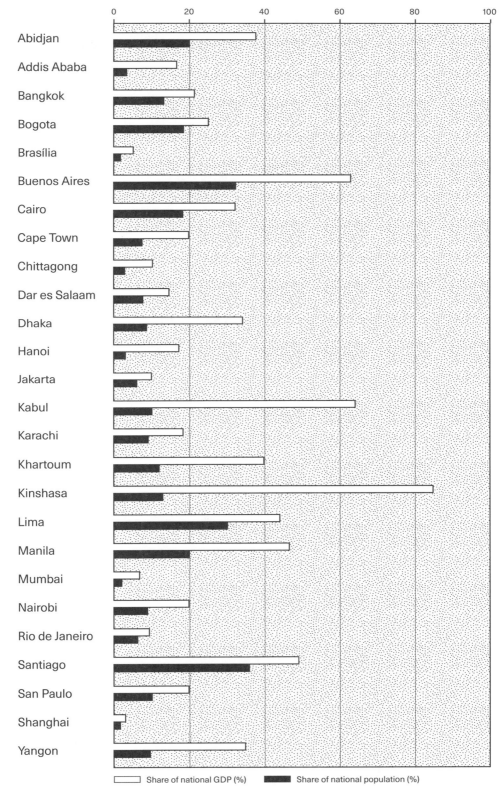

	0	20	40	60	80	100
Abidjan						
Addis Ababa						
Bangkok						
Bogota						
Brasília						
Buenos Aires						
Cairo						
Cape Town						
Chittagong						
Dar es Salaam						
Dhaka						
Hanoi						
Jakarta						
Kabul						
Karachi						
Khartoum						
Kinshasa						
Lima						
Manila						
Mumbai						
Nairobi						
Rio de Janeiro						
Santiago						
San Paulo						
Shanghai						
Yangon						

☐ Share of national GDP (%)   ■ Share of national population (%)

Fig. 5   (Left page) Share of GDP and national population in selected cities (developed countries).

Fig. 6   Share of national population and GDP in selected cities (developing countries).

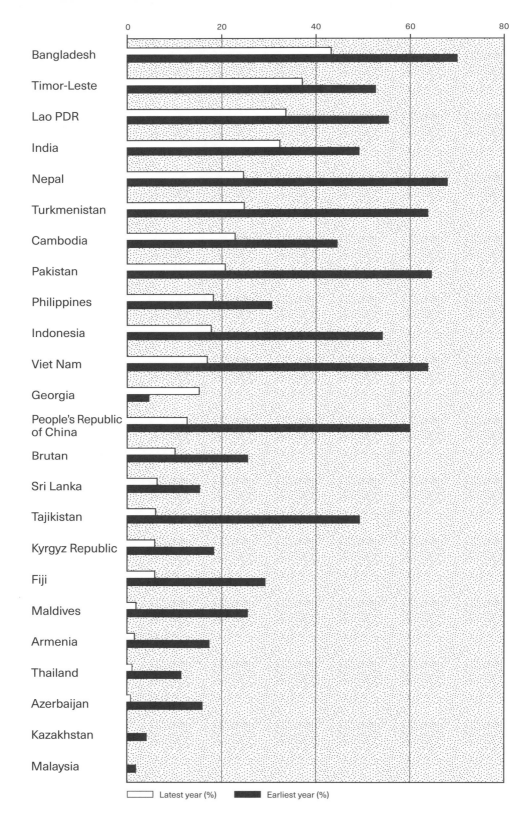

| | Latest year (%) | Earliest year (%) |

Urbanisation Indicators

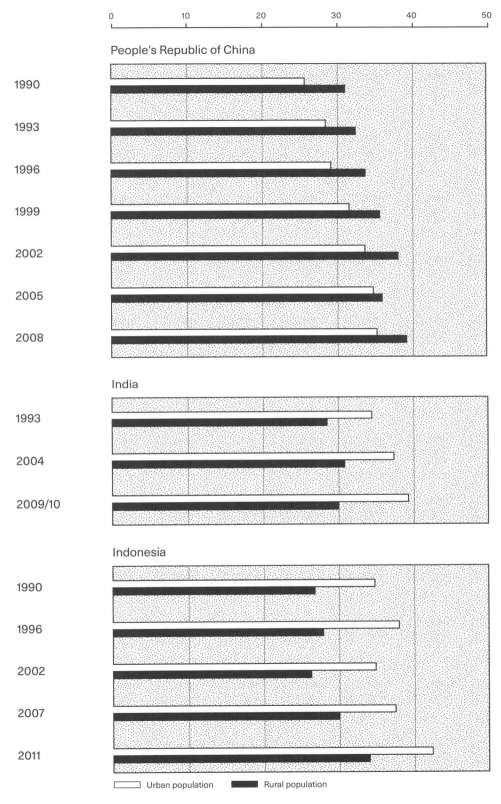

Fig. 7   (Left page) Proportion of population living on less than $1.25 a day, earliest
          (1990–2003) and latest (1996–2010) years (per cent).
Fig. 8   Urban and rural inequality in the PRC, India, and Indonesia, 1990s–2000s.

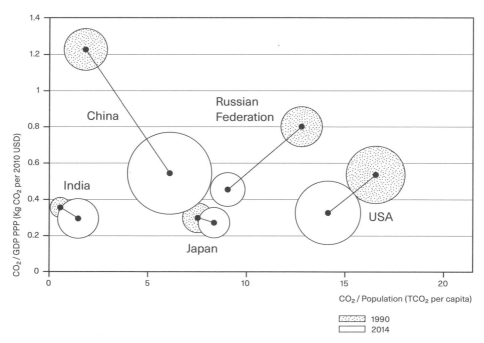

Fig. 9   Trends in CO$_2$ emission intensities for the top five emitting countries (the size of the circle represents the total CO$_2$ emissions from the country in that year).

Economic Growth and Inequality

Cities have always almost been drivers of economic growth. Today they generate more than 80 per cent of gross domestic product worldwide (GDP) (World Bank 2015). The economic power of cities is indicated in selected figures for cities in developed countries (by UN definitions) such as Auckland, London, New York, Paris, Sydney, Tokyo and Zürich (Figure 5). In all of these cases the share of GDP is higher in cities than the share of national population. In some cases (Auckland), the difference is substantial; in others it is not so great (Zürich). This selection of cities in developed countries is within a range of two to 15 per cent higher than their share of their respective national populations.

In the case of cities in developing countries (by UN definition), the differences are much larger on the whole (Figure 6). Cities such as Abidjan (18 per cent), Manila (24 per cent), Yangon (30 per cent), Kinshasa (70 per cent) are stark indicators of uneven development, where cities account for much larger proportion of economic growth than their population proportions suggest.

Although poverty (by UN definition) decreased from 43 per cent to 21 per cent between 1990 and 2010 worldwide, and the middle class grew by 450 million people, income inequality rose over the same period.

In the Asia-Pacific region populations defined as living in extreme poverty dropped significantly between 1990 and 2010, although eight of the region's economies retained rates above 20 per cent, including three of the most populous—Bangladesh (43.3 per cent), India (32.7 per cent) and Pakistan (21 per cent) (Figure 7). China represented the sharpest reduction in the total number of extremely poor people region-wide with annual decreases of 28.3 million (2.6 per cent) followed by India with annual decreases of 4.2 million (one per cent) (ADB 2012b).

At the same time, inequality in the Asia-Pacific region rose by seven per cent of Gini coefficient between the early 1990s to the late 2000s (ADB 2012a). Furthermore, the economic powerhouses of China, India and Indonesia saw urban and rural inequalities deteriorating by 10 and nine per cent, five and one per cent, and eight and five per cent respectively (Figure 8).

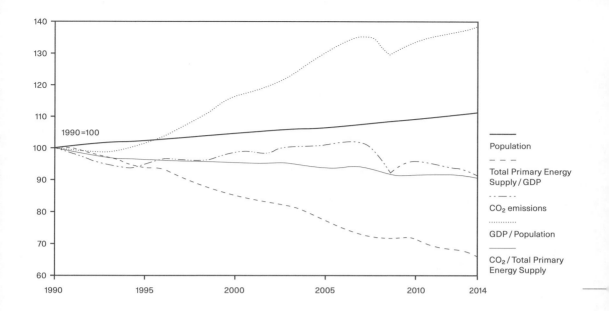

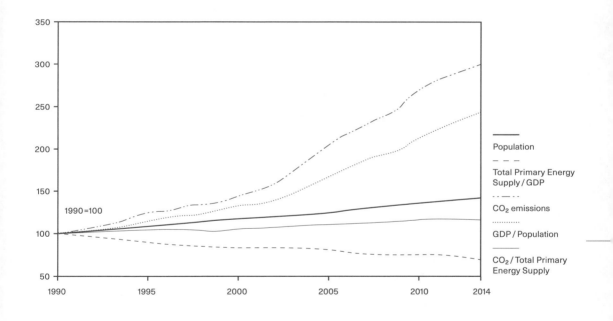

Fig. 10   (a) Annex I CO$_2$ emissions and drivers (Kaya decomposition).
'Annex I' countries by the UN Framework Convention on Climate Change [UNFCCC]
include: Australia, Austria, Canada, Croatia, Denmark, Sweden, Switzerland,
Russian Federation, United Kingdom, United States and countries in the European
Economic Community.
(b) Non-Annex I CO$_2$ emissions and drivers (Kaya decomposition).
'Non-Annex I' countries by the UN Framework Convention on Climate Change
[UNFCCC] include: Algeria, Botswana, Cameroon, Ethiopia, Pakistan, Bangladesh,
India, Indonesia, Philippines, Vietnam, China, Argentina, Brazil and Bolivia.

CO$_2$ Emissions and 'Decoupling'

Cities consume almost two-thirds of energy and generate more than 70 per cent of the CO$_2$ emissions worldwide (UNEP 2015).

Globally, per-capita CO$_2$ emissions grew by 16 per cent between 1990 and 2014, with China tripling, and India doubling their respective per-capita emissions (Figure 9). This correlates with strong per-capita GDP growth in those countries. The Russian Federation and the United States decreased their per-capita emissions by 30 per cent and the 16 per cent, respectively (IEA 2016).

CO$_2$ emissions in 2014 were eight per cent lower than in 1990 in countries in the developed world (called 'Annex I' countries by the UN Framework Convention on Climate Change [UNFCCC], which include: Australia, Austria, Canada, Croatia, Denmark, European Economic Community, Sweden, Switzerland, Russian Federation, United Kingdom and United States). This indicates a significant localised decoupling of energy consumption from economic activity (Total Primary Energy Supply (TPES)/GDP: -34 per cent). However, per-capita economic output (GDP/population) and population grew by 39 per cent and 11 per cent respectively and the energy sector's carbon intensity (CO$_2$/TPES) declined by nine per cent in Annex I countries.

In 2014, countries in the developing world (so-called non-Annex I countries), represented 58 per cent of global CO$_2$ emissions in 2014, while Annex I countries represented 39 per cent.

The CO$_2$ emissions in non-Annex I countries tripled over between 1990 and 2014, combined with a large growth in per-capita economic output (+145 per cent) and population (+45 per cent).

The energy sector's carbon intensity (CO$_2$/TPES) increased slowly until 1999, before reaching +18 per cent as a result of the increase in coal consumption; these increases were moderated by a significant decrease in the energy intensity of the economic activity (TPES/GDP: -28 per cent) (IEA 2016).

Bibliography

ADB (2012a). *Asian Development Outlook 2012. Confronting Rising Inequality in Asia.* Mandaluyong City, Philippines: Asian Development Bank.

ADB (2012b). *Key Indicators for Asia and the Pacific 2012.* Mandaluyong City, Philippines: Asian Development Bank.

Brenner, Neil and Christian Schmid (2011). 'Planetary urbanization', in *Urban Constellations: An Overview of Contemporary Urban Discourse*, ed. Mathew Gandy, 10–13. Berlin: Jovis Verlag.

IEA (2016). *Key CO$_2$ Emissions Trends', Expert from CO$_2$ Emissions from Fuel Combustion.* Available from <https://www.iea.org/publications/freepublications/publication/KeyCO2EmissionsTrends.pdf> Accessed on 10 November 2016.

Steffen, Will, Wendy Broadgate, Lisa Deutsch, Owen Gaffney and Cornelia Ludwig (2015). 'The trajectory of the anthropocene: The great acceleration', *The Anthropocene Review* 2(1): 81–98.

Steffen, Will, Regina Angelina Sanderson, Peter D Tyson, Jill Jäger, Pamela A Matson, Berrien Moore III, Frank Oldfield, Katherine Richardson, Hans Joachim Schellnhuber, Billie L Turner, Robert J Wasson (2004). *Global Change and the Earth System: A Planet under Pressure.* Berlin: Springer.

UN Department of Economic and Social Affairs (2014). *The 2014 Revision, Key Findings and Advance Tables. World Population Prospects.* New York: United Nations.

UN Department of Economic and Social Affairs (2008). *World Urbanization Prospects: The 2007 Revision. World Population Prospects.* New York: United Nations.

UN Habitat (2016). *Urbanization and Development: Emerging Futures. World Cities Report* Nairobi, Kenya.

UN Habitat and CAF (Development Bank of Latin America) (2015). *Construction of More Equitable Cities: Public Policies for Inclusion in Latin America.* Nairobi, Kenya.

UNEP (2015). *District Energy in Cities: Unlocking the Potential of Energy Efficiency and Renewable Energy.* Available from <www.unep.org/energy/portals/50177/DES_District_Energy_Report_full_02_d.pdf> Accessed on 10 November 2016.

United Nations, Department of Economic and Social Affairs, Population Division (2015). *World Population Prospects: The 2015 Revision, Key Findings and Advance Tables.* Working Paper No. ESA/P/WP.241.

Wackernagel, Mathis and William Rees (1996). *Our Ecological Footprint: Reducing Human Impact on the Earth.* Gabriola Island, BC: New Society Publishers.

World Bank (2015). *Urban Development: Overview.* Available from <http://www.worldbank.org/en/topic/urbandevelopment/overview> Accessed on 10 November 2016.

High Density Living in Asian Cities

Tokyo, Hong Kong and Singapore are among Asia's most successful cities — globally connected, economically competitive and offering high standards of living to residents and visitors alike. Each one has emerged over the past 50 years to encapsulate many of the qualities of an advanced Asian urbanism: comprehensive public transportation networks, efficient logistical systems, energetic business districts, vibrant cultural districts and rich offerings for leisure are energised by vertical urban forms and high population densities. The urban complexity and intensity of these cities is unprecedented. Now, in the second decade of the twenty-first century, each city has begun to face new challenges: managing ageing populations, labour-market shortages, economic inequalities, expanding environmental footprints, demand for even higher quality living at higher densities, and integrating automation into everyday life. All of these challenges take shape in a complex and shifting geo-political setting.

Caleb Ming is a Singaporean photographer whose work examines urban living in contemporary cities. He addresses the themes of public space, everyday life and event space in documentary mode. He is also a close observer of Singapore and neighbouring Asian cities.

Chinatown,
Singapore

Little India,
Singapore

Shibuya,
Tokyo

Sai Ying Pun,
Hong Kong

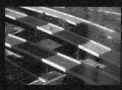

Connaught Road West,
Hong Kong

High Density Living in Asian Cities

A

High-Density Mixed-Use Cities

Large-scale urban projects have become major drivers of urban renewal in cities around the globe. [...] In places where land resources are limited and/or the urban population is increasing expeditiously, large-scale, high-density projects are regarded as a viable way for advancing urban development. These large-scale, master-planned projects—here referred to as *Grand Projet*—may hold answers to some of the emerging challenges related to the future of our cities.

While individual countries and human society as a whole need to understand and prepare for a warmer world over the coming decades, cities will need to adapt to even higher temperatures, and perhaps also to greater risks of flooding. Against this background, it becomes urgent to find ways of increasing the resilience of cities and making them less vulnerable to the potentially catastrophic effects of global change. Design concepts using plants and vegetation can contribute greatly to this effort, reducing urban temperatures and the risk of flooding, and also increasing the liveability of cities, improving public health and enhancing biodiversity.

When it comes to developing strategies for energy efficiency in cities, working at the scale of the individual building is too limited and that of the entire city is too complex and perhaps abstract. The scale of the neighbourhood and district, however, bears an interesting potential to increase energy efficiency, which means delivering the same services with less energy.

We have ceded the possibility of the city being a part of *nature* in favour of *naturalising* it into our technological and architectural repertoire. This specific ecological turn is not to suggest a 'return to nature' but instead a more sustained attempt to transpose the benefits of mass and massiveness from the scale of material to the scale of architecture.

A   High-Density Mixed-Use Cities

Cities are often said to deliver social, ecological, and economic benefits, along with higher standards of living. The key to this argument is the notion of proximity. The proximity of people, things and places enables inhabitants of cities to live productive, enjoyable and stimulating lives. Proximity by itself, however, is not enough to deliver environmentally sustainable, economically vibrant and socially coherent future cities (Glaeser 2011). Proximity must be organised to enable complex relationships of interdependence between people, activities, places, buildings and the wider territories of cities. We call this condition, the high-density, mixed-use city.

For most of human history cities have supported relatively high population densities, and rich functional mixes. This long history was interrupted by industrialisation and the failure of historic city fabrics to cope with its effects. Modernist doctrines of functional segregation, designed to remedy such failures, were damaging too. Functionalism in urban planning was, of course, heavily critiqued. Urban activist Jane Jacobs observed that the segregation of functions destroyed the original qualities of the city. She campaigned to protect and re-establish links with what she called the 'ubiquitous principles' of urban planning, namely: 'the need of cities for a most intricate and close grained diversity of uses that give each other constant mutual support, both economically and socially. The components of this diversity can differ enormously but they must supplement each other in certain concrete ways' (Jacobs 1961, 14).

This chapter introduces research on the concept of the high-density, mixed-use city. It argues that shaping such cities requires a design process that better understands the interdependencies between the component parts of cities and their actors, as well as an openness to different disciplinary expertise and institutional capacities that are responsible for city making.

Five Challenges

The planning and design of high-density, mixed-use cities presents a broad range of issues, questions and difficulties which can be summarised under five general challenges. The first is to understand how higher densities can make better use of urban land and build more vital communities (Rogers 2000). The second is to rethink rigid zoning policies, particularly in response to segregations between living and working, where commuting creates congestion and crowding. A third great challenge is how to achieve a better understanding of the interdependencies between different aspirations of the related disciplines—in a scientific manner. The fourth is to develop methods for effective collaboration between different disciplines, citizens and stakeholders. The fifth challenge is to articulate a specific planning ambition and to define the priorities and urgencies involved. Each challenge is elaborated below.

1   Does Density have a Limit?

There are many social, environmental and economic reasons for the densification of physical space and physiological flows. Limited land and a growing population require new concepts for reducing footprints, distances, congestions and crowding. More research on the typologies of high-density urban living that can address these emerging needs for the support of social inter-action or economic networks is needed. Today, high-density urban districts are often planned mono-functionally. They often lack distinctiveness. Vibrant local neighbourhoods and communities, however, are central to achieving a liveable city. Suburbanisation and car-based living on the urban edge inspired by the wish for more living space will likely continue for many years. Yet there is already evidence, particularly in Asia, to show that high-density city-based developments are offering alternatives (Yuen and Yeh 2011; Ng 2009). One reason for this is the ongoing desire for face-to-face human interactions in a variety of vital communities. High-density urban environments can much better support such aspiration. Since the quality of common spaces defines the char-acter of the city, and many face-to-face meetings happen there, the importance of common spaces in high-density environments becomes even more relevant.

2   Rethinking Co-existence

Population density is directly linked to a concentration of activities and flows in and through a place. The concept of mixed-uses makes these activities and flows even more vital and exuberant.

Rethinking the usage patterns of working and living spaces can contribute to more social interaction and innovation (Duffy 2008). While the advantage of mixing uses is increasingly rec-ognised, functional segregation remains a common feature in many cities around the world. The desire for tranquil neighbour-hoods with reduced noise pollution and without conflicting impacts from co-existing functions is the main consideration behind mono-functional residential areas.

Population counts rarely include the commuters who enter cities during weekdays, or the hundreds of thousands of visitors to city hospitals, universities, and to nightlife venues. Due to high property prices, average income earners often cannot live in centrally located neighbourhoods that offer better connectivity and public facilities. Future-oriented high-density, mixed-use districts should not only include a variety of different programmes but also consciously include low-cost rental models for better social mixture and integration.

The capacities of mixed-use planning to deliver higher economic, social, and environmental synergies are apparent (Ng 2009). They create more vibrant, attractive and secure environments, and better quality city centres. Moreover, the notion of mixed-use creates freedom and opportunities, less need to travel, less reliance on cars and more public transport usage. Architects Juan Abalos and Iñaki Herreros state that 'as a result of these multiple factors from new theories to the logic of the real estate market, theorists and planners began to focus on the need to revise the topological schematism of the modernist city and its commercial centre' (Abalos and Herreros 2003). They further note 'as an organisational mechanism, stratification was capable of totally altering the hierarchical and functionally compartmentalised architectural models that served the business sector in its early stages. Today this mechanism is beginning to shape a new kind of urban topology'. They conclude that 'ultimately, the practice of designing and erecting high-rise structures has generated a flood of new ideas about the topology of built space and the city'. This discourse leads to the conclusion that the high-density, mixed-use city model necessarily engages in defining new spatial relationships between different activities, and concerns how such relationships create new synergies in a three-dimensional environment.

3   Transdisciplinary Aspirations

High-density city concepts can succeed or fail depending on how their designs are spatially translated, and how resulting built form is managed. To explore the various forces that influence the transformation of urban life styles and the fundamental spatial patterns that emerge in response to urban growth trends, one needs to look into the dynamics between human activities and the form of high-density environments.

There is strong interconnectivity between life and form in cities: forms shape, inhibit, enable, curtail, facilitate and respond to people's needs. What interest observers is the relationship between public behaviour and the form of architecture and the city. Amos Rappaport identifies 'the need for people's involvement in the environment and the relationship of activity and form' (Rappaport 1977, 7). Further, he states 'after discussing urban design as the organisation of space, time, meaning and communication, it considers the nature of the environment, cultural differences, role of values and the concept of environmental perception as it is currently used' (Rappaport 1977, 6).

There are practical experiences that we can learn from. What is missing is a sound scientific understanding of interdependencies between different disciplinary aspirations and their effects on the overall quality of life. Unfortunately, some believe that when every discipline brings their smartest solution into a multidisciplinary setting, and that the sum of all those smart solutions will result in the highest quality of urban life. This however, is rarely the case; such a utopian image would assume that there is always full consensus between the disciplines.

46

The question of whether high-density living is generally better for the overall quality of life has not been answered yet, but a quick look at its possible environmental benefits may suggest so. A systematic study of the interrelationships between people and their built environment is needed. What are the effects of high-density cities on human behaviour, mood or well-being? In general, technology and digitalisation are the strongest drivers and probably the two most significant trends influencing future urban forms. They appear to be leading towards either a dispersed urban pattern with lower densities or a more centralised pattern with higher densities, 'accommodating a variety of types and sizes of micro-public spaces and encouraging diversity, proximity, complexity, spontaneity, and civility of collective human experience' (Pressman 1985, 359).

4   Designing the Process

Contemporary research techniques and analytical tools have enhanced our capacity to describe cities and their underlying structures. But how we might challenge those structures, adapt or radically rethink them, or propose alternatives is less clear. This suggests that the planning and design of urban environments with a higher degree of three- and four-dimensionality urgently calls for more efficient and fruitful methods of collaboration between different disciplines. Such a collaboration would likely take the form of a network of interconnected disciplinary experts, stakeholders, citizens supported by cyber-physical systems and mediated by information technology and efficient knowledge and data flows. This transdisciplinary approach thrives on open-ended and temporally fluid rather than linear processes —similar to the work of a simultaneous interpreter, such processes keep the conversation in continuous flow. Certain degrees of control and freedom alternate within a large number of feedback loops and keep the transdisciplinary discourse open.

The advantages of having interfaces between agents and reality seem to be obvious in urban research and design processes, between agents and computational devices (De Landa 1997). The approach needs, however, to be tested with regards to the complexity of optimisation processes, and the production of alternating solutions within a framework of properties.

For this research on and the development of the design framework of high-density, mixed-use cities in FCL we focus on four areas. They include the exploration of characteristics and mechanisms of large urban projects as agents of development and redevelopment in contemporary cities (The *Grand Projet*: Towards Adaptable and Liveable Urban Megaprojects); the understanding of how we can better design urban green spaces to provide ecosystem services to people (Ecosystem Services in Urban Landscapes); the leveraging of synergies between urban development, urban design and energy systems for the efficient and sustainable supply of energy in cities (Multi-Scale Energy Systems for Low Carbon Cities); and the study of environmental, social, economic and design benefits of dense and green building typologies in high-density urban contexts (Dense and Green Building Typologies).

5   Real World Projects

We believe that scientific research in urbanism needs to critically inform urban design practice and vice versa. Ultimately, research findings cannot be simulated and implemented in abstract environments, but need to be tested in concrete urban situations. Juan Busquets notes 'such precedent gives great importance to the idea of "the project" within urbanism, in its implementation as either a long term vision or an immediate action able to decanter more to the point improvements than what a large scale, holistic project could achieve'. Further, he continues, 'the "urbanistic project" appears as the entity that acts as a vehicle between theory and practice, since only through the urbanistic project can certain theoretical points be tested and converted into actions' (Busquets 2010, 1).

The high-density, mixed-use cities scenario at the FCL follows this thinking by developing the 'urbanistic project' for Singapore's Southern Waterfront in Tanjong Pagar. Together with the Urban Redevelopment Authority (URA) we identified this area as a perfect test field for the implementation of new research-based strategies. This project not only informs the research and tests its findings, but it also supports the development of new design tools and methods. Key features of this project—such as design, modelling, big-data processing, new visualisation techniques, and the cross fertilisation between different disciplines —characterise it as a knowledge incubator. It stimulates new forms of collaboration and new approaches towards successful high-density, mixed-use cities.

Conclusion

We have detailed five general challenges facing a transdisciplinary research and design process for high-density, mixed-use cities. In conclusion, we want to take up the issue of a transdisciplinary methodology in urban design. Our basic contention is that although urban design should certainly give more attention to scientific analysis and empirics, the profession still needs to continue deepening its critical and evidence-based design process and analytical frameworks, particularly along the lines of the five challenges outlined above.

Bibliography

Abalos, Inaki and Juan
Herreros (2003). *Tower
and Office: From
Modernist Theory to
Contemporary Practice*.
London, MA: MIT Press
Cambridge.

Busquets, Joan (2010).
Defining Urban Design.
Available from <http://
www.gsd.harvard.edu/
person/joan-busquets/
courses> Accessed
on 28 November 2016.

De Landa, Manuel (1997).
Meshrooms. Bern: Benteli
Verlags AG.

Duffy, Francis (2008).
Work and the City.
London: Black Dog.

Glaeser, Edward (2011).
*Triumph of the City: How
Our Greatest Invention
Makes Us Richer, Smarter,
Greener, Healthier,
and Happier*. New York:
Penguin Press.

Jacobs, Jane (1961). *The
Death and Life of Great
American Cities*. New York:
Random House.

Pressman N (1985). 'Forces
for spatial change', in *The
Future of Urban Form: The
Impact of New Technology*,
eds. J F Brotchie,
P Newton, P Hall and
P Nijkamp. London:
London Croom Helm.

Rappaport, Amos (1977).
*Human Aspects of Urban
Form: Towards a
Man-Environment
Approach to Urban Form
and Design*. Oxford:
Pergamon Press.

Rogers, Richard (2000).
'City of density: Towards
an urban renaissance',
Foyer, pp. 8–9.

Yuen, Belinda and Anthony
Gar-On Yeh (eds) (2011).
*High-rise living in Asian
cities*. Berlin: Springer.

Ng, Edward (2009).
*Designing High-Density
Cities for Social
and Environmental
Sustainability*.
London: Earthscan.

High-Density Mixed-Use Cities

Kees Christiaanse, Anna Gasco,
Naomi Hanakata

The *Grand Projet*: Towards Adaptable and Liveable Urban Megaprojects

Large-scale urban projects have become major drivers of urban renewal in cities around the globe. High-density, mixed uses and transit-connectivity are increasingly seen as positive attributes in a liveable city from social, economic as well as environmental perspectives. Notably in places where land resources are limited and/or the urban population is increasing expeditiously, large-scale, high-density projects are regarded as a viable way for advancing urban development. These large-scale, master-planned projects —here referred to as *Grand Projet*—may hold answers to some of the emerging challenges related to the future of our cities.

At the same time, Grands Projets have been criticised as overly top-down in their programme, design and implementation process. They can appear to be compartmented in mono-functional zones, with poor public spaces, and lack the spatial and programmatic diversity designed to foster social, economic and cultural interaction. With respect to their investment partnerships or programme arrangements, many Grands Projets are global in their orientation. Examples looked at include the greater Marina Bay area in Singapore, HafenCity in Hamburg, King's Cross in London, La Défense in Paris, Lujiazui in Shanghai, Marunouchi in Tokyo, and West Kowloon in Hong Kong.

Due to the combination of centrality, intensity, diversity and connectivity, the impact of Grands Projets can go beyond their perimeter on a regional scale. The topic of *Grand Projet* therefore deserves special attention and investigation. Within the Future Cities Laboratory the characteristics and mechanisms of large-scale urban projects are currently being explored with a focus on Asian and European cases. This study investigates how such projects are conceived, initiated, elaborated and implemented and how they influence their immediate surroundings and their larger metropolitan context. Central to this study are the following questions: How can Grands Projets be better conceptualised, designed and implemented in a sustainable way and provide additional value to an existing urban situation and the larger metropolitan context? And given their global character, how can Grands Projets develop specific qualities, which positively contribute to the local identity of a place?

The aim of this study is to understand *Grand Projet* based on in-depth case studies, analysis and to use the generated body of knowledge to assess and evaluate other projects based on a set of developed criteria.

Challenges in Studying *Grand Projet*

The complexity of Grands Projets in their design, implementation and management processes presents challenges when it comes to studying them. The sheer size of Grands Projets often leads to organisational challenges as they are often completed in several phases, in which rearrangements, corrections, additions, and errors occur, frequently with cost overruns. This often leads to the perception that their planning and construction processes are opaque (del Cerro Santamaría 2013). In addition, their conceptualisation, realisation, and viability are susceptible to market preferences, demographic shifts, financial issues, and changing government agendas (Hall 2014). The study therefore needs to make inherent complexities transparent and readable in order to be able to develop productive evaluation tools.

Due to its complexity, any Grand Projet necessitates a particular research methodology that is able to address its multi-dimensionality. The large-scale of a Grand Projet makes it particularly conducive to, and dependent on, multiple parameters of a socioeconomic, political and spatial nature. Grands Projets

FCL INDICIA 01 A HIGH-DENSITY MIXED-USE CITIES

are formed by an interdependency of various procedural and geographical interlinked processes. These parameters are considered key for the social acceptance, economic success, as well as long-term sustainability and liveability of such Grands Projets. Hence, an analysis of Grand Projet requires an approach from multiple angles. Grands Projets need to be comprehensively analysed in order to evaluate and assess them today, and for future reference.

Over the last decades, sustainability, adaptability, and liveability have become central themes in research and practice related to the urban condition (Marcotullio 2001; Evans 2002; Maynard 2008; Cilona 2016). The sheer size of Grands Projets coupled with their comprehensive planning effort over a considerable period of time make it a particularly interesting test bed to study such qualities. This study would need to identify which parameters are decisive in the planning process and evaluation of Grands Projets in order to attain a sustainable, adaptable, and liveable urban environment.

We consider 'sustainability' as an aim that will meet contemporary requirements in the development without compromising future needs (Brundtland et al. 1987), while 'adaptability' is taken as the ability to adapt to changing circumstances such as economic trends, power relations or user preferences. Likewise, 'liveability' addresses the ability to offer highly qualitative, healthy and resilient environments that can accommodate a variety of uses and users. In the past, Grands Projets were mainly top-down mono-functional projects. Over the last decades, however, we can observe a paradigm shift away from these characteristics towards more integrated, stakeholder-managed and mixed-use developments. In Asia, this change in approach has barely begun. Nevertheless, we can clearly see a general trend away from a static design-approach towards a strategic and open-ended one.

On the ground, the qualities of 'sustainability', 'adaptability' and 'liveability' are highly interdependent. For an analysis of Grands Projets, it is necessary to understand the extent to which they have been incorporated in the design strategy and to what extent they have evolved through the dynamics of the project, and between the project and its surrounding. La Défense, for example, was conceived as a conventional, mono-functional Central Business District (CBD), but over time it expanded and evolved into a more diverse environment that included residential areas.

More recent Grands Projets have reacted to the problems of earlier cases by incorporating continuous adaptation processes, offering a mixed-use development from the start, with diverse building types and complex forms of ownership and management. Examples include King's Cross in London, and HafenCity in Hamburg. These projects involved skilled and multi-disciplinary project teams supported by open stakeholder management strategies.

Contextualising *Grand Projet*
in the Current Academic Discourse

The development of Grands Projets is a process accelerating in quantity and speed in different geographical locations. Contextualising Grands Projets on a global scale enables us to read them as physical manifestations of global trends shaping our urban centres—such as expanding economic networks, multi-national stakeholders, or globally applied planning practices. Furthermore, an analysis of Grands Projets enables us to examine these trends and discuss their implication for processes on the ground: reading Grands Projets as paradigmatic indicators for globally advancing processes allows us to identify and address the challenges they face when confronted with local realities.

One of these developments is urbanisation itself. As a process transcending any physical border, political jurisdiction and social sphere, urbanisation has become a planetary phenomenon (Brenner and Schmid 2015). As well as a sharp increase in speed and scale of urbanisation over the last decades, the relation and dynamics within and between urban areas has also shifted. This shift has created new forces of attraction and exclusion, of explosion and implosion (Schmid et al. 2012), putting large-scale inner city Grands Projets developments at the core of the debate.

Processes of neoliberalisation are another trend which impinge upon the conceptualisation and manifestation of Grands Projets. A regulatory transformation of the globally dominant neoliberal economic system, which prioritises market-based and market-oriented responses to regulatory problems, is reflected in the financing, development and marketing of many Grands Projets (Kemper and Vogelpohl 2013). Stakeholders as well as financing and developer partnerships are often dominated by the private sector,

The *Grand Projet*: Towards Adaptable and
Liveable Urban Megaprojects

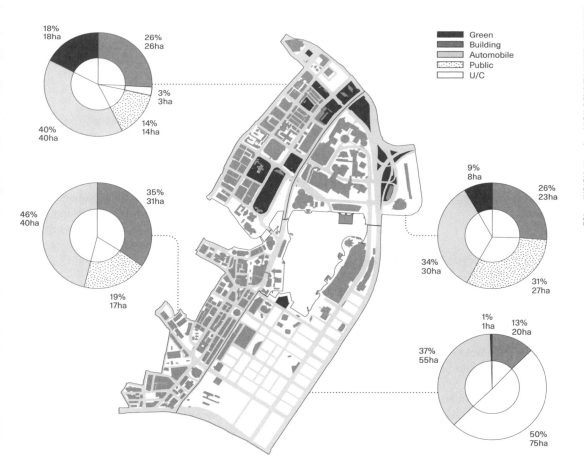

Green
Building
Automobile
Public
U/C

18%
18ha

26%
26ha

3%
3ha

14%
14ha

40%
40ha

35%
31ha

46%
40ha

19%
17ha

9%
8ha

26%
23ha

34%
30ha

31%
27ha

1%
1ha

13%
20ha

37%
55ha

50%
75ha

Fig. 1   8 Case Studies.
(Top) Marunouchi, Tokyo; Downtown Core, Singapore; Lujiazui, Shanghai;
West Kowloon, Hong Kong.
(Bottom) King's Cross, London; 22@, Barcelona; Hafencity, Hamburg;
La Défense, Paris.

Fig. 2   Downtown Core, Singapore: Ground level public space distribution.

using the competitive advantages of private interests on a global scale. This process further corroborates the expansion and consolidation of global economic networks, whereby geographic hierarchies of decision-making are established and physically manifested in Grands Projets as key spatial nodes of a globalised economy.

The commonly stated motivation for promoting large-scale urban projects, either by local governments or private investors and developers, is their ability to attract real estate investment. The benefits are not limited to developers but are projected to trickle down to inhabitants through the provision of infrastructure, public space, cultural amenities, and improved international image (Ponzini 2013). However, such benefits may require higher than anticipated public investments, or may demand increased flexibility in planning instruments and city administration (Lobo 2013).

The implementation of Grands Projets often means revisiting structural plans, introducing special district legislation, and altering previous city visions (Ponzini 2013; Lobo 2013). Public attention is drawn to this type of project when their development is preceded by land readjustment and/or a consolidation of multiple landholdings such as in Roppongi Hills in Tokyo. This can also occur when Grands Projets impact regional urban dynamics through the introduction of a new centrality, or through the diversion of resources from an existing one—such as in West Kowloon in relation to central Hong Kong, and the associated high-speed rail link to Hong Kong International Airport.

Initial Findings on *Grand Projet*

Initial analysis of 'processes', 'urban design' and 'management' aspects in the previously listed in-depth case studies of *Grand Projet* shows how the physical materialisation of such projects are significantly defined by factors such as land ownership, governance, process, and open space.

Land Ownership
Landownership and stakeholder management are fundamental parameters for the planning and implementation of Grands Projets. Their role and constellation however vary extensively between the case studies analysed, showing that despite globalisation, landowners have specific arrangements depending on the context.

In the Grands Projets analysed in London, complex public and private partnerships have evolved over time and landowners are now located in different locations of the global economy. Over 50 per cent of the area of King's Cross has been owned by an Australian pension fund since 2016. In Canary Wharf, most of the shareholders were from Canada in the 1980s, before shifting to US shareholders in early 2000, and more recently to Qatari investors. This globalisation of land ownership poses, amongst others, challenges related to different cultures of management practice of the privately owned public realm.

In Tokyo, on the other hand, the notion of land ownership remains very local. Land is usually owned, planned and developed by local stakeholders. In particular, larger, inner city development projects are owned and developed by a large Japanese conglomerate or railway company and provide exemplary case studies of Transit Oriented Developments (TODs). In the case of Marunouchi, the Mitsubishi Estate Group owns about one third of the 120 hectare area, which it acquired at the end of the nineteenth century and turned into the capital's central business district.

In Shanghai Lujiazu, despite the appearance of a globalised built environment, many of the buildings' developers are products of the Chinese State's planned economy. The earliest towers were the manifestation of investments by state-owned enterprises such as the China Marine Group. Private enterprises located in Lujiazui have strong state backing, such as the headquarters of Huaneng Group—an enterprise owned by the son of former Chinese Premier Li.

Governance
A study of governance processes illustrates how Grands Projets often reflect the political and economic agendas of their times. Investigating the King's Cross area in London in relation to other cases study references in the city shows how evolving modes of governance have supported the contrasting spatial materialisations of Grands Projets from the 1980s onwards.

Canary Wharf for example, demonstrates the centralisation of power under the 1980's Thatcher government. The Local Government, Planning and Land Act, introduced in 1980, created a shift of power from local boroughs to the central government. The

'Public Request to Order Disposal' entitled the government to force local authorities to sell publicly owned land. This led to the introduction of Urban Enterprise Zones—such as the one at Canary Wharf —with tax concessions and reduced regulations designed to attract private investors. The Canary Wharf scheme was overseen by the London Dockland Development Corporation, masterplanned by American architects and developed by a Canadian developer. It was built on a layout disconnected from the adjacent neighbourhoods, with upper middle class inhabitants working and living next to an area of lower income housing and lower wage earners.

From the mid 1990s onwards, the decentralisation of UK political power came with a clear focus on the metropolitan level, with power devolved to the borough and cross-borough level. This shift was supported by various British government policies that encouraged developers to promote inclusive urban regenerations. In comparison to Canary Wharf, the development of King's Cross falls into this period of decentralised decision-making practices, with the surrounding boroughs and communities involved in the planning process. From the beginning of the project Camden Borough joined forces with the developer, Argent, and various private and public stakeholders to shape a clear vision for the site.

The inclusive attitude of the developer towards the local community also played a key role in enabling an open-ended consultation process, which in turn lead to a detailed brief for the site's master planners. King's Cross development portrays a high integration within its local area, and acceptance by the surrounding residents. The fact that all stakeholders felt included in shaping the future of the area is one of the main lessons to take away from the King's Cross development. This contrasts with examples of rapidly developing Grands Projets in Asian city contexts, where governance and master-planning methods remain mainly centralised.

In the case of Marunouchi, modes of governance are defined by the dominant stakeholder of the area: the Mitsubishi Estate Group. While privatisation of large, inner city areas is a process increasingly found in many cities around the globe (Harvey 2007), this has historical roots in the case of Marunouchi and Mitsubishi. At the same time, this very stable tenure situation allowed for a continuous planning with gradual adaptations, in comparison to the processes of 'scrap and build' that

characterise the urban transformation of other parts of Tokyo.

The incremental adaptation of Marunouchi for more than 100 years has also produced a diverse set of building typologies. The area is managed by a council[1] consisting of all property owners and steered by a committee made up of the main stakeholders in the area. This council is in charge of planning and building maintenance, and of overall coordination including events in the public spaces. The allocation of further area management duties such as area cleaning to a non-governmental organisation (NGO) comprising local property owners, rather than the municipal or city government, is a common practice in Japan. It contributes to a collective effort and communal sense within a district and can also be found in other reference case studies in Tokyo, namely Roppongi Hills, Shibuya Station and West Shinjuku.

The participation of multiple stakeholders in the process, design and management of a Grand Projet is a complex procedure. It is characterised by tensions related to defining who the community is, and how to avoid single-issue politics that can dominate debates (Imrie et al., 2009). Therefore, a consultative approach requires a specific framework, which includes creating a common understanding of the plan for all stakeholders involved.

Process

The temporal dimension of Grands Projets offers another angle to investigate challenges related to design, development, and management of large-scale urban projects.

At King's Cross, within the relatively short span of time from the planning phase—seven years —to the actual start of construction in 2007, the development partnership paid particular attention to the temporal strategy. This is reflected in the phasing of the open-space developments and in the introduction of various temporary uses for plots yet to be developed. The key priority was to ensure public accessibility from the start of the construction; public spaces were planned and finished in the first phases, allowing integration into the surrounding area even before the first buildings were completed. In addition, temporary uses include a community garden and a swimming pond where local users and neighbouring

---

1   Council for Are Development and Management of Otemachi, Marunouchi, and Yurakucho.

The *Grand Projet*: Towards Adaptable and Liveable Urban Megaprojects

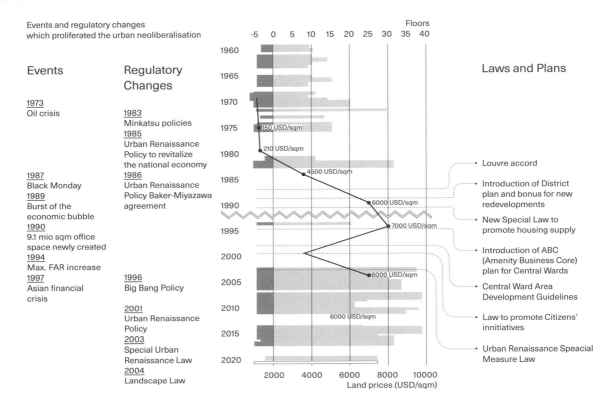

Events and regulatory changes
which proliferated the urban neoliberalisation

Floors
-5 0 5 10 15 20 25 30 35 40

Events

1973
Oil crisis

1987
Black Monday
1989
Burst of the
economic bubble
1990
9.1 mio sqm office
space newly created
1994
Max. FAR increase
1997
Asian financial
crisis

Regulatory Changes

1983
Minkatsu policies
1985
Urban Renaissance
Policy to revitalize
the national economy
1986
Urban Renaissance
Policy Baker-Miyazawa
agreement

1996
Big Bang Policy

2001
Urban Renaissance
Policy
2003
Special Urban
Renaissance Law
2004
Landscape Law

1960
1965
1970
1975   150 USD/sqm
1980   210 USD/sqm
1985   4500 USD/sqm
1990   6000 USD/sqm
1995   7000 USD/sqm
2000
2005   6000 USD/sqm
2010   6000 USD/sqm
2015
2020

2000   4000   6000   8000   10000
Land prices (USD/sqm)

Laws and Plans

• Louvre accord

• Introduction of District
plan and bonus for new
redevelopments

• New Special Law to
promote housing supply

• Introduction of ABC
(Amenity Business Core)
plan for Central Wards

• Central Ward Area
Development Guidelines

• Law to promote Citizens'
innitiatives

• Urban Renaissance Speacial
Measure Law

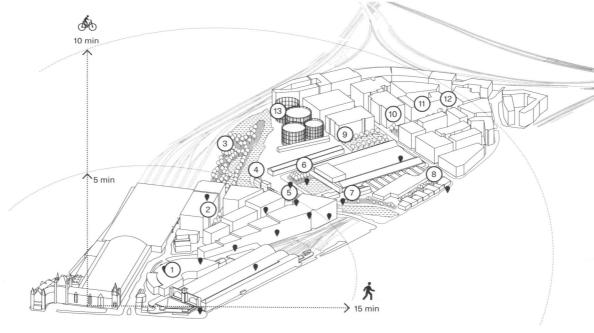

10 min

5 min

15 min

Bycicle Stations	4 Viaduct	8 Handyside Gardens	12 Skip Garden
1 King's Cross Square	5 Canalside Square	9 Lewis Cubitt Square	13 Gasholder park
2 Pancras Square	6 Granary Square	10 Lewis Cubitt Park	
3 Camley Street Natural Park	7 Wharf Road Gardens	11 Pond Club	

Fig. 3   Marunouchi, Tokyo: Development of building stock and open spaces in relation
to Urban Renaissance Policies, 1958–2020.
Fig. 4   King's Cross, London: Open Spaces Framework and Soft Mobility Network.

residents could interact. This allowed new and surrounding communities to become attached to the temporary spaces. Developers are looking into adapting the plan to incorporate these facilities as permanent programmes.

The case study of Marunouchi in Tokyo provides a long temporal span of processes to study as the site has been developed based on a comprehensive plan for over 125 years.

A significant moment in the recent history of the city was the collapse of the bubble economy at the beginning of the 1990s. Up until then, the Marunouchi area was characterised by mono-functional zones with little street activity. In the early 1990s, in response to rising property prices, new strategies were sought to restructure the mono-functional program of the business core, and to secure a high letting ratio. The result was a new phase characterised by program diversification and multiple stakeholder involvement, supported by the introduction of a new open space network that connected both open and indoor spaces above and below ground.

Similarly, in Singapore, the Downtown Core area has developed over a long period. From the first phase governed by Raffles' Plan in the 1820s, the area has gradually expanded through various land-reclamations until today. The spatial diversity of building typologies and open space networks reflect the different implementation phases and 'ages of land', such as the Padang (1819), Marina Bay (1992) and Marina South (under construction). These spatial expansions are followed by an evolving planning vision for this area: from political and financial centrality at first, the newly reclaimed areas are now gradually moving towards a more mixed-use condition.

Open Space

In Singapore, the Downtown Core also offers interesting insights into a particular public realm typology: the underground open spaces network. In order to mitigate Singapore's tropical weather conditions, some of the Mass Rapid Transport (MRT) rail stations are connected to existing commercial basement spaces. In order to further expand this underground network, developers can apply for cash grants from March 2004, as well as take up options to add additional (yet limited) money-generating activities in the underground spaces.

The Marina Bay Development, an agency set up by Singapore's Urban Redevelopment Authority (URA), manages and rents various pockets of public space within the area. The range of events results in a variety of atmospheres throughout the year, from morning workout sessions to night festivals and monthly cultural performances. These all encourage residents and users from all walks of life to interact. The Formula One race held in the Downtown Core since 2008 also acts as a magnet for tourists and residents alike.

Conclusion

This contribution sought to provide some insights into the many challenges that Grands Projets face in their design, management and implementation process. Despite the current emphasis on qualitative urban design, the role of designers, their agency in the stakeholder network and the significance of a good design rationale are issues that have received little academic attention. Through the analyses of the eight case studies—and their related secondary case studies in each city—the research aims to provide insights into causes, manifestations and implications of key urban Grands Projets.

In doing so, the research will focus on specific qualities which appear increasingly crucial as properties to be identified and strengthened in the planning and development process. Furthermore, the study will provide a framework to assess the sustainability, long- and short-term adaptability, as well as the liveability of Grands Projets.

The *Grand Projet*: Towards Adaptable and Liveable Urban Megaprojects

Bibliography

Brenner, Neil and Christian Schmid (2015). 'Towards a new epistemology of the urban?', *City* 19(2–3): 151–82.

Brundtland, Gru, Mansour Khalid, Susanna Agnelli, Sali Al-Athel, Bernard Chidzero, Lamina Fadika, Volker Hauff, Istvan Lang, Ma Shijun, Margarita Morino de Botero and others (1987). 'Our common future'.

del Cerro Santamaría, Gerardo (ed.) (2013). *Urban Megaprojects: A Worldwide View*. Bingley: Emerald Group Publishing.

Cilona, Teresa (2016). 'Future cities urban transformation and sustainable development', in *Computational Science and Its Applications— ICCSA 2016, Lecture Notes in Computer Science*, eds. Osvaldo Gervasi, Beniamino Murgante, Sanjay Misra, Ana Maria A C Rocha, Carmelo M Torre, David Taniar, Bernady O Apduhan, Elena Stankova, and Shangguang Wang, 183–97. Springer International Publishing.

Evans, Peter B (2002). *Livable Cities?: Urban Struggles for Livelihood and Sustainability*. Berkeley: University of California Press.

Hall, Peter (2014). *Cities of Tomorrow: An Intellectual History of Urban Planning and Design since 1880*. Chichester: John Wiley & Sons.

Harvey, David (2007). 'Neoliberalism and the city', in *Studies in Social Justice* 1(1): 1–2.

Imrie, Rob, Loretta Lees and Mike Raco (2009). *Regenerating London: Governance, Sustainability and Community in a Global City*. London: Routledge.

Kemper, Jan and Anne Vogelpohl (2013). 'Paradoxes of the neoliberal city', *Geographische Zeitschrift* 101(3–4): 218–34.

Lobo, Bruno (2013). 'Urban megaprojects and local planning frameworks in New York City, Paris, and Sao Paulo', in *Urban Megaprojects: A Worldwide View,* ed. Gerardo del Cerro Santamaria, 131–58. Bingley: Emerald Group Publishing.

Marcotullio, Peter J (2001). 'Asian urban sustainability in the era of globalization', *Habitat International* 25(4): 577–98.

Maynard, Lee (2008). 'Sustainable Cities'. Available from < http://leecmaynard.synthasite.com/resources/sustainable+cities.pdf> Accessed on 23 December 2016.

Ponzini, Davide (2013). 'Branded megaprojects and fading urban structure in contemporary cities', in *Urban Megaprojects: A Worldwide View*, ed. Gerardo del Cerro Santamaria, 107–29. Bingley: Emerald Group Publishing.

Schmid, Christian, Josep Acebillo and Jacques Lévy (2012). *Globalization of Urbanity*. Barcelona: Actar.

The *Grand Projet*: Towards Adaptable and Liveable Urban Megaprojects

Peter Edwards, Daniel Richards

Reconciling Urbanisation with Ecology

Ecological Challenges Facing Urban Landscapes

Rapid urbanisation over the past 50 years has disrupted the integrity of natural habitats and reduced biodiversity in many parts of the world (Sodhi et al. 2004; Yaakub et al. 2014). As established ecosystems are replaced by built infrastructure, environmental problems such as flooding (Gupta 2000; Chow et al. 2016) and high urban temperatures—often referred to as the 'urban heat island' (Chow and Roth, 2006)—tend to increase.

Especially under the high rainfall conditions in tropical and subtropical cities, a high coverage with impervious surfaces increases stormwater runoff, which can cause flash-flooding (Gupta 2000). In Singapore, for example, intense rain and flooding have increased markedly during the past few decades, which can be linked to urban expansion (Chow et al. 2016). In other tropical cities, including Bangkok, recent flooding has caused considerable loss of life and huge financial damage (Ziegler et al. 2012).

Tropical cities are particularly susceptible to the negative impacts of the urban heat island effect because tropical regions experience relatively high temperatures throughout the year. The magnitude of this effect varies depending on the season, city size and population density (Roth 2007).

Whereas temperatures in relatively small cities such as Gaborone are rarely more than 1°C higher than the surrounding countryside (Jonsson 2004), the difference may be 5°C or more in larger cities such as Mexico City (Jauregui 1997) and Singapore (Chow and Roth 2006). In climates that are already hot, these elevated temperatures can have negative effects upon people's health and well-being, as well as leading to greater energy use for cooling.

In addition to these 'self-made' problems, cities are confronted with environmental changes that are not directly (or solely) of their making. Models of climate change forecast that global average temperatures will increase by at least two degrees by the end of the century. Associated with this warming will be major changes in the patterns of rainfall.

Although more difficult to forecast than changes in temperature, global models indicate that average precipitation will increase, with storms and extreme events becoming more frequent and less predictable. It is already clear that these effects will exacerbate the problems of the urban heat island effect and increased runoff.

While individual countries and human society as a whole need to understand and prepare for a warmer world over the coming decades, cities will need to adapt to even higher temperatures, and perhaps also to greater risks of flooding.

Against this background, it becomes urgent to find ways of increasing the resilience of cities and making them less vulnerable to the potentially catastrophic effects of global change. Design concepts using plants and vegetation can contribute greatly to this effort, reducing urban temperatures and the risk of flooding, and also increasing the liveability of cities, improving public health and enhancing biodiversity.

The term 'ecosystem services' is widely used to denote the many benefits that people obtain from functioning ecosystems, including green areas within cities. These services are often considered under four main categories (MEA 2005) as outlined:

- *Provisioning ecosystem services* are those that provide useable goods such as food, building materials and fuel. Functioning ecosystems can also enhance the provision of clean water and air.
- *Regulating ecosystem services* maintain environmental conditions within safe or comfortable limits; for example, vegetation in urban green spaces can influence urban microclimates and contribute to mitigating urban heat islands. Similarly, by temporarily retaining rainwater, vegetation and unsealed land can help prevent floods following heavy rain (Breuste et al. 2013).

- *Socio-cultural ecosystem services* affect human psychology and culture; for example, trees and gardens can increase the amenity and attractiveness of the urban environment (Kleerekoper et al. 2012), and nearly all green spaces offer recreational potential (Breuste et al. 2013). Urban green spaces have been proved to directly influence human physical activity, recreation and both physical and mental health (Kaplan 1998; Nassauer et al., 2009; Tzoulas et al. 2007). As places where people meet, rest and play, public green spaces can foster social and cultural integration (Maas et al. 2009), especially among children and young adults (Seeland et al. 2009; Kazmierczak 2013).
- *Supporting services* underlie the provision of the other three categories and increase resilience to changes in environmental or social conditions. Key supporting services include pollination, which helps to maintain plant populations and biodiversity, which can increase the resilience of an ecosystem in providing services. Biodiversity can be supported in urban green spaces (Marzluff and Rodewald 2008).

Research Challenges in Using Ecological Knowledge in Urban Design

The contribution that urban green spaces make to urban transformation has long been recognised (Swanwick et al. 2003). However, most research has been in regions with a temperate climate, including in North America, Europe and China (Haase et al. 2014; Luederitz et al. 2015). Much less is known about the role of green spaces in cities of tropical Southeast Asia, where the climate is usually hotter and wetter. It is therefore important to quantify urban ecosystem services in Southeast Asia cities, and understand how these services depend upon particular plant species, vegetation types, and management practices.

To gain the greatest benefit from plants and vegetation in urban areas, information about ecosystem services needs to be readily accessible to planners and developers. Several 'toolboxes' have been developed that enable a user to map or model ecosystem services under different landscape scenarios. These include InVEST (Nelson et al. 2009), TESSA (Peh et al. 2013), and i-Tree (Nowak et al. 2002). However, none of these models were developed in Southeast Asian, or even in a tropical region, and they are typically not easy for designers to use. It is therefore desirable to develop collaborative platforms that allow the ecosystem service impacts of different design scenarios to be visualised in real time. Such tools would allow planners to make iterative amendments to existing designs, and determine the likely benefits in terms of environmental performance.

Cities in the humid tropics differ both climatically and socially from those in temperate regions (Gupta 2002; Roth 2007). Humid tropical cities generally experience higher average temperatures, and a larger proportion of the annual rainfall occurs in heavy bursts (Chang and Lau 1993). Additionally, many temperate cities are located in economically developed countries, while many tropical cities are still developing; economically, in terms of population size, and in urban density (Gupta 2002).

Using Ecosystem Services to Design Future Cities

An Overview of Ecosystem Services Research

The study of ecosystem services has developed from what was originally an economic exercise aimed at determining the value of nature (Costanza et al. 1997), to a more nuanced conceptual approach to understanding the full range of benefits that we obtain from ecosystems (Tallis and Polasky 2009; Potschin and Haines-Young 2011). Central to this approach are the trade-offs between ecosystem services, which determine the optimal use of vegetation in a particular situation. For example, a planting regime that maximises the cooling effect of vegetation may not be the best kind of green space for recreational use. Characterising ecosystem service trade-offs and examining the extent to which they can be resolved will therefore be the key to designing sustainable cities that benefit from a range of ecosystem services.

The characteristics of a plant species that influence how it grows or reproduces are known as plant functional traits. These traits, which include reproductive strategy, leaf area index, or growth rate, can be useful in understanding how particular species or groups of species influence ecosystem properties. Plant functional traits therefore offer a potential to link community structures to ecosystem functioning.

Fig. 1   Tropical cities must integrate forests and managed green spaces with the built environment, to provide ecosystem services to residents.

Fig. 2   Trees provide shade and cool the air through evapotranspiration, providing a comfortable thermal environment and spaces to relax.

Fig. 3   Public green spaces can provide great opportunities for recreation.

Recently, some researchers have attempted to quantify the connections between ecological structures and ecosystem services at small spatial and temporal scales that are relevant for ecosystem management (Quétier et al. 2007; deBello et al. 2010). This approach may help in predicting how changes in the composition of vegetation due to management could affect ecosystem services (Quétier et al. 2007), and in understanding the associated trade-offs between different services (Lavorel et al. 2011).

In principle, this approach could be used to design better management strategies for urban ecosystems (Bennet et al. 2009). For this purpose we would require information about the plant species present in different urban habitats, and their plant functional traits. If such information could be included in a three-dimensional (3D) visualisation of land management types, it would provide a powerful tool that enable planners and policy makers to quantify the benefits from different ecosystem services and weigh the trade-offs.

Used as part of a participatory decision-making process, this tool could demonstrate the value of ecosystem services such as social and cultural ecosystem services, which are commonly overlooked. This, in turn, might enable these services to be more effectively incorporated into design scenarios.

Research into Cooling and Water Regulation by Urban Vegetation

Plants cool the environment in two ways: by absorbing and reflecting radiation, and by taking up water, which evaporates through pores in their leaves and thereby taking up latent heat. Several recent studies (Lin and Lin 2010; Armson et al. 2012; Declet-Barreto et al. 2013) have shown that urban vegetation can reduce surface temperatures considerably (by as much as 9°C), and ambient air temperatures are reduced by up to 2.5°C, not only beneath trees, but also in the vicinity of wooded areas.

However, trees vary considerably in their capacity for cooling depending on factors such as foliage density, leaf thickness, leaf texture and leaf

Reconciling Urbanisation with Ecology

Fig. 4   Trees have featured heavily in Singapore's urban development for over 40 years, with green spaces provided even in some of the earliest public housing blocks.

Fig. 5   Future cities will provide ecosystem services through placing vegetation on top of and within buildings, as well as at ground level.

colour (Lin and Lin 2010). Variation in the cooling effect provided by Southeast Asian tree species or functional trait groups has not been studied in detail, limiting the potential for designers to consider this particular ecosystem service in urban areas. Similarly, while the local microclimate effects of vegetation are generally well known, we do not yet know how these local effects contribute to impact conditions across larger urban areas.

The presence of vegetation moderates runoff and reduces the risk of flooding. In particular, the tree canopy and the litter layer beneath it intercept large amounts of precipitation (amounting to several millimetres), which either evaporates from the surface or is returned to the atmosphere by transpiration, or moves slowly into the drainage system. In addition, water usually infiltrates more readily into the soil beneath vegetation than in bare areas and the higher organic content of vegetated soil increases its water-holding capacity.

As a consequence, trees in urban areas can reduce surface runoff by as much as 60 per cent compared with asphalt surfaces (Armson et al. 2012). Even treeless ecosystems with a much lower biomass such as grasslands and wetlands are important in mitigating floods as well as reducing the quantities of sediments and dissolved chemicals that move into waterways.

Water-related ecosystem services are intimately related, even in urban environments, to the local hydrological and hydraulic conditions. The risk of floods can be lessened by replacing the usual culverts and drains with 'greener' designs that use vegetation to absorb water and moderate flows. It is a disadvantage of traditional flood risk measures that severe damage usually results during large floods, especially since these measures are typically designed for relatively frequent forcing events (e.g. every 10–15 years). In contrast, an urban drainage system that incorporates ecosystem services can exhibit a more gradual response that allows a better control of damage and increases the system's resilience (e.g. Wagner and Breil 2013). Restored urban river corridors where the riparian vegetation is in dynamic equilibrium with the river can be effective to this purpose besides contributing to aesthetic and recreational ecosystem services.

Enhancing Ecosystem Services in Humid Tropical Cities

Tropical cities must utilise ecosystem services better in the future. As well as providing spaces for recreation and relaxation, green spaces within the urban fabric can contribute to the cooling of the city and reduce the risk of flooding. However, getting the greatest benefit from green areas is complicated because we know too little about how different plant species contribute to ecosystem services, and how individual trees contribute to city-wide networks of greenery.

To allow architects and urban planners to utilise ecosystem services effectively in design, we must first understand the benefits provided by different tree species, for a range of tree sizes and at different times of the year. Measurements taken from individual trees can be scaled up to estimate ecosystem service provision across a whole landscape, for example by using remote-sensing of satellite images (Friess et al. 2015), or mechanistic ecohydrological modelling based on land cover data (Fatichi et al. 2012).

Information on ecosystem service provision is only useful if it can be successfully translated into design. To enable designers to make use of data on ecosystem services, these data must be presented in a way that is understandable to non-specialists. Furthermore, designers are more likely to find an optimal solution if they can compare a range of scenarios in real time, for example using 3D interactive platforms (Grêt-Regamey et al. 2013).

Singapore as an Example of Tropical Urbanisation

Singapore is a prosperous island city-state with a population of some 5.3 million. Like many other large cities, the urban heat island effect is considerable, reaching as much as 7°C in the city centre at certain times of the day (Chow and Roth 2006).

However, the densely urban areas in Singapore are balanced with areas of green space, and over 50 per cent of the land area is covered in vegetation (Yee et al. 2011). Since the 1970s, greening has been a priority, and the island holds a botanic gardens, many nature reserves, parks and green corridors (Briffett et al. 2004).

'Gardening in the sky' is also increasingly practised, with the Housing and Development Board promoting roof-top gardens and green walls (Tan 2013). An important concept that has guided the recent development of Singapore has been the 'city in a garden'. This expresses more than a general wish for a pleasant, leafy city with abundant trees, but is the basis for detailed design and planning decisions. Similarly, there has been recent interest in more environmentally friendly design, particularly relating to water resources. The ABC (Active, Beautiful, and Clean) Waters programme has encouraged projects that aim to restore ecological functions to urban waterways, most notably in the case of a river restoration project in the Bishan public park (NParks 2016).

Ecosystem services are typically associated with natural and semi-natural vegetation types, but 27 per cent of Singapore is covered with managed vegetation (Yee et al. 2010). Although urban parks, secondary forests and green corridors are the prominent elements within the urban area, the smaller green areas—including gardens, roadside verges, vertical gardens, and roof-top vegetation—may also contribute to ecosystem services.

To grow sustainably in the future, Singapore, like other tropical cities, must improve the delivery of ecosystem services by appropriate management of green areas. Demand for these services is likely to increase in the future as the pressures of climate change and a growing urban population persist. The population is expected to grow from 5.3 to 6.9 million by 2030 (Prime Minister's Office 2013), which will put further pressures on the limited green space on the island (MND 2013). Until now, efforts to create a green environment in Singapore have focused on the aesthetic and recreational value of plants and vegetation, and their contribution to biodiversity (Tan et al. 2010). Little is known about the role of urban green spaces in providing other ecosystem services, making it difficult to make quantitative predictions about the impacts of new developments.

Singapore is the most economically developed country in Southeast Asia and it has sometimes been cited to illustrate the negative impacts that rapid urbanisation can have on biodiversity and ecosystem integrity (Sodhi et al. 2004). However, other cities in the region continue to urbanise, and will soon face the challenge of reconciling urbanisation with demand for ecosystem services. Other rapidly growing cities in Southeast Asia may thus be able to learn from Singapore's experiences, both positive and negative, helping them to protect existing ecosystem services and develop new urban typologies that enhance the provision of ecosystem services.

Bibliography

Armson D, P Stringer, and R Ennos (2013). 'The effect of street trees and amenity grass on urban surface water runoff in Manchester, UK', *Urban Forestry & Urban Greening*, 12: 282–86.

Bennett, Elena M, Garry D Peterson, and Line J Gordon (2009). 'Understanding relationships among multiple ecosystem services', *Ecology Letters*, 12: 1394–1404.

Breuste J, D Haase, T Elmqvist (2013). 'Urban landscapes and ecosystem services', in *Ecosystem Services in Agricultural and Urban Landscapes*, ed. S Wratten, H Sandhu, R Cullen, R Costanza, 83–104. Chichester: Wiley-Blackwell.

Chang J H, and L S Lau (2005). 'Appendix a—Definition of the humid tropics', *Hydrology and Water Management in the Humid Tropics*. Cambridge: Cambridge University Press.

Chow, W T L, Cheong, B D, and Ho B H (2016). 'A multimethod approach towards assessing urban flood patterns and its associated vulnerabilities in Singapore', *Advances in Meteorology*. DOI: 10.1155/2016/7159132

Chow, Winston T L, and Matthias Roth (2006). 'Temporal dynamics of the urban heat island of Singapore', *International Journal of Climatology*, 26: 2243–60.

Costanza, Robert, Ralph d'Arge, Rudolf de Groot, Stephen Farber, Monica Grasso, Bruce Hannon, and others (1997). 'The value of the world's ecosystem services and natural capital', *Nature*, 387: 253–60.

de Bello F, S Lavorel, S Diaz, R Harrington, J H C Cornelissen, R D Bardgett, M P Berg, P Cipriotti, C K Feld, D Hering,

P M da Silva, S G Potts, L Sandin, J P Sousa, J Storkey, D A Wardle, P A Harrison (2010). 'Towards an assessment of multiple ecosystem processes and services via functional traits', *Biodiversity and Conservation*. 19: 2873–93.

Declet-Barreto, Juan, Anthony J Brazel, Chris A Martin, Winston T L Chow, and Sharon L Harlan (2013). 'Creating the park cool island in an inner-city neighborhood: Heat mitigation strategy for Phoenix, AZ', *Urban Ecosystems*, 16: 617–35.

Fatichi S, V Y Ivanov, and E Caporali (2012). 'A mechanistic ecohydrological model to investigate complex interactions in cold and warm water-controlled environments: 2. Spatiotemporal analyses', *Journal of Advances in Modelling Earth Systems*, 4: 1–31.

Friess, Daniel A, Daniel R Richards, and Valerie X H Phang (2015). 'Mangrove forests store high densities of carbon across the tropical urban landscape of Singapore', *Urban Ecosystems*, DOI: 10.1007/s11252-015-0511-3

Grêt-Regamey, Adrienne, Enrico Celio, Thomas M Klein, and Ulrike Wissen Hayek, (2013). 'Understanding ecosystem services trade-offs with interactive procedural modeling for sustainable urban planning', *Landscape and Urban Planning*, 109: 107–16.

Gupta A (2002). 'Geoindicators for tropical urbanisation', *Environmental Geology*, 42: 736–42.

Haase, Dagmar, Neele Larondelle, Erik Andersson, Martina Artmann, Sara Borgström, Jürgen Breuste, and others (2014). 'A quantitative review of urban ecosystem service assessments: Concepts, models, and implementation', *Ambio*, 43: 413–33.

FCL INDICIA 01 A HIGH-DENSITY MIXED-USE CITIES

Jauregui E (1997). 'Heat island development in Mexico City', *Atmospheric Environment*, 31: 3821–31.

Jonsson P (2004). 'Vegetation as an urban climate control in the subtropical city of Gaborone, Botswana', *International Journal of Climatology*. 24: 1307–22.

Kaplan R S Kaplan and R L Ryan (1998). *With People in Mind: Design and Management of Everyday Nature*. Washington DC: Island Press.

Kazmierczak, A (2013). 'The contribution of local parks to neighbourhood social ties', *Landscape and Urban Planning,* 109 (1): 31–44.

Kleerekoper L, M van Esch, T B Salcedo (2012). 'How to make a city climate-proof, addressing the urban heat island effect', *Resources Conservation and Recycling*, 64: 30–8.

Lavorel S, K Grigulis, P Lamarque, M-P Colace, D Garden, J Girel, and others (2011). 'Using plant functional traits to understand the landscape distribution of multiple ecosystem services', *Journal of Ecology*, 99: 135–47.

Lin, Bau Show, and Yann J Lin (2010). 'Cooling effect of shade trees with different characteristics in a subtropical urban park', *HortScience*, 45: 83–6.

Luederitz, Christopher, Ebba Brink, Fabienne Gralla, Verena Hermeling-meier, Moritz Meyer, Lisa Niven, and others (2015). 'A review of urban ecosystem services: Six key challenges for future research', *Ecosystem Services*, 14: 98–112.

Maas J, S M E van Dillen, R A Verheij and P P Groenewegen (2009). 'Social contacts as a possible mechanism behind the relation between green space and health', *Health and Place* 15: 586–95.

Marzluff J M, A D Rodewald (2008). 'Conserving biodiversity in urbanizing areas: nontraditional views from a bird's perspective', *Cities and the Environment* 1 (2): 6–25.

Millennium Ecosystem Assessment (2005). *Ecosystems and Human Well-being. Health Synthesis*. Washington DC: Island Press.

MND 2013. *Land Use Plan*. Ministry of National Development. Available from: <http://www.mnd.gov.sg/landuseplan/> Accessed on August 2016.

Nassauer, J I, Z Wang and E Dayrell (2009). 'What will the neighbors think? Cultural norms and ecological design', *Landscape and Urban Planning* 92: 282–92.

Nelson, Erik, Guillermo Mendoza, James Regetz, Stephen Polasky, Heather Tallis, D Richard Cameron, and others (2009). 'Modelling multiple ecosystem services, biodiversity conservation, commodity production, and tradeoffs at landscape scales', *Frontiers in Ecology and the Environment*, 7: 4–11.

Nowak, David J, Daniel E Crane, Jack C Stevens, and Myriam Ibarra (2002). 'Brooklyn's Urban Forest', *United States Department of Agriculture General Technical Report NE-290*.

NParks (2016). *Your Guide to Bishan-Ang Mo Kio Park*. Available from <https://www.nparks.gov.sg/~/media/nparks-real-content/gardens-parks-and-nature/diy-walk/diy-walk-pdf-files/bishan-amk-park.pdf> Accessed on 16 August 2016.

Peh, Kelvin S H, Andrew Balmford, Richard B Bradbury, Claire Brown, Stuart H M Butchart, Francine M R Hughes, and others (2013). 'TESSA: A toolkit for rapid assessment of ecosystem services at sites of biodiversity conservation importance', *Ecosystem Services,* 5: 51–7.

Potschin M B, and R H Haines-Young (2011). 'Ecosystem services: Exploring a geographical perspective', *Progress in Physical Geography*, 35: 575–94.

Prime Minister's Office (2013). *A Sustainable Population for a Dynamic Singapore*. Government of Singapore.

Quétier F, S Lavorel, W Thuiller, I Davies (2007). Plant-trait-based modeling assessment of ecosystem-service sensitivity to land-use change. *Ecological Applications* 17: 2377–86.

Roth M (2007). Review of urban climate research in (sub)tropical regions. *International Journal of Climatology* 27: 1859–73.

Seeland K, S Dübendorfer and R Hansmann (2009). 'Making friends in Zürich's urban forests and parks: The role of public green space for social inclusion of youths from different cultures', *Forest Policy and Economics* 11: 10–17.

Sodhi, Navjot S, Lian Pin Koh, Barry W Brook, and Peter K L Ng (2004). 'Southeast Asian biodiversity: An impending disaster', *Trends in Ecology & Evolution*, 19: 654–60.

Swanwick C, N Dunnett, H Woolley (2003). 'Nature, role and value of green space in towns and cities: An overview', *Built Environment,* 29 (2): 94–106.

Tallis, Heather, and Stephen Polasky (2009). 'Mapping and valuing ecosystem services as an approach for conservation and natural-resource management', *Annals of the New York Academy of Sciences*, 1162: 265–83.

Tan P Y (2013). *A Vertical Garden City, Singapore*. Singapore: Straits Times Press.

Tan P Y, R T Corlett and Hugh T W Tan (eds) (2010). *A Field Guide to the Native Garden @ Hortpark: An Urban Oasis of the Native*

Flora and Fauna of Singapore. Singapore: Centre for Urban Greenery and Ecology, National Parks Board, and National University of Singapore.

Tzoulas K, K Korpela, S Venn, V Yli-Pelkonen, A Kazmierczak, J Niemela, J and P James (2007). 'Promoting ecosystem and human health in urban areas using green Infrastructure: A literature review', *Landscape and Urban Planning* 81: 167–78.

Wagner I, and P Breil (2013). 'The role of ecohydrology in creating more resilient cities', *Ecohydrology and Hydrobiology* 13 (2): 113–34.

Yaakub S M, McKenzie L J, Erftemeijer P L A, Bouma T, Todd P A (2014). 'Courage under fire: Seagrass persistence adjacent to a highly urbanised city-state', *Marine Pollution Bulletin*, 83: 417–24.

Yee A T K, Richard T Corlett, S C Liew, and Hugh T W Tan (2011). 'The vegetation of Singapore—An updated map', *Gardens' Bulletin Singapore*, 63: 205–12.

Ziegler A D, Lim H S, Tantasarin C, Jachowski N R, Wasson R (2012). 'Floods, false hope, and the future', *Hydrological Processes*, 26: 1747–50.

Arno Schlueter, Jimeno A. Fonseca, Gabriel Happle, Shanshan Hsieh, Zhongming Shi

Multi-Scale Energy Systems for Low-Carbon Cities

The Intergovernmental Panel on Climate Change (IPCC) highlights the influence of the built environment on global energy consumption and climate change. Buildings account for 32 per cent of the global energy consumption, causing 19 per cent of greenhouse gas emissions. Today, 75 per cent of primary energy is consumed in urban areas. Energy consumption projections in buildings range from double to triple by 2050 (Lucon et al. 2014) which prize cities for the transition towards a low-carbon society.

Even though the knowledge, practice and technology to make the transition exist, many barriers prevent the application of cost-efficient measures to increase energy efficiency and reduce carbon emissions of the built environment. Due to their long life cycles, buildings that are not transformed and cities that are not designed to operate with low-carbon emissions endanger meeting the global goals for climate change mitigation.

Historically, the availability of renewable energy sources has been an important parameter for the establishment, growth and prosperity of cities. The access to energy has been described as even more important for stability than the access to food (Schott 1997). When only renewable energy sources were available, the spatial vicinity to these resources has influenced the location, size, functions and form of cities. With available, powerful, cheap and manageable energy from fossil fuels, this relation has changed, leading to detached and centralised energy infrastructures.

While developing nations still struggle to establish such a reliable infrastructure, industrialized nations face the challenge of transitioning towards a new energy system by reintroducing renewable energy at large scale.

Energy Consumption and Comfort

Thermal comfort is a complex notion affected by temperature, humidity, air velocity and heat exchange with the environment. To feel comfortable means to be satisfied with the thermal environment (American Society of Heating Refrigerating and Air-Conditioning Engineers 2013).

Buildings can be described as active agents of comfort in the urban environment. Their primary function is to provide shelter for work and living. Elements of architecture at interplay with technical systems influence and balance the indoor conditions of temperature, air, humidity and light to desired levels. In tropical (hot and humid) climates, buildings can contribute additionally to outdoor thermal comfort by providing shading, a cooler microclimate and even providing outdoor air conditioning services (Figure 1).

Buildings, however, can also have a negative effect on urban comfort. Air-conditioning systems in buildings, for example, add noise and reject heat to the outdoor environment. Additionally, the surfaces of buildings warm up and store heat, which radiates back into streets and exterior places. When buildings obstruct natural wind flows, they mitigate the removal of heat. Such effects contribute to the increase of air temperature in cities, provoking a greater demand for cooling, which then increases the amount of energy consumed in urban areas. The resulting uncomfortable conditions of the exterior endanger the health of city dwellers and inhibit more activities that could have taken place outdoors (Figure 2).

Challenges related to human comfort and energy consumption in cities have to be addressed in a holistic, multi-scale approach. Such an approach should discuss the intelligent planning of buildings and open spaces, and novel strategies for energy efficiency. To do it though, the exact role of the building as an active agent of thermal comfort in future low carbon cities has yet to be defined.

How can buildings actively contribute to indoor and outdoor comfort without compromising the energy needs of the future? How does this interact with urban planning and design?

Efficiency and Local Energy Production

When it comes to developing strategies for energy efficiency in cities, working at the scale of the individual building is too limited and that of the entire city is too complex and perhaps abstract. The scale of the neighbourhood and district, however, bears an interesting potential to increase energy efficiency, which means delivering the same services with less energy.

Energy efficiency can be achieved through a variety of strategies: by designing buildings for cooling demand, identifying efficient energy conversion technologies, coupling consumers and producers of energy and by using efficient appliances. District scale energy systems open up the opportunity to exploit local renewable sources and to use efficienct large-scale technology and thus provide efficient pathways of energy production (Figure 3). They have proven to be a cost-effective choice for reducing the carbon footprint of cities (The UP-RES consortium 2013). District networks tap into multiple local energy sources such as renewable energy and waste heat, distributing energy to multiple customers in the vicinity. Examples of such applications in Singapore (Kee 2010) and Hong Kong (Chow et al. 2004) reveal the benefits of more space, efficiency, reliability and cost-effectiveness.

New technologies bear the potential to further improve efficiency and cost-benefits of district energy systems. For instance, refrigerant-based district networks could cut up to 40 per cent the size of the distribution network, save up to 80 per cent of energy when connecting heating (industrial) and cooling customers (residential, commercial), and reduce upfront costs significantly (Henchoz, et al 2015). Building technologies such as those used in the 3for2 approach, which features decentralised ventilation and high-temperature sensible cooling, are able to drastically reduce the operational energy needed as well as to reduce space and material consumption in buildings (Schlueter et al. 2016).

To foster such technological advances at district scale, new city developments should integrate the design of energy infrastructure to interact with the shape, form and quality of urban space. This is important as urban design does not only define the demand but also the technical and spatial options for the sustainable delivery of energy in cities.

The programme and morphology of buildings define the available space for clean technology (e.g. roof-top area for photovoltaic panels), the sources of waste heat (e.g. excess heat from data centres and industry), the connectivity rules between energy networks, and the investment costs for energy generation (Fonseca and Schlueter 2015; Fonseca et al. 2016a). With this in mind, the important research questions to advance energy efficiency in cities are: Which future district scale concepts and technology allow further increases in energy efficiency in tropical cities? How can potential synergies between energy systems and urban design be identified, leveraged and synthesised?

Systems Integration into Urban Design

As interdisciplinary research is gaining importance, it is common to find professionals from engineering, economics, and sociology touching the ground of architecture, urban design and city planning. Similarly, architects, urban designers and city planners are complementing their work with green technologies, human comfort and economic considerations. To achieve a higher energy performance, neither designers nor energy engineers can work in an isolated manner.

The architectural historian and critic Colin Rowe and Professor Fred Koetter borrowed the *Theory of the Hedgehog and the Fox* from Isaiah Berlin to explain the monism (the hedgehog) and pluralism (the fox) of buildings and cities in *Collage City* (Rowe and Koetter 1978). A hedgehog knows only one great topic and links everything else to that while, in contrast, a fox knows many topics and pursues diverse goals.

A city is not a make of individual components but a system of elements interacting with each other. All issues in cities require more of a 'fox-like' thinking. Synergy is beyond the sum of professionals of different disciplines. It requires systematic collaboration. In synergy, urban design and energy systems work synchronously instead of successively; in other words, they make the whole greater than the sum of its parts.

Multi-Scale Energy Systems
for Low-Carbon Cities

Fig. 1   Shading and air-conditioning installations in Clarke Quay, Singapore.
Fig. 2   Illustrative example depicting the thermal influence of air conditioning units
         in buildings to outdoor comfort.

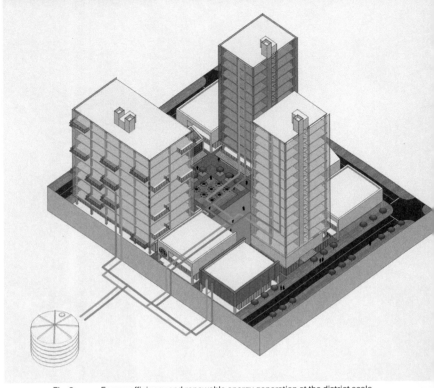

Fig. 3   Energy efficiency and renewable energy generation at the district scale.

Like pipes buried underground, the energy infrastructure is always hidden beneath the surface of the city. Though seldom noticed, the invention and incorporation of new technologies shape our cities. For example, automobiles brought highways to the city; steel structures raised the height of buildings and mobile phones kicked phone booths out of the streets. A district cooling plant, instead of individual cooling facilities for each building, saves the building roof-tops for gardens and improves the energy performance of large areas.

From individual buildings to an urban block, from several districts to a larger region, a synergetic approach requires a multi-scale consideration and integration of urban design and energy systems engineering. To allow such a holistic approach, research on building technology needs to shift from high-performing components to high-performing systems interacting with local infrastructure. For example, a green building does not necessarily add a positive effect on its adjacent environment as it might miss out on the opportunity to receive clean energy from more effective and alternative sources.

In this order of ideas, high-performing components may make up mediocre (even poor) performing systems when just viewed as a single entity. How can we bring high-performing systems to the agenda of urban design in cities? How can this be achieved for the benefit of social, economic and environmental sustainability?

Dealing with Uncertainty

When discussing the future of cities it is relevant to obtain an understanding how certain, plausible or possible this future might be. This is especially so in respect to changes in technology, economy, climate and population which over the past few years have shifted the agenda of urban development.

Today, plans of energy infrastructure in cities depend on long-term projections of fuel prices, demands and resource availability of up to half a century ahead. These projections are influenced by urban planning policies, local socioeconomics and technology. When these projections are highly speculative,

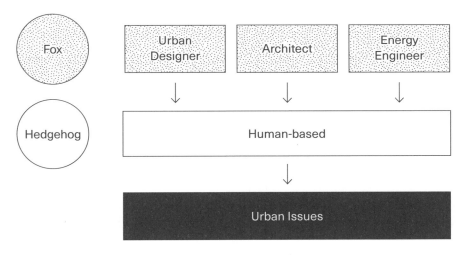

Fig. 4   Theory of the hedgehog and the fox problem in energy systems integration.

the financial and environmental risks of energy infrastructure increase.

A classic example of this phenomenon is the series of predictions of energy consumption made in 1960s for the new millennium. In these predictions, Morgan and Keith found the estimates of most energy agencies to be up to three times more than the real demand held during 2000 (Morgan and Keith 2008).

In energy systems design, we know what we know—the materials, components, machines and physics of operation. There are also known unknowns—future states of demands, prices and policies—and unknown unknowns such as unpredictable events that lead to a failure or disruption. On the other hand, there are unknown knowns—or things that are over-looked when addressing the problem from a single perspective (i.e. urban, economic, technical etc.).

Today's way to handle uncertainty in energy systems design is focused on uncovering the known unknowns. These are plausible events or states that may well affect the carbon emissions, energy efficiency and financial costs of infrastructure. We design energy systems to achieve a targeted performance and to be robust to variations of known factors. Such variations are at their best described by a probability of occurrence, which is our best representation of the (unknown) future from what we know today (a statistical extrapolation of historical facts). This way

of dealing with uncertainty might not apply to the unknown unknowns, which expose a higher risk for operation and performance as we cannot predict them.

Scenario analysis is a technique widely used to create plausible alternatives of the future (Stwart et al., 2004). This involves a possible future point in the space of all possibilities. These are storylines made of 'cause and effect' relation or 'what-if, then' cases in the story of a future city. In principle, it is an interesting technique to explore unknown unknowns including potential chain reactions. However, these scenarios lack a measure of the likelihood of the events leading to that plausible future as they normally omit any use of probability.

Future design of district energy systems might incorporate the trajectory of future events at the pace of the urban development of the district. Such an approach may translate in studies of uncertainty, which break down a scenario in time intervals with accumulative probabilities of occurrence. The approach may well measure the probability of the unknown unknowns based on the evolution of known unknowns over time.

This potential approach is, nonetheless, based on the classical assumption of what energy systems should be. That is, systems that do the 'extra mile' of energy production and cash flow. If this concept is the aim, can we therefore propose systems and components that better adapt to changes in urban

Multi-Scale Energy Systems
for Low-Carbon Cities

development and thus decrease the risk of techno-logical and economic failure? How do we best handle uncertainty in designing future district energy systems?

Advanced, Integrated Design Tools

The analysis and design of future synergetic district energy systems implies a new generation of computational models that incorporate energy efficiency strategies with the morphology of buildings and districts. Such models need to identify interdependencies, synergies and thresholds that influence the design of the cities and their energy infrastructure as part of an integrated process.

From the academic perspective, such tools should allow researchers to model under uncertainty how future trajectories of development might influence energy systems performance. Practitioners might find these set of tools useful to improve the energy efficiency of urban areas. The process requires a new concept of operations that exploits and integrates urban and energy systems decisions into practice. This aspect might even require a new generation of professionals with adequate knowledge in these areas.

Until this new generation of professionals arises, these tools could be valuable presently in aiding city planners with impact analysis of their designs on the overall performance of an area. It is in their hands to define and optimise the variables that influence the demand and supply of energy in cities such as building typology, building use and street patterns.

Future users of toolsets such as the City Energy Analyst (CEA) under research and development at ETH Zürich (Figure 5) are able to investigate the trade-offs between different urban forms to the type, dimension, spatial configuration and associated investment risks of energy infrastructure (Fonseca et al. 2016b). The challenge remains: how can such tools be used effectively in design practice and decision making? Who are the users and what do they need to know to be able to use them?

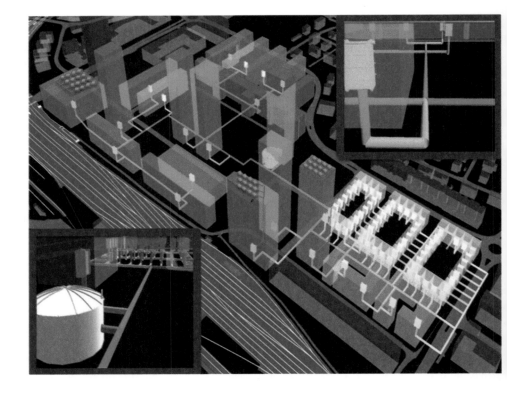

Fig. 5   Representation of energy demand and energy infrastructure in a simulation tool.

Conclusions

Mitigating climate change demands a redefinition of the relationship between city and its energy systems in terms of assessing and controlling future demands, developing systems for renewable energy supply, human comfort and well-being. Similarly, adapting to climate change requires a strong definition of the way we discuss the uncertainty, especially the known unknowns and the unknown knowns that appear within a 'fox-like' thinking.

District-scale energy systems open up many opportunities to increase energy efficiency, reduce carbon emissions and increase comfort of city dwellers. Future research needs to address the aforementioned questions to reshape future energy systems in urban areas. As it is not possible to look at energy systems in a detached manner from the environment for which they were designed, the goal is to identify and leverage the interactions and synergies between urban design and energy systems that facilitate the design of future low-carbon cities.

New computational tools can help to analyse these phenomena and develop a deeper understanding of quantities, qualities and interactions of city dynamics. Still, to make an impact, these tools need to be designed and incorporated into urban design decision making and planning practice.

Bibliography

American Society of Heating Refrigerating and Air-Conditioning Engineers (2013). *ASHRAE Handbook—Fundamentals*. Atlanta: ASHRAE.

Bruelisauer, Marcel, Sonja Berthold, Lei-Ya Wong, Zuliandi Azli, Cheng-kai Wang, Christian Ribback and Matthias Mast (2015). *Reclaiming Backlanes. Design Vision for Increasing Building Performance and Reprogramming Public Space*, eds. Marcel Bruelisauer and Sonja Berthold. Singapore: World Scientific.

Chow T T, W H Au, Raymond Yau, Vincent Cheng, Apple Chan and K F Fong (2004). 'Applying district-cooling technology in Hong Kong', *Applied Energy* 79(3): 275–89.

Fonseca, Jimeno A, Thuy-An Nguyen, Arno Schlueter and Francois Marechal (2016a). 'City Energy Analyst (CEA): Integrated framework for analysis and optimization of building energy systems in neighborhoods and city districts', *Energy and Buildings* 113: 202–26.

Fonseca, Jimeno A and Arno Schlueter (2015). 'Integrated model for characterization of spatiotemporal building energy consumption patterns in neighborhoods and city districts', *Applied Energy* 142: 247–65.

Fonseca, Jimeno A, Daren Thomas, Anja Willmann, Amr Elesawy and Arno Schlueter (2016b). 'The city energy analyst toolbox V0.1', in *Proccedings of SBE 2016*, 1–6, Zurich.

Henchoz, Samuel, Céline Weber, François Maréchal, and Daniel Favrat (2015). 'Performance and profitability perspectives of a CO_2 based district energy network in Geneva's city centre', *Energy* 85 (June): 221–35. DOI: 10.1016/j.energy. 2015.03.079.

Kee, Tey Peng (2010). 'District cooling as an energy and economically efficient urban utility—its implementation at Marina Bay business district in Singapore'. Available from <http://www. singaporepower.com.sg> Accessed on 19 December 2016.

Lucon O D Ürge-Vorsatz, A Zain Ahmed, H Akbari, P Bertoldi, L F Cabeza, N Eyre, A Gadgil, L D D Harvey, Y Jiang, E Liphoto, S Mirasgedis, S Murakami, J Parikh, C Pyke and M V Vilariño (2014). 'Buildings', in *Climate Change 2014: Mitigation of Climate Change: Contribution of Working Group III to the Fifth Assessment Report of the Intergovernmental Panel on Climate Change*, eds. Marilin Brown and Tamas Palvolgyi, 1–44. Intergovernmental Panel on Climate Change.

Morgan M Granger and David W Keith (2008). 'Improving the way we think about projecting future energy use and emissions of carbon dioxide', *Climatic Change* 90(3): 189–215.

Rowe, Colin and Fred Koetter (1978). *Collage City*. Cambridge, Massachusetts: MIT press.

Schlueter, Arno, Adam Rysanek, Clayton Miller, Jovan Pantelic, Forrest Meggers, Matthias Mast, Marcel Bruelisauer and Chen Kian Wee (2016). '3for2 : Realizing spatial, material, and energy savings through integrated design', *CTBUH Journal* (II): 40–5.

Schott, Dieter (1997). 'Energie und stadt in Europa: Von der vorindustriellen 'Holznot' bis zur ölkrise der 1970er jahre'. Franz Steiner Verlag.

The UP-RES consortium (2013). *Energy Distribution: District Heating and Cooling—DHC*.

Weber, Céline and Daniel Favrat (2010). 'Conventional and advanced CO_2 based district energy systems', *Energy* 35(12): 5070–81.

Multi-Scale Energy Systems for Low-Carbon Cities

Thomas Schroepfer

Dense and Green Building Typologies

A Paradigm of Paradigms

The global rapid urbanisation is, by now, an incontrovertible reality. From Lagos to Lahore, Seoul to São Paulo, economic, political, and social dynamics are driving people into cities in great numbers (UN DESA 2008; see also Urbanisation Indicators, this volume). The accompanying continual and radical recasting of the form of our urban environments is often considered as a process of unadulterated metastasis which, depending on a host of variables, tends to result in sprawl that maintains the preceding human density or even increases not only the net area of human population centres, but also their density.

Problems associated with density include urban heat island effects and excessive waste, poorer ecosystem quality, loss of privacy and direct sunlight, and reductions in our physical and mental wellbeing (Boyko 2014). Density, however, as many leading architects of the twentieth century have demonstrated, can be designed and designed well. It can be the ultimate test of intelligent design and, at its best, generate compact and liveable urban environments that make our lives more practical, manageable and urbane.

In the midst of the current ecological turn, one cannot omit from the list of desirable benefits the value of being in greater sync with the natural environment. To be sure, density has the potential to bring a certain amount of marked ecological benefits, chief among them being the consolidation of resources. These are more likely to be economically utilised,

be they fossil fuels or food. Yet like urbanisation, the process of becoming ecological in a dense world can happen with design volition. Design, on the other hand, appears to be more integral to becoming more ecological than it is to becoming denser. In other words, being dense and being 'green' are not synonymous to the extent that they have often thought to be. This essay advocates for an integrative understanding of the two as well as a more holistic formulation of a twenty-first century architecture and urban design paradigm.

The effort to define such a paradigm and to set forth templates and examples for it, while new in itself, emerges organically from earlier paradigms that began to coalesce in the wake of the environmentalist and re-urbanisation movements of the 1960s. A particularly critical moment was the publication of Reyner Banham's *Architecture of the Well-Tempered Environment* in 1969. While many seeking to contextualise ecological thinking in architecture have duly looked to his 1971 publication *Los Angeles: The Architecture of Four Ecologies,* Banham's articulation of the so-called 'well-tempered' environment was not as divorced from urban issues as has hitherto been thought and it is perhaps even more instructive as a metathesis.

The *Well-Tempered Environment* makes the compelling case that the harmonisation of major population centres with architecture is a question of mass. Banham explains how physical massiveness in architecture emerged from antiquity as the Western's architectural tradition's foremost preoccupation. Massiveness comprised not only the advantages of 'perdurable' shelter but also the symbolic power of technological achievement vis-à-vis monumentality (Banham 1969).

Banham's observation makes clear the dramatic paradigm shift wrought on our relationship with nature by the rise of the machine and explains it as primarily a question of the level of density, more precisely of material density. Rammed earth, massive stone and bulky wood construction techniques would give way to the balloon frame, cast iron and lightweight steel with the beginning of the modern era. Along with this shift from relatively heavy to relatively light materials came a higher mediation with mechanised systems integrated to the lightweight architectural mainframe. Buildings became apparatuses of minimised physical appearance for 'perfect' environments in general and cities in particular, where

75   Fig. 1   Sky gardens at PARKROYAL on Pickering by WOHA, Singapore.
Fig. 2   Roof terrace of Villa Savoye by Le Corbusier, Poissy, France, 1931.

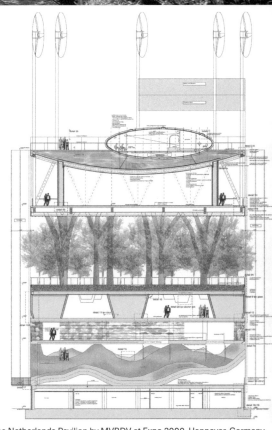

Fig. 3   The interior of the Netherlands Pavilion by MVRDV at Expo 2000, Hannover, Germany.

Fig. 4   Section of the Netherlands Pavilion by MVRDV at Expo 2000, Hannover, Germany.

Fig. 5   Rendering of Ateliers Jean Nouvel, 10000 Santa Monica Boulevard (Green Blade), Los Angeles, California, USA.

they were most commonly staged—a 'sub nature', as David Gissen described it (2009). This transformation furnished unprecedented human comfort that went along with an alienation from the natural world, which until recently was thought of as lamentable only by the postmodern and poetic sensibilities.

However, in recent decades it has become clear that more was lost in this process than just a romantic vista and the smell of flowers (or of brick or even concrete). We have ceded the possibility of the city being a part of *nature* in favour of *naturalising* it into our technological, and consequently architectural, repertoire. This specific ecological turn is not to suggest a 'return to nature' but instead a more sustained attempt to transpose the benefits of mass and massiveness from the scale of material to the scale of architecture. We can achieve ecological balance in today's cities comparable to the way we once had at the scale of the building. To do so, it is necessary to retool our understanding of human density to become a question of the massivity of scale, not of large size and in turn see our cities as places where being dense *and* green holds the promise of paradigms that

have been difficult to achieve through the trials and errors of the twentieth century.

One can find antecedents for this shift in thinking in many historical examples: from the Hanging Gardens of Babylon via the tight knitting of Medieval European cities to Le Corbusier's subtle but critical placement of the 'landscape' atop, rather than next to, the Villa Savoye in 1931. Yet the issues at stake are ultimately specific to our time, negotiating the technological and population conditions in which we have found ourselves in recent decades.

The New Dense and Green Paradigm

A host of buildings completed mostly since the turn of the millennium offer important insights into the ways in which the diverse channels have rallied around an almost subconscious movement, which we are only just beginning to recognise.

An important moment in the evolution of the dense and green paradigm is the Netherlands Pavilion at the Expo 2000 in Hannover. The pavilion has largely been considered the Expo's most successful and likely the most adapt interlocutor of the overall themes of the exposition: 'man, nature and technology' (Flamme-Jaspers 2000). The fair's programming stressed the capacity for design to mediate a balance between those three entities through exploring the best practices for global human coexistence. Design company MVRDV's interpretation of the task in the context of the Netherlands Pavilion consisted of a densely stacked, airy building comprising six distinct levels and exhibition features that signify distinct ecosystems of the Dutch landscape. A main ground level, conceived as a grotto, hoists the structure aloft through three root-like pillars and is in turn topped by layers addressing the themes of agriculture, oysters, forest, rain and water.

The tightly stacked plates and the didactic and immersive environments that they contain pay tribute to Dutch successes in negotiating one of the world's most densely populated nations with a progressive design culture. Each level creatively demonstrates or proposes architectural solutions to the problem of the day. While the structure's character is primarily one of a demonstrative showpiece, it also has a number of synthetic and original architectonic qualities. For one, the pavilion bears out the supposition that varying ecological strategies for buildings can be juxtaposed, as opposed to integrated, and that this can be a point of aesthetic interest, not discord. Moreover, the apparent 'trick' of the densification and overlay of the programs further spur the possibilities of thinking of a 'green' architecture as one that could just as easily be oriented vertically as it could be horizontally.

Many recent works by Jean Nouvel are emblematic of how the dense and green paradigm has been brought to term by architects who did not originate their careers with the ideas of ecological design. Nouvel's own shifts have been gradual and to some extent demonstrate the uneasy marriage of 'autonomous' formal concerns in architecture and the contingent conditions of both ecological and density-driven design. Nouvel's 2008 design for a residential tower in Los Angeles' Century City, nicknamed the 'Green Blade', is a case in point. Sitting on a 2.4 acre site and rising 45 storeys, Nouvel's design appears at first glance to be a rather typical high-rise luxury condominium development. Upon closer inspection of the design, however, a number of subtle and innovative adaptations make themselves evident, in

Fig. 6   Bosco Verticale by Stefano Boeri Architetti, Milan, Italy.
Fig. 7   The Office of Riyue Nishizawa, Vertical Garden House, Tokyo, Japan.

Fig. 8   Aerial view of the Interlace by OMA/Büro Ole Scheeren/RSP, Singapore.

particular the building's very thin profile and its extremely reductive treatment of the façade, which is rendered as not much more than scaffolding with affixed glass sheet. The building's profile is intended to create a floor-through plan, which eliminates the need for artificial light entirely during daytime, while the façade construction is intended to furnish the application of an extensive programme of planters, which cover the building with a display of plant life indigenous to southern California.

In Milan, Stefano Boeri, Gianandrea Barreca and Giovanni La Varra's Bosco Verticale is a veritable celebration of architecture as an organism. The architects have collaborated closely with botanists and horticulturalists in their design of 119-metre residential towers in the rehabilitated industrial district of Porta Nuova, focusing on the science of the plants installed on each successive level's perimeter to determine what can best mitigate the smog of the area and increase the air quality of its inhabitants. Epitomising the 'furry' green building, the architects are fully aware and not afraid of the cliché, proving that the literal greening of the building envelope is more than a visual stunt—a true test for one of Europe's most polluted urban areas.

Ryue Nishizawa's Vertical Garden House in Tokyo of 2011, a four-storey private residence, tucked into an impossibly narrow site in the heart of the city, is stripped of all glazing apart from one component at ground level, presumably for security purposes, rejecting what the architect has described as a 'true façade' (Zancan 2011).

Instead, a simple palette of full-height windows, curtains, benches, and planters function as dividers within the interior space as well as between the building envelope and the exterior. What is left are white floor plates that accentuate the building's compositional appearance as a shelf with discrete objects resting on it, lyrically conveying a sense of a still-life painting come to life in three dimensions. The project represents the dense and green paradigm at its most elemental, where density is derived by the urban site condition and green is derived from the relinquishing of complex enclosure systems and the poetic, almost sublime reification of the quotidian houseplant.

Dense and Green Building Typologies

At the other end of the scale range of dense and green housing typologies is OMA's/Büro Ole Scheeren's/RSP's Interlace project in Singapore, an expansive, 170,000 square metre, 1,000-unit residential development in a city known for its experimentation with dense and green design. The project consists of 31 apartment blocks of identical length, each six storeys in height. These block-like horizontal components are stacked in a hexagonal arrangement. In between the blocks are spacious courtyards. The overlay of the units creates a network of nodal moments of connection, forming a continuous vertical corridor between the units that facilitates access for both shared and private elevated garden spaces. The project, sited in an already verdant neighbourhood, completes a long evolving green belt of municipal parks, recreation and residential spaces. In a best practice approach to environmental concerns, the project employs strategic systems based on the careful study of the sun, wind and microclimatic conditions of Singapore in general and the site in particular. Backing those, advanced passive energy strategies exist.

Learning from Singapore

A number of fortuitous and strategic conditions have made Singapore a leader in dense and green typologies for the tropics. Projects like WOHA's School of the Arts (completed in 2010) and PARKROYAL on Pickering (completed in 2013) have led the way in design with visionary leadership. Asia in general and Singapore in particular have great potential for the further exploration of dense and green as well as liveability principles. The breath-taking scale of many of the new developments here captures the attention of politicians and developers and the imagination of its citizens.

As a small island state with limited land and natural resources, Singapore's developmental approach has been guided by 'green' agendas, even before the term became a buzzword. The former Prime Minister of Singapore Mr Lee Kuan Yew had the vision of transforming Singapore into a 'Garden City'. It was a revolutionary concept at that time because no one else in Singapore talked about 'going green' or climate change (Ng 2012).

Since then, Singapore has recognised the importance and benefits of a green environment. Even as the city state embarked rapidly on industrialisation and urbanisation programmes to provide jobs and

housing for its people, the natural environment was high on the government's agenda. Today, Singapore's vision has evolved from 'Garden City' to 'City in a Garden'. This concept is seen to strengthen Singapore's brand as a distinctive, liveable city. The new vision also embodies ideas of conserving and nurturing biodiversity in the urban context, an area where Singapore has contributed scientifically through the Singapore Index (for urban biodiversity).

As Singapore's population continues to grow and with limited land available, developing a compact city with extensive greenery and highly liveable environments will continue to be an important strategy. Singapore has identified three key strategies for further pursuing its 'City in a Garden' vision: using pervasive greenery from the ground to the façade and rooftops of buildings, infusing biodiversity into urban landscapes and fostering community involvement as active participation. Ownership and pride among the community are seen as factors that will sustain the 'City in a Garden' vision (Poon 2012).

Since the early 2000s, Singapore has pursued a number of research studies and small demonstrations that explore the integration of green spaces in buildings. These projects led to a number of policies and initiatives such as GFA Exemption for Communal Sky Terraces, GFA Exemption for Communal Planter Boxes, Skyrise Greenery Scheme, Landscape for Urban Spaces and High-rises (LUSH), as well as the Landscape Excellence Assessment Framework (LEAF). These have been instrumental for the subsequent experimentation with dense and green building typologies.

Many property developments in Singapore employ marketing phrases such as 'near a park', 'rooftop greenery', or 'vertical greenery'. The quantifiable benefit of such features is land value appreciation. At the same time, dense and green building typologies can also be seen as having a potential alleviating effect on land use competition as they are able to layer horizontal city functions vertically, thereby optimising land use in Singapore. At the same time, Singapore increasingly recognises the unquantifiable benefits of living within or near natural areas with rich biodiversity that can result in improved physical and mental health and mitigate some of the negative effects associated with high-density urban environments (Tan 2012).

Further, pockets of green spaces are not just visual delights nor simply for human use but can also function as part of a larger urban ecosystem. For example, in Singapore's efforts to promote a greater biodiversity in its urban environment, dense and green building typologies can function as high quality habitats for flora and fauna. The combination of buildings with green spaces such as green corridors, parks, nature areas and nature reserves can form an interconnected matrix that becomes part of a larger ecosystem.

Dense and green building typologies can mitigate the negative effects of high density areas and improve urban environments by incorporating the environmental, social, architectural and economic aspects of living.

Singapore offers a wealth of case studies for dense and green building typologies research. The information at hand and knowledge gleaned from these can enable similar typologies to be applied to other cities. This helps improve urban environments there as well, steering the new dense and green paradigm from its current status to an integrated and tacit element of architecture as well as urban design and planning in the coming decades in that density and liveability are not seen as contradictory but rather as mutually dependent and synergistic.

Bibliography

Banham, Reyner (1969). *The Architecture of the Well-Tempered Environment*. Chicago: University of Chicago Press.

Boyko, Chris (2014). 'Misunderstanding density: Why we are building the wrong sort of cities', *The Guardian*. Available from <https://www.theguardian.com/housing-network/2014/jul/29/cities-density-building> Accessed on 15 August 2016.

Flamme-Jaspers, Martina (2000). *Expo 2000 Hannover: Architecture*. Ostfildern: Hatje Cantz.

Gissen, David (2009). *Subnature: Architecture's Other Environments*. Princeton: Princeton Architectural Press.

Ng, Lang (2012). 'Singapore—Capital city of vertical green' (interview), in Ed. N Yoshida. *Architecture and Urbanism*. Special Edition May 2012. Tokyo and Singapore: A+U Publishing.

Poon, Hong Yuen (2012). 'Singapore—Capital city of vertical green' (interview), in Ed. N Yoshida. *Architecture and Urbanism*. Special Edition May 2012. Tokyo and Singapore: A+U Publishing.

Tan, Puay Yok (2012). 'What does vertical green mean', in Ed. N Yoshida. *Architecture and Urbanism*. Special Edition May 2012. Tokyo and Singapore: A+U Publishing.

United Nations, Department of Economic and Social Affairs, Population Division (2008). 'Comprehensive tables', in *World Urbanization Prospects. The 2007 Revision*, vol. 1. Available from <http://www.un.org/esa/population/publications/wup2007/2007WUP_Highlights_web.pdf>. Accessed on 3 August 2013.

Zancan, Roberto (2011). 'Tokyo's vertical thresholds #2: Ryue Nishizawa', in *Domus,* December 2011.

Richard Hassell, Naomi Hanakata,
Aurel von Richthofen

Conversation on Designing Future Cities with Measures for a New Urban Agenda with Richard Hassell

Richard Hassell (RH) is the co-founder of WOHA Architects—Singapore. In an interview with Naomi Hanakata (NH) and Aurel von Richthofen (AVR) (Future Cities Laboratory) in September 2016, he discusses his approaches to measuring city characteristics and how this can support a more complex view of designing in cities.

NH   *Could you tell us a little bit about how you adopt technology in your daily architectural practice?*

RH   We are very quick to adopt new technologies. When you are designing and you want to communicate something or explore something, then you might like to use whatever new tools that are available because they are so exciting and you can do so much more with them. This is also the moment when we develop our own tools in the field of communication, simulation and so on. Design work is quite fast moving and when we want to explore an idea, we need new methods and we need them to be fast; there is a real need for quick and dirty tools. We should be aiming for statistical and 'fuzzy' improvements in performance—instead of highly optimised and calibrated solutions—because over-optimised solutions are not 'real world' in both data and practice. At the time of design we have too few parameters, and we can only guess how the end-users will interact with a building, yet many software solutions try to optimise the results based on this patchy and inaccurate information as if it were a simple equation.

AVR   *Your work has been driven by 'green' ideas from the beginning. Could you tell us how you started that?*

RH   We have been driving an ethical desire to create a sustainable world and could see that architects seem to be the only people who are in a position to make sustainable solutions actually happen. The reason behind this is architects are generalists—we have to operate across all kinds of domains and fields, and we come face-to-face with all kinds of specialists. Somehow we have to stir them together into a kind of soup where we achieve a desired outcome. In fact, the world is getting into a situation where we can only survive with very complex sustainable solutions that integrate many different processes. We will need more and more of these specialists in all sorts of projects, not just architectural projects, yet the specialists are quite helpless to contribute unless they are placed into a broad framework and strategy so that interests are aligned and there can be movement towards an integrated solution. So, our idea was to develop a broader context in our writings and publications that set up this framework. Looking back 20 years ago, we saw very little interest in sustainability in Singapore. There was the belief that energy solves the climate problem.

AVR   *How did you translate the idea of eco-consciousness into practice?*

RH   We had to smuggle in our design research by tagging the sustainable elements with additional attributes that were desired by the client. We argued 'how nice would it be if your home had less air conditioning? It could be like a resort and you could really enjoy the garden!' We had to frame questions in the right way so that the answers were positive.

NH   *To what extent does the Singapore institutional framework facilitate your urban experiments?*

RH   Singapore is one of the few places in the world that does have the integration of governmental departments, including a sense of a common mission to make these things happen. And once they happen here as a prototype, they are more likely to be adopted by other cities. I believe Singapore is difficult in many

RATING
CITIES

Sociable architecture and sustainable cities have now become the 21st century priorities, and building developments need to be assessed in terms of their contribution to social and environmental sustainability, as well as their economic viability.

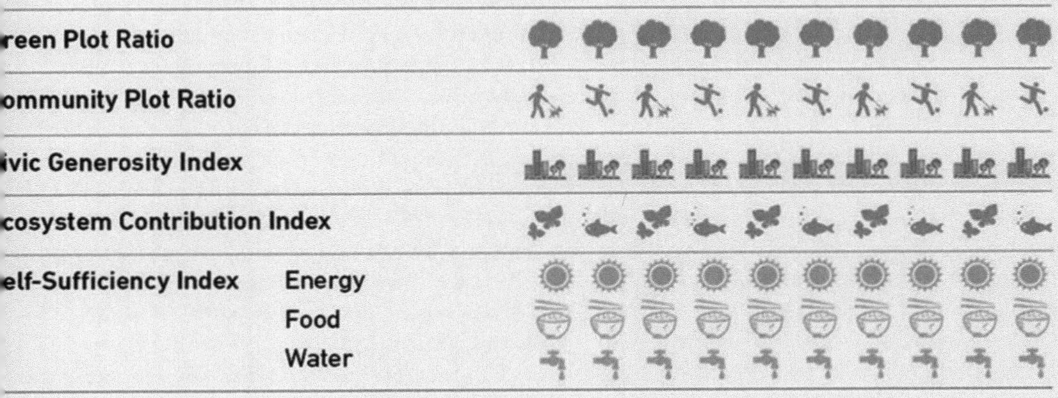

Green Plot Ratio		
Community Plot Ratio		
Civic Generosity Index		
Ecosystem Contribution Index		
Self-Sufficiency Index	Energy	
	Food	
	Water	

83

Fig. 1   Five measures for a new urban agenda (WOHA)

ways and easier in some others. The high cost of land is actually really good for doing slightly experimental buildings. Because the investment in land cost is so high—it far exceeds the construction budget—the incremental cost of doing small experiments within the building budget adds little to the overall development budget. I think that is why there has been a flourishing of experimental buildings here. Singapore has a really challenging tropical climate for sustainability, because it has a very steady state condition that is slightly outside comfort levels. In Singapore, you cannot rely on a cool night to average out your temperature. You cannot dig a hole into the basement to use thermal cooling because the earth is of the same temperature as the air. Also there is very little wind and the sky is often overcast. There are big challenges to designing sustainable, comfortable and efficient buildings here.

AVR   *The Future Cities Laboratory is constantly seeking to redefine the understanding of urbanisation to better address current urban problems. In your opinion, where are we now?*

RH   People are moving to cities, and apparently, we have crossed the halfway point of urban/rural population. So I think we have maybe moved beyond urbanism; we now live in a hybrid virtual and real world where a wave of technology affects architecture and has swept over urbanism too. The danger is the disconnection that people feel from the world beyond the city. There's also a lack of relevance felt by people who have lived all their lives in the city to a wilderness area, for example. They don't know it or value it, so why would they protect it?

AVR   *Does technology facilitate this hybrid condition?*

RH   I see that the Anthropocene era could be the moment when wireless internet is available everywhere throughout the rainforests and wilderness areas; people would not have to move to the city to be urbanised. They would quite happily be posting Instagram of themselves with orangutans out in the rainforest. In the digital infrastructure era, people cluster around technology access as they used to cluster around water sources.

AVR   *Your architectural and urban projects convey design principles for tropical cities. Could you elaborate on these principles that you distilled from your previous competition and design projects?*

RH   We developed five measures for a new urban agenda (Figure 1), which we thought were missing in conversations with urban designers and developers. We named the first one Green Building Ratio (GBR). According to our calculation method our highest ratio so far is the 1100 per cent replacement of green spaces in our Oasia Hotel Downtown project. For us, this is a super exciting measure, since you can argue that one building can compensate for ten other buildings around it. For us, GBR ratios are something that should be known, tracked, even made mandatory, and cities need to compare, discuss and enforce green replacement as a key tool to stop vegetation from being lost as cities grow—Singapore authorities have again taken the lead in requiring at least 100 per cent green replacement rate. The potential of these new green areas to then start functioning as a habitat led us to an ecosystem school of thinking; plants perform many kinds of ecosystem services in terms of oxygen and carbon dioxide exchange, water storage and so on, but these green areas can do much more in terms of supporting animal and insect life, and preserving the biosphere.

NH   *How do ecosystem services and related ecological-economic evaluation criteria inform your architectural designs?*

RH   We are in the Anthropocene era, and in a funny way it is easier for cities to achieve protected ecosystems. Outside the cities, there isn't the sort of stakeholders and caretakers who might invest into or protect ecosystem services. But in the city, there are literally millions of stakeholders who are potential champions and protectors of nature, particularly if it is right in front of them. In Singapore, otters and people co-exist and many people love the otters and Instagram them, so they have a huge digital impact on the citizens. We all know what is up with the otters as we can follow them easily on social media. We think the idea of having designed ecosystems in the city is really interesting. Many traditional hunter gatherer tribes had protected sacred areas where hunting was taboo and these acted as a haven for wildlife and ensured their conservation, even in tough times of famine or drought. We need these kinds of protected havens more now than ever, and cities may have a big role. Cities are protected from wildfires, and from drought, in that there is a lot of wastewater from human activities. These qualities could be very important in future.

NH   *And how do you integrate these into an urban project?*

RH   Once you have all this greenery, you start to work in systems rather than as isolated pockets. How can you connect them? In the future maybe the city will start generating its own rain if we can induce a cycle of transpiration microclimate and hydrology into the design of the city. So this sort of performative ecosystem measure could be really interesting. We decided to put a score in there as well. The full score of this performative ecosystem measure means that you have a new ecosystem that can be as complex as the site would have had before the city was built. I do not like a scoring system where you can easily achieve 100 per cent. Instead we felt it was important to have measures where 100 per cent was not a relative, but an absolute score: if you achieve 100 per cent we would be in a kind of unspoiled paradise! So we graded it from simple green to green that can support animals, flying animals, crawling animals and then just sort of add diversity until it reaches something that would be fantastic — the equivalent of an untouched wilderness in diversity and productivity — coexisting with the city.

AVR   *A city is made of people as well as architecture. How would you include social aspects as important values in dense places like Singapore?*

RH   Our next measure is Civic Generosity Index (CGI). We start off by asking 'if you were to characterise a building like a person, what would its character be?' Would it be someone that was a fine, upstanding citizen? Or would it be like a psychopath, just grabbing things? A few years ago, a study analysed corporations as if they were people and found that most corporations behaved like psychopaths. And we thought — actually most buildings behave like that too. We believe that having a CGI score would help encourage the development of buildings that behave like good citizens. If we are aiming for the city as a sustainable system, buildings need to start acting like civil-minded people — the kind who separate their waste, don't disturb their neighbours, offer someone a drink of water or a place to sit — and in return this would make the city — the community of buildings — a more generous and civil place to live in.

AVR   *Civic generosity could also translate into benefits for the community. How can you include this to make Singapore's public spaces more attractive to the community?*

RH   There is the Community Plot Ratio (CPR). This is in response to developers who are always trying to eliminate as much as possible the common space; this is a ratio in contrast to pure productive space. Urban planners have accepted developer efficiency of net-to-gross efficiency as a good thing; it sounds good but it is really bad for the community, and it makes density bad. Once the community plot ratio is tracked, planners can use the Community Plot Ratio data to tune up exactly how much community space is necessary for a high amenity and convivial environment. It is surprising how little is known about this, so even measuring it would be a huge advance. Once you can say — this area feels good, it has a ratio of X, so we should aim for that in this new masterplan and it would be very high amenity, I think you would have great community buy-in. Within our project SkyVille @ Dawson we had over 100 per cent of community plot ratio. When you are there, it feels like a place that is very civic and community-based.

NH   *The ideas of civic generosity and community plot ratio put a strong focus on 'public space'. How do you enhance the existing cultural spaces in Singapore?*

RH   Our last measure is the Self Sufficiency Index (SSI). Singapore particularly makes you think about this aspect, because the city has no hinterland. Singapore is very fragile; it has to import almost all of its food, energy and some of its water. An ideal situation for Singapore — to achieve complete security — would be to shrink its food, energy and water footprint to the size of the island. If you want the city to do that, you need to track how each component — each building performs in terms of self-sufficiency. You could then compensate for the missing parts through infrastructure, common areas and public spaces. It's not enough to aim for LEED Platinum rating if your design is nowhere near self-sufficient and still relies on having a big footprint somewhere else. LEED is relative — buildings that are doing better than other buildings — but our measure is absolute and gives an indication of how far we are from achieving the ultimate aim of self sufficiency.

AVR   *Can you be sure that your architecture lives up to these high aims and expectations?*

RH   Many of our own project scores are terrible from a self-sufficiency point of view. Yet, we were sick of our buildings being solely judged by their elegant sculptural form when that is really not what they were about. We wanted to create a beautiful environment yet address environmental issues at the same time. In our practice, we challenge ourselves based on our way of understanding buildings and we challenge other architects as well by asking 'How well does your building perform against these critical measures?'

NH   *So you came up with the CPR, CGI and SSI criteria to assess and validate your design practice in the Singapore context?*

RH   Yes. We realised that buildings in themselves cannot achieve all of these aims and what is difficult is that it is necessary to rethink and redesign the city as well—a very complex process. Urban design necessarily involves the political process as the government needs to balance the cost and benefit of adopting additional socio-ecological measures. These tools, however, are quite simple and easy to implement and administer, yet they lock in very important objectives and values, which makes them quite powerful.

NH   *Do you aim to redesign the city of the future by introducing a way to assess or value parameters such as self-sufficiency or civic generosity?*

RH   Yes. Some of our measures could be market driven, others might have to adhere to governmental requirements, but if the assessments are done and the results are to be made public, it would be very interesting to see how they could affect the development of the city. Would cities that score higher be better places to live? I suspect so. Since cities have become very competitive and if Singapore were to adopt, for instance, the community plot ratio, I suspect many other cities would quickly follow suit. If we value quality of life, we need to measure the factors that contribute to this.

NH   *Very inspiring. Thank you so much for this interview!*

Werner Sobek, Naomi Hanakata

Conversation on Research and Technological Innovation with Werner Sobek

Werner Sobek (ws) is professor for Architecture and Structural Engineering at the University of Stuttgart and founder of the ILEK Institute for Lightweight Structures and Conceptual Design. In an interview with Naomi Hanakata (NH) of Future Cities Laboratory in November 2016, he shares his views on the main challenges of metropolisation and sustainable building approaches today.

NH   *You are deeply embedded in practice but also conduct your own research on sustainable design and engineering. How do you link your research with practice?*

ws   There is no clear description. It is a process of continuous modification and change. We have certain scientific questions and a set of ethical boundaries. We combine these with two main objectives that guide us throughout our work: first, we have to build for more people with less material. Second, we have to avoid the use of fossil-based energy. The question of which technologies and materials will help us to achieve these objectives, however, still needs to be solved. The main issue is (and this is something most people who talk about sustainability do not really understand) due to the dramatic increase of the global population, we have to build for many more people with far less material than hitherto. Lightweight structures and recyclability are essential prerequisites for achieving these objectives.

NH   *In your practice, how much are you exploring new technologies to achieve these goals?*

ws   Permanently. Both in my office and at the ILEK (*Institut für Leichtbau Entwerfen und Konstruieren* = Institute for Lightweight Structures and Conceptual Design) we constantly explore new terrains. ILEK is one of the biggest research institutes in the field of architecture in Germany.
Clients come to our consultancy because they consider us to offer results of the highest quality and precision. In order to safeguard our advance, we have to be innovative. Our innovations are very bold, but still they are innovations for tomorrow only. At the University we research innovations for the day *after* tomorrow. Therefore, these innovations can be bolder and riskier—risky in the sense that we might fail, that we may not reach our target. In my view it is sad to see that most university professors are no longer doing any research where there is a real risk of failure. I think the noblest part of a professor's job is to take a few steps ahead into the unknown field, the *terra incognita*, to find out if something makes sense or if it is on the wrong path. The so called 'applied research' where you have to know the results even before you start in order to a research grant, in my opinion, does not really belong to a university. University research should address the needs of the day *after* tomorrow. Research for today or for tomorrow should be addressed by the research department of a company.

NH   *You mentioned continuous change, modification and adaptability as core elements of your work. You also mentioned the challenge of having to build for more people in a sustainable way. Working towards that goal are you also considering the potential demographic shifts in the opposite direction? If we look at the demographic trends and predictions, for example in Japan or Germany, we have to assume a decline of inhabitants.*

ws   Definitely, but most of our colleagues are not talking about this. Neither are the politicians. Germany will soon experience a serious population decline—without having the money to pay for all her retired people. After 2030 our population pyramid will dramatically invert, a scenario that takes already place in Japan. But what happens in Japan is not really discussed in Germany. It is something that happens far away, on TV. Architects, engineers and urban designers have to address this issue. Today there are 270 million job-holders in Europe (including Russia). Due to the population decline and inversion of the pyramid there will only be 160 million employees in 2040. If there is no population influx based on immigration, we will lose 40 per cent of our workforce. You cannot overcome this by increasing productivity alone, certainly not by 40 per cent. A hairdresser cannot cut twice as fast. That is absolutely impossible. There will be a dramatic lack of employable people, especially those in the business of caring for the elderly.

NH *And how do you address these challenges in your work?*

WS I am not an urban designer, so I'm not *planning* the big picture. I'm *thinking* in the big picture. The overarching theme is something easily named: the trend towards metropolisation. A trend that may have a catastrophic end. It is destroying the rural areas where we commonly find the most valuable natural resources such as agricultural land, mineral resources, wind turbines or water based power, and so on. If we make the countryside unattractive, who will manage those resources? Or do we want to hand over control to robots? On the other hand, a high density urban environment is, in my opinion, not the best place for kids to grow up. Kids that grow up in an area like Manhattan, which is not even a super high density city, have never seen a cow, played in a creek or river or cut a tree in their entire life. Since they have no idea about any of these things, then how should they be able to understand nature?

NH *When you say we have to rethink the role of rural areas, is it more a matter of re-evaluating the way we approach these areas? And that we have to conceive them as part of a large and complex urban system rather than marginal territories?*

WS Yes, absolutely. Rural and urban areas are two sides of the same medal, of the one environment in which we live. At the end it is what human beings and society are about. Ultimately this also leads us to the question about the system in which we live and work. I am definitely not a communist, and I'm not a capitalist either. But in my opinion the capitalist system misguides society. We can already see some ruptures and they will become more dramatic if we do not stop this process of metropolisation.

Furthermore, all of these so-called new industries: what does it really mean? When confronted with a choice between human and machine interaction, the human will lose by default because a human makes errors and mistakes. This is an essential part of the *conditio humana*. But what does it mean if humans are not allowed to make mistakes and errors anymore? We do not allow them to be human beings. We are trying to create a perfect living machine, which is impossible. And un the end we could probably lose the potential to discover new ideas and directions by accident or by error.

NH *At the same time, in research as well as in practice, we have to think about the social implications of all these technological innovations, something that is often not considered. Do you consider it as part of the same problem in your work?*

WS The technological progress, which is driven by engineers, researchers and architects, makes up only one wheel of the car. Social developments, the way we live together, our objectives in life are things we have to discuss more than we do now. Technology is nothing else than the oil in the gearbox. Technology has to sit in the engine room and not in the driver's seat. But what is in the driver's seat? What is the direction we are heading to? This is what I meant when I said that society has to overcome capitalism. We have to find new solutions for the problems resulting from the inversion of the population pyramid, the explosion of population or global warming.

NH *Let's elaborate more on your car metaphor and the differentiation between the engine and the steering wheel. In many cases, we let the car be driven by its engine; we don't spend much time thinking about what should be in the driver's seat instead, and in which direction we should really be heading.*

WS Especially in our field there has always been a fascination with technology. Remember the fascination Le Corbusier had for steamships and hence his designs of buildings as such? We were all fascinated by aircrafts and spaceships. The fascination for new typologies will help us overcome capitalist restrictions. Thereby we will be able to overcome the problems resulting from the inversion of the population pyramid and the population explosion. If we really intend to overcome metropolisation we do not need to talk about the future of the metropolis in technical terms.

Fig. 1   Active House B10 (Stuttgart 2014) is part of a research project examining how innovative materials, structural designs and technologies can improve our built environment in a sustainable manner. It combines mobile and permanent infrastructures for an integrated and decentralized power supply to serve the needs of both electro-mobility and the built environment.

NH   *Regarding your activities in many different regions around the world, how do you take your guiding principles into those regions? Do you develop place-specific responses in all of them?*

WS   Yes, we have to. People's value systems differ to a great extent. This has something to do with their cultural background, their educational background, the density of population etc. Car emissions are not a point of discussion in Kazakhstan. But they are an important point of discussion in Stuttgart or in New York. The technical ability to develop solutions also differs. As a result, the urgency to overcome certain issues and to develop common solutions is highly different from country to country.

When we designed a high-rise building in Manhattan, I proposed to use triple glazing. The client said: 'No. Let's install single glazing. If we need more heating energy, who cares? There's enough energy out there.' And when I told him about global warming he said: 'I don't believe it.' People in Siberia may have the same approach. They don't have any problem burning 100 litres of gasoline — but there are 1,000 square kilometres of empty space around them. So the situation and perceptions around the world differ greatly.

What we have to create is a high sense of responsibility within our profession. We have to define the problems we should be working on more clearly; this is something we don't even do in Central Europe.

NH   *Looking at the big challenges faced by our urban society, how do you evaluate the various strategies and responses that governments are pursuing?*

WS   The Swiss, Austrian and German governments definitely pursue the wrong path; under the title of energy efficiency, they prescribe specific U values and G values for buildings. But we know that the overall CO_2 emission does not really decline, since the average number of square meters per person has nearly doubled over the last 40 years (at least in Germany). So we have to be more radical. As a society we should demand energy that is completely free of fossil or nuclear origin. This is what we should be talking about. How to reach that? For instance, you could wear three layers of pullovers or install 200 square meters of solar panels — there are different solutions out there and I think we should leave it up to individuals' responsibility as well as the architects and engineers to find the solution best suited — as long as they fulfil the requirement of zero fossil-based energy.

NH   *Taking these ideas back into your practice: what are the key elements in your dialogue with your clients in developing specific solutions based on your guiding principles?*

WS   I frankly admit that in many cases I do not reach my objectives. But I try. The easiest part is reducing the amount of building material. If you tell clients that for a 200 metre high-rise we would normally need 150,000 tonnes of concrete but that we are able to do it with 100,000 tonnes instead, they would sign the deal. This not only does something positive for the environment, but also saves a lot of money. However, if you tell them that using non fossil-based energy necessitates the integration of photovoltaic elements into the façade, in many cases you cannot get them to sign the contract because there could be too many obstacles and financial hurdles. Based on energy saving codes in Germany, municipal regulations require facades to be stone or plastered. They also require the façade to have an opening of maximum 40 per cent. This rule does not take into consideration where the building stands—whether on the north or south side of a hill, in northern or southern Germany. I believe the only requirement we should impose on buildings is zero fossil-based energy. The big problem is that the governments issue laws, restrictions, and guidelines that are based on consultancy with so-called experts—what they propose are tools and methods such as U values, G values, percentage of façade transparency and so on. But nobody talks about the actual objectives that we should be aiming for in practice.

NH   *Professor Sobek, thank you so much for your time.*

B

Responsive Cities

Gerhard Schmitt

Big Data-Informed Urban Design
[...] aims to extend the smart city
concept to strengthen the human
dimension and to move the citizen
to the centre by incorporating
a wider and more complex set of
urban governance, planning
and design concerns. Big data can
support evidence-based,
high-quality decisions and help
simulate the impact of new design
and governance scenarios on
the performance and liveability
of cities.

The replacement of all ageing infrastructure is not sustainable, not cost effective, not convenient, not safe, and sometimes not possible. Fortunately, civil infrastructure often has much reserve capacity since behavior models at the design stage, prior to construction, are necessarily conservative. Sensing and advanced data-interpretation methodologies lead to more accurate estimates of real behaviour once infrastructure is in service.

Walking and cycling must be considered a multi-sensory experience which includes vision, auditory, somatic sensation, olfaction and vestibular stimulation. Conducting survey work to understand the perception of various street design options based on static pictures only can be restrictive. To fundamentally understand the relationship between the built environment and its ability to make active transport modes a positive experience, one needs to study the cognitive processes used while walking and cycling.

Christoph Hoelscher

How to investigate the manner in which people perceive and mentally process their urban environments? Specifically, we are interested in densely populated urban quarters that are characterised by the presence and movement of large numbers of pedestrians. In this context, the research identifies and models spatial information processes such as pedestrian orientation and navigation choices within and between connected building structures.

Heiko Aydt, Gerhard Schmitt, Bige Tuncer, Markus Schlaepfer,
Ian Smith, Alexander Erath, Christoph Hoelscher

B   Challenges for Responsive Cities

When was the last time your city hall or town's administrative office interacted with you? What was it about? A fine? A tax? New garbage collection arrangements? Whatever their content, such interactions generally take the form of requests, instructions or communiqués. City hall is typically the sender and the citizen the recipient. There is little room for dialogue. It is true that all city governments around the world are held accountable in other ways. The media reports on government policy, decisions and their effectiveness. Periodical elections of government officials give voice to citizens.

Many governments try to do much more and strive to engage citizens in the running of cities, be it planning, service delivery, housing, budgeting or education. As early as 1999, UN-Habitat recognised the importance such policies had on the well-being of city residents, and launched its Global Campaign on Urban Governance. Since then, various feedback mechanisms and efforts to enhance transparency have become commonplace. Citizen report cards, service delivery reports, performance targets, ombuds-men, complaint offices and public petitioning procedures have become standard tools of good urban governance.

Nevertheless, for all these advances, exchanges with city hall remain rudimentary. It is rare that we, as city residents, engage in a dialogue with city hall. It is even more unusual to fold exchanges that include fellow citizens and community groups into such a dialogue. And the diverse 'voices' of inanimate structures of the city—the water infrastructure, the transport system, the energy network and more—are usually present only through the technical reports of engineers.

The term 'responsive city' describes a city whose inhabitants and authorities respond constructively to each other's' needs, desires and aspirations in the context of current and future capacities of infrastructure and material systems. The responsive city connects people, places and things in dynamic relationships to support liveability, resilience and sustainability of cities. It does so in time, be it the flux of day-to-day life, seasonal cycles of change, as well as less predictable disruptions and even disasters. As Goldsmith and Crawford (2014) point out, engaging citizens in the governing of a city can help to significantly improve the way a city operates. This is a point that is also widely reflected in literature on urban planning and design (see De Lange and De Waal 2013; Neuhaus et al. 2015).

Heightening the responsiveness of a city is made possible by cultivating a fertile relationship between the principles of public participation in urban governance and recent advances in information and communication technology, such as wireless broadband internet, smartphones and apps, sensing and data analytics. These and other technologies, conventionally clustered under the heading 'smart city' technology, help to make cities more efficient. Planning such technologies intelligently can enhance the capacity of cities to be responsive to an unprecedented degree. Furthermore, it can also support increased levels of transparency. Ordinary citizens can have much better appreciation of what is happening in their city, raising awareness among citizens and giving them a means to voice their opinion.

The distinction between 'smart' and 'responsive' cities is important. Smart cities derive their 'smartness' from technology. The liveability, sustainability, efficiency and resilience of cities have all been claimed to be enhanced by the application of smart technologies. While some aspects of liveability can indeed be improved by technology, planners, policy-makers and citizens alike are mostly aware that a concept as multi-layered as 'liveability' is not attainable by the mere application of technology. We know that progress towards all such aspirational concepts must include planning, design, management, science and technology. A good example is the improvement of traffic systems. Technology can help to make existing traffic systems more efficient to reduce congestion. However, in most cases, this is merely treating the symptoms. The underlying cause, for instance, the need for long commute to work every day cannot simply be addressed by technology. Instead this requires urban planning and design interventions.

Responsive cities, by contrast, focus on the ability to respond to wider urban challenges. A responsive city is based on the premise that liveability can be enhanced by providing timely and adequate responses to changes and disturbances. The means of facilitating such a response could very well be technology based. Nevertheless, urban planning, design and citizen engagement play an equally important role. This helps to shift the focus to a three-way relationship between the city administration, the city's inhabitants and its material infrastructure. While technological development is fast paced, the rate at which the urban environment can adapt is limited by the fact that urban fabrics, buildings and civil infrastructure is typically built to last several decades. It is important that urban planning and design processes take this into consideration in order to achieve a responsive city. Responsive cities are sensitive to catalytic relationships between technology, people and principles of good governance.

With respect to cities' responsiveness in relation to urban planning and design, there are many challenges. At the intersection between urban planning and design, human behaviour and civil infrastructure, the following challenges are highlighted:

Fig. 1   Interface design tool highlighting a network of cities and power plants.
Fig. 2   Responsive cities word-cloud.

Challenge 1
How can urban planning and design better respond
to the needs and requirements of residents?

Responsiveness in urban planning and design requires planners and designers to be well informed about the states of urban
environment and the needs of its (future) residents. With the capabilities offered by smart-city technologies (e.g., sensors, big-data
analytics), high-performance computational models and simulations, designers and planners now have potentially sophisticated
and powerful tools at their fingertips. These tools can be used to
evaluate planning and design alternatives at an unprecedented
degree of fidelity. In principal, that allows planners and designers
to respond more effectively by addressing issues and concerns
with solutions that are tailored to the specific requirements posed
by the given urban environment and, in particular, its residents.
New forms of collecting citizen feedback through e-participation
and the wealth of data provided by large numbers of residents,
sensors and other data sources, clearly have the ability to substantially enhance conventional feedback mechanisms such as town
hall meetings and case-specific survey efforts. The challenge is to
extract useful information from the data and ultimately use this
information in combination with models to generate knowledge
that can be used to improve the planning and design process.

Challenge 2
How can existing infrastructure be better utilised
to support responsiveness?

Urban infrastructure and civil infrastructure in particular
are built to last for several decades. Furthermore, infrastructure

elements are planned and designed for specific purposes. As urban economies and societies evolve over time and cities are confronted with various challenges such as densification, aging and migration. As a result, existing infrastructure may have to be either extended or repurposed to suit new needs and requirements. Simply replacing aging infrastructure is often not an option as it could be not sustainable, too costly, impractical or outright impossible. One way of responding to changing requirements is to repurpose existing infrastructure. This is challenging—partially due to the fact that it can only be modified within certain limits—but also, and perhaps more importantly, because it is difficult to estimate reliably how repurposing would affect remaining lives. Being able to determine the current state of the infrastructure and to predict remaining lives under changing conditions would make it possible for infrastructures to be used longer and more efficiently.

Challenge 3
How can urban planning and design respond to changing needs, preferences and behaviour of citizens?

Urban environments can be made more accessible and accommodating to residents' needs by explicitly considering individual and collective behaviour in the planning and design phase. Just as urban planning and design paradigms evolve over time to accommodate changing needs and preferences, so does human behaviour adapt to the changing urban environment. It is important to understand how human behaviour is affected by design and how behaviour adapts to the urban environment. However, while it is possible to study human behaviour in existing environments, studying human behaviour in environments that are yet to be built is challenging.

Challenge 4
How can urban planning and design respond
to challenges such as urban mobility?

Changing the way we commute is crucial to improve liveability in densely populated urban environments. While it is necessary to consider explicitly the infrastructure for engaging
mobility (e.g. cycling) in planning and designing urban environments, inhabitants need to adapt and embrace alternative transport modes such as cycling and walking. Infrastructure can be
developed with alternative transport modes in mind. Convincing
commuters to change their habits—on the other hand—is far
more challenging. For a city to respond to the challenges of mobility, they need to find ways that allow for responsive and adaptive
interaction between infrastructure and behaviour.

References

De Lange, Michiel and
Martijn De Waal (2013).
'Owning the city:
New media and citizen
engagement in urban
design' in First Monday.
Available from <http://
journals.uic.edu/ojs/index.
php/fm/article/
view/4954/3786>
Accessed on 07 June 2016.

Goldsmith, Stephen and
Susan Crawford (2014)
The Responsive City:
Engaging Communities
through Data-Smart
Governance. Chicester:
John Wiley & Sons.

Neuhaus, Fabian,
Hans-Joerg Stark and
Matthias Drilling (2015).
ATLAS ePartizipation:
Demokratische
Stadtentwicklung.
Available from <https://
issuu.com/urbantick/docs/
atlas_epartizipation/1>
Accessed on 7 June 2016.

Challenges for Responsive Cities

Gerhard Schmitt, Bernhard Klein,
Reinhard Koenig, Markus Schlaepfer,
Bige Tuncer, Peter Bus

Big Data-Informed Urban Design

Big Data in Future Cities and Urban Planning

The impacts of drastic population increase and rapid urbanisation in Asian cities in the last few decades on local and regional density is unprecedented (see Urbanisation Indicators, this volume). These impacts outstretch the capacity of traditional planning methods and instruments. Constructing more road infrastructure, public transportation, healthcare facilities, childcare, schools and housing facilities may make cities more liveable and strengthen local and regional businesses, but it brings little innovation to help cities deal with long-term new complexity. Urban planners, designers, managers and leaders' knowledge of the requirements of the emerging dynamic of such urban systems is limited.

Transforming and improving the capacity of urban governance and planning is necessary, as the impacts of rapid growth threaten the liveability and resilience of cities. Such side effects are traffic jams, pollution (up to 70 per cent of global CO_2 emissions originate in cities according to Tollefson 2012), urban heat islands (eight to 15 degrees for tropical clouds over land, Lensky and Driori 2007) and burgeoning urban waste (up to three per cent increase per year in high-income countries, despite recycling efforts according to a report from the UN Human Settlements Programme). Facing these challenges, cities go through continuous transformation processes.

Cities are investing in digitalisation and smart city technologies to improve safety and asset management at all levels. They can become smarter through distributed sensor technologies that collect data from urban infrastructure, transport systems, citizens and devices to relay information about what is happening in the city. Data mining and data analytics deliver information about events or opinions, phone data, surveillance scenarios like emergency and crime detection, and open data from government agencies such as air pollution, meteorology, land use and different kinds of geometric and spatial resources.

This technocratic perspective however assumes that everything can be measured and technologically solved and ignores that cities are complex human habitats, represented as complex urban systems with emergent dynamics. Urban challenges such as air pollution, traffic congestion, and local climate zone disturbances have multiple causes and side effects. Integrated thinking, planning and decision making processes that make use of the citizens' observation capacity, experience, problem solving skills and creativity are urgently needed.

Responsive Cities can help urban planning practitioners to deal with these challenges. Cities like Singapore and Zürich, which have excellent data situations and prioritise the interest of citizens in the further development of their respective cities, have the potential to become Responsive Cities. To achieve this potential, more citizen engagement and evidence-based decision making are necessary. Based on Smart Cities technology, big data and machine learning can help to produce this evidence, which in turn can drive cognitive design computing, urban complexity science and citizen design science. These can eventually inform urban design and the transformation of urban governance.

Big Data-Informed Urban Design therefore aims to extend the smart city concept by incorporating a wider and more complex set of urban governance, planning and design concerns, to strengthen the human dimension and to move the citizen in the centre. Big data can lead to evidence-based high-quality decisions and help simulate the impact of new design and governance scenarios on the performance and liveability of cities. Big Data-Informed Urban Design can therefore lead to new urban planning, design and management processes. It offers a departure from fixed and static approaches towards flexible and dynamic approaches. In the course of this development, advanced data analytics, cognitive design computing and citizen design science processes will emerge. Big Data-Informed Urban Design can also contribute to the responsiveness of a city; it represents the common base for the collaboration between government and citizens, and an increasingly engineered and automated infrastructure.

Five Research Challenges
in Big Data and Urban Design

Big Data-Informed Urban Design is not a goal in itself but a means to achieve more liveable cities. With this being the overarching aim, five major research challenges emerge. These challenges emerge from exploring the potential of big data and data science in: addressing wicked urban problems with consequences for urban governance; augmentation of design and decision making processes with human cognition; identification of common principles behind the organisation of cities through complexity science; systematic inclusion of knowledge from citizens, stakeholders and experts in controlled design processes; and the correlation of urban form and behavioural models.

Addressing Wicked Urban Problems:
Big Data and Urban Governance
Urban systems are full of wicked problems on every level. These are situations with many stakeholders in which an alleged solution might create a multitude of new or additional problems. Think of private urban transportation, wider streets and more parking spaces. While benefiting some, there is a high social cost associated with traditional expansion solutions. Future transportation will change radically with more autonomous vehicles and multi-modal systems. Accordingly, future urban governance needs to anticipate these dynamic developments and their side effects. The fact that adjacent European countries such as Germany and the Netherlands have opposite policies with regard to commuting shows the dimension of the problem.

Clearly, changes in technology or lifestyle alone—two drivers that determine urban systems—cannot solve those wicked problems. Policy measures and possibly adjustments in governance become essential to take necessary long-term actions towards urban sustainability and resilience that are beyond the immediate time or technology horizon.

Governments use policies with positive or negative incentives as control mechanisms to steer urban behaviour. Modern car toll systems, for instance, can be used to regulate traffic and reduce pollution. Although policies are often used to address such problems, they are prone to fail in the long run as they tend to be static and seldom offer the appropriate scale of intervention. The major research question is *how policies can be better focused, more broadly applicable and more adaptive to respond better to ever evolving cities*.

From the viewpoint of the urban metabolism as a system of stocks and flows, it is not feasible to strictly control individual stocks but rather to constrain their flow in a way that their goals will be reached by exploiting synergies or eliminating disturbances as much as possible. The availability of sensor data (see Figure 1) and voluntary citizen data can reduce the complexity of a decision making process, by augmenting the impacts of urban policies, or more specifically urban flows with evidence.

According to Bar-Yam (2015), big data could play an important role to reveal the unwanted side effects of urban policies and therefore help to formulate more focused responses. Modern computer technologies offer significant opportunities to simplify and automate policy making. Stream processing frameworks as proposed by Kiran et al. (2015) allow the generation of urban behaviour models from sensor data using machine learning techniques. Puppim de Oliveira et al. (2015) studied the opportunities of more holistic mitigation strategies by applying 'system of systems' modelling approaches as an instrument for collaborative policy making. However, noisy data and missing semantic concepts often represent a barrier for machines to extract models that a human can easily interpret. The system developed by Wetz et al. (2014) that links continuous environment sensor data with open government data is one step in this direction, as it provides additional contextual information crucial to draw significant conclusions. However little has been done to support citizens in identifying complex event patterns automatically and to correlate them with human interpretable performance indicators in order to verify policy success.

Additional questions arising with regard to big data and governance are new and fundamental: what is needed in terms of policy measures and analysis methods to enhance the resilience of urban systems, such as the capability to respond to changing conditions or recover from environmental threats that bring potential damage to public safety, health and security? How can governance system accountabilities

Fig. 1   DataCanvas weather time-lapse video.

be strengthened to support improved responsiveness? Can we analyse times series data for certain patterns, such as phases of stability or chaotic changes? As time series data are necessary for calibrating and validating dynamic analysis or simulation models, will those datasets be available for a few decades on a low aggregation level? Can a pattern only be found in one data set or also in multiple sets for different aspects of the same area, or even in other data sets for different areas but similar configurations? Can meaningful aggregated and combined measures on a higher level be constructed by combining individual basic measures? And how could these emergent high-level features be easily interpreted?

Augmenting Design and Decision Making Processes with Human Cognition: Cognitive Design Computing

In the past, urban simulations were often used for large scale models that were not sensitive to small scale urban planning problems. Furthermore, urban analysis methods are used mainly to evaluate completed designs, such as independent tools based on the space syntax theory (Hillier & Hanson 1984; Hillier, Leaman, Stansall and Bedford 1976). Alternatively, there are sophisticated methods to generate designs but they are not coupled systematically with urban analysis methods. A well-known example represents the CityEngine that uses procedural methods to create road networks and building configurations (Parish and Müller 2001). This indicates there is a gap between the analysis and the synthesis of designs, which can be addressed with *Cognitive Design Computing.*

Cognitive Design Computing is a combination of the excellence of human cognition with the power of modern computing technology. We aim to mimic the way a designer's brain works by combining state-of-the-art optimisation with machine learning approaches and available simulation methods. Given the complex nature of urban design problems, an additional aspect is the provision of models for human-computation interaction. Since urban design tasks cannot be fully automated, the computational burden of an urban design problem needs to be distributed between computer and designer.

A key approach in which digital tools can support designers is by generating design alternatives as a creative input for proposal making. Evolutionary multi-criteria optimisation methods allow the exploration of a multidimensional design space and provide a basis for the designer to evaluate contradicting requirements: a task that urban planners are faced with frequently. The vision for a cognitive design

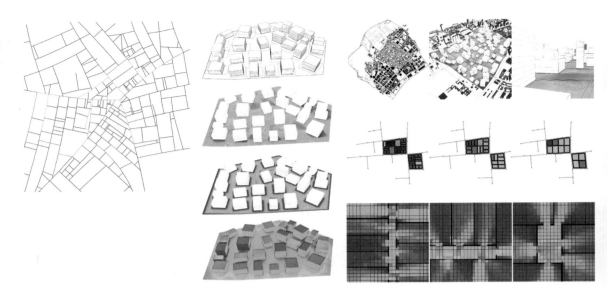

Fig. 2   Performance measures for various spatial configurations including street networks,
parcels/buildings and floorplans.

computing system is to enable an urban planner to treat a planning problem as a back-casting problem by defining what performance a design solution should achieve, and to automatically query or synthesise a set of best possible solutions.

Another important aspect of this approach is that researchers can gain insights into the nature of the design process by employing machine learning methods. This helps the understanding of how designers use such computational design support systems in combination with manual design strategies to deal with complex urban planning problems. By observing how designers work, it is possible to derive more complex artificial solution strategies that can help computers make better suggestions in the future.

König (2015) developed a library of design synthesis and evaluation methods that is published on the website of the computational planning group CPlan. This framework integrates urban data in urban design tools via model containers. In the context of data analysis, existing methods can be divided into two main groups, corresponding to the particular kinds of compared data: either the comparison of shape-determining rules instead of a shape itself (Stiny and Mitchell 1978); the comparison of characteristic values computed as shape features of a design (Derix and Jagannath 2014; Dillenburger 2010); or topology

informed labels (Langenhan, Weber, Petzold, and Dengel 2011). Beside using existing urban designs or manually creating them, another crucial part of the cognitive design computing framework is to synthesise designs. The basic technique that we use for this purpose is Evolutionary Algorithms (EA), due to their flexibility with regard to problem representation as well as their robustness. Combining geometry synthesis with the labelling method (see Figure 2) described earlier, we propose an inverse design process that can fulfil formalisable design requirements.

The main research questions for the development of a Cognitive Design Computing method are: What are the most suitable models representing urban space and function and their complex interactions? To what extent urban models need to become integrated to achieve best possible analysis power without paying too much for computational effort? These lead to the question of what are the most essential information sets needed for the design and planning of new urban areas. Related to big data we need to explore which data sets can be used theoretically for which urban design conclusions. Finally, we need to ask if and how meaningful aggregated measures can be constructed on a higher level by combining individual basic measures, as well as how these emergent high-level features can be interpreted.

106

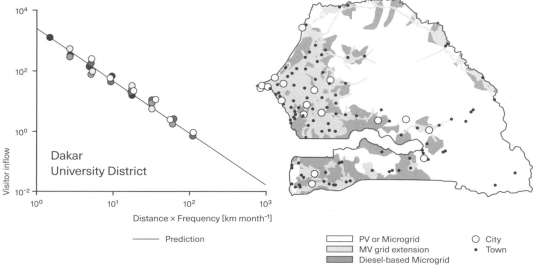

▭ PV or Microgrid	○ City
▭ MV grid extension	• Town
▭ Diesel-based Microgrid	

Fig. 3   (Left) Number of individuals visiting the university district in Dakar, Senegal, as a function of their home distance and visiting frequency. The different symbols are empirical values and denote different visiting frequencies. The straight line is the theoretical prediction of the people flows.

Fig. 4   (Right) Optimal electrification options in Senegal based on the predicted people flows and resulting energy demand (MV=medium voltage, PV=photovoltaics). The same approach can also be applied to assess the efficiency and resilience of existing energy supply systems in cities.

Revealing Common Principles of Cities: Urban Complexity

Cities are prime examples of complex systems: they are made up of many interwoven social, economic and infrastructural features that are subject to a multitude of individual and collective decisions. These interdependencies render cities prone to 'emergent' phenomena that cannot be predicted by a simple decomposition of the urban system into independently acting components. As a consequence, urban planners and designers face a hardly manageable amount of uncertainties, which are further exacerbated by the ongoing urbanisation worldwide. A prominent warning example of the resulting risk of unforeseen and potentially detrimental planning outcomes is Beijing's recent failure to implement a multi-centred urban form that has led to counterintuitive people flows, significant traffic congestion and air pollution (United Nations 2013).

Complexity science offers a promising 'big picture view' to elucidate such interdependencies by applying statistical physics and network theory modelling techniques. Importantly, it allows us to better anticipate systemic behaviour that result from the many interactions of all the components that make up a city (including people, infrastructures and more). Indeed, complexity science has recently proven to provide fundamental insights into the underlying principles of cities. Examples are urban scaling laws that are able to predict socioeconomic outputs of cities such as wages, patents or social interactions based on population size (Bettencourt 2013; Schläpfer 2014), or cellular automata for the simulation of urban growth (Batty 2013a).

The overall challenge is to enrich existing approaches of complexity science with new possibilities from big data in order to become directly applicable within the urban planning and design process. Mobile phone records, geo-referenced social network data and many other types of big data provide us with more and more details of how people actually make use of urban space. In a first step, these new empirical insights can be used for the development of simple mathematical models that are able to predict the overall performance of cities based on very local considerations.

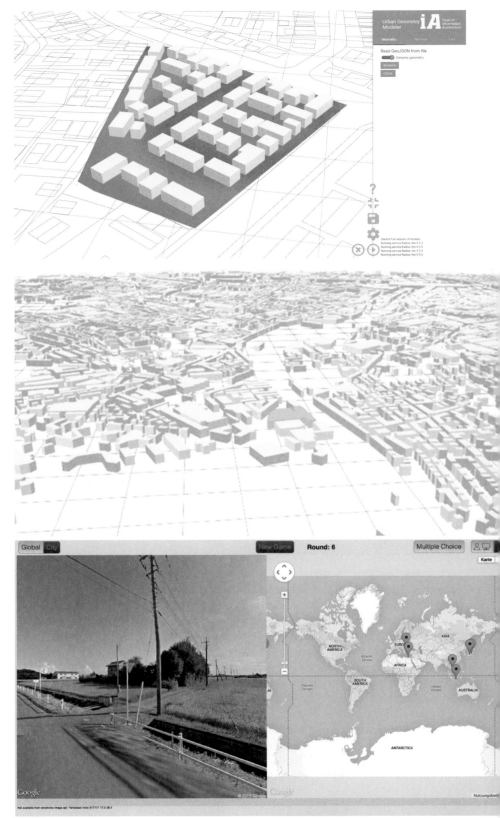

Fig. 5 (a–c) Web-viewer and modeller developed by Artem Chirkin (top and middle image) and image evaluation framework developed by Lukas Treyer (bottom image).

It is this high spatial and temporal granularity that will eventually make it possible to inform urban planners and designers of the city-wide consequences of local planning measures. As an illustrative example, mobile phone records allow us to track the movements of millions of people in cities, while complexity science offers the appropriate mathematical framework to model and eventually predict such collective flows to different urban centres (see Figure 3). These predictions, in turn, will provide urban planners and designers with the possibility to anticipate changes in the city-wide traffic flows when planning a new urban centre.

In a second step, the quantification and prediction of how people make use of urban space can be utilised to better understand the complex interplay between human activities and the performance of urban infrastructures. To that end, detailed bottom-up models of infrastructure demands can be developed and deployed for an adequate assessment of the efficiency and resilience of existing and future infrastructure networks. As an example, the insights into people flows in cities will allow the prediction of spatio-temporal energy demands, helping to identify the optimal design of energy supply networks (Figure 4).

Out of this come the main research questions: What are the statistical regularities behind the spatial organisation of cities, in terms of how people make use of urban space? Can such potentially 'universal' principles in the urban spatial organisation be harnessed to predict the future development of cities? And finally, what is the interplay between the spatial organisation of cities and the performance of urban infrastructures in terms of efficiency and resilience?

Combining Citizen Science and Participatory Design: Citizen Design Science

Prudent governments have always included citizens in the design and management of their cities. Yet specialisation and delegation in urban functions and governance have limited citizens' participation in spite of better technical communication and the availability of big data.

As a consequence, there is a huge, unexploited potential for citizen participation in the future urban planning process. Crowdsourcing and citizen science are processes for obtaining content by soliciting contributions from a large group of people. Citizens provide their view of the city, volunteer data

on their daily routines and give detailed insights on a level that survey based data collection can never provide. *The Wisdom of Crowds* (Surowieck 2004) suggests that the collective opinion may increasingly replace experts, and for lower costs. Yet the biggest potential rests in each citizen's design competence and design interest, if triggered and encouraged. The new concept of *Citizen Design Science* offers inhabitants and stakeholders the possibility of actively taking part in the design process.

To achieve this, different ways of public participation in urban planning must be considered; ones which provide intuitive and yet powerful tools for generating reasonable design proposals for non-expert users. A collaborative interface between citizens and urban planners, designers and managers represents a major challenge. It requires deeper research on efficient human-computer interaction technologies that combine laypersons' intuition with data science. Researchers at ETH Zürich, in cooperation with the Future Cities Laboratory, have developed two prototypes (see Figure 5) that function as web-based citizen design science tools. The first is a game-like approach where citizens have to decide which urban scenes shown in a photo belong to which city. Successfully selected images are afterwards clustered to identify visual properties that characterise a given city. The methodology follows the original idea of the streetscore project conducted by Naik and Philipoom (2014) to predict safety of streetscapes from photos. The second prototype supports functions for creating, editing, visualising and evaluating spatial configurations at various scales (König et al. 2015). This can be used to provide a design challenge and to observe the strategy a citizen designer applies to finding a spatial solution. These strategies can then be taken as input for a learning mechanism with the aim of applying it independently to new and similar design tasks. Data analysis methods provide instant feedback to citizens by measuring qualities of an existing or a new urban design, depending on social, cultural and functional contexts.

However, experience shows that the majority of citizens will not actively participate in such processes (Nielsen 2006); or when they do they deliver results with varying quality, therefore measures for citizen engagement and quality assessment have to be investigated. Considering the potentially large number of citizen contributions, different consent-making strategies need to be explored for aggregating design knowledge of citizens and the validity of transferring

Big Data-Informed Urban Design

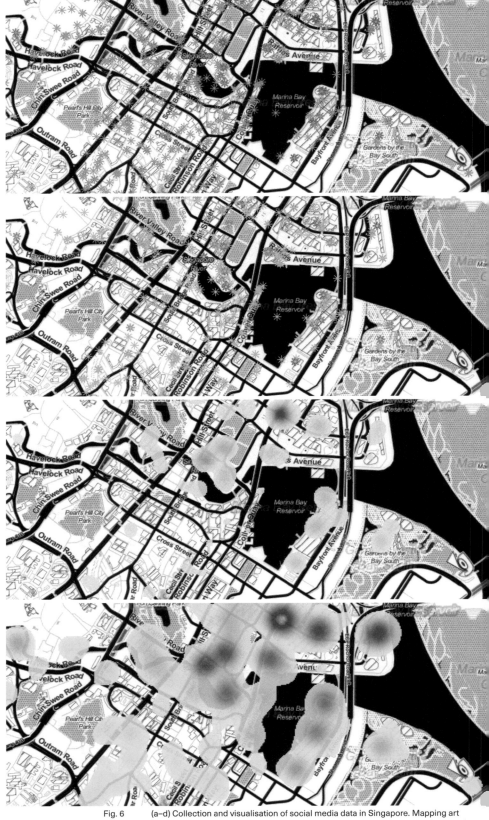

Fig. 6 (a–d) Collection and visualisation of social media data in Singapore. Mapping art locations by geo-localised data, and comparing planning decisions with the actual use of spaces.

insights to other cities with the goal of raising their liveability. For this, characteristic patterns need to be extracted and various urban metrics like the attractiveness of given areas need to be defined. By combining crowdsourced ideas with urban design standards, citizen design science has the potential to enhance and move smart cities towards responsive cities.

This promising development poses formidable research questions: How can city governments motivate a wide range of citizens to participate in the urban planning process? Is crowdsourcing representative enough or would it make more sense to work with citizens' initiatives? Do citizens decide on the design solutions that are the best for the city? Or is there a significant difference between propositions desired by the neighbourhood, and those of other citizens? Can we generalise the ideas of citizens and try to transfer the proposals to similar categorised areas?

Correlating Urban Form and Behaviour Models: Evidence Informed Urban Design and Planning Processes

The final product of an urban planning and design process, however dynamic, is still a physical environment: a city, a neighbourhood or a public place. Designing for responsive urban environments requires a shift away from conventional to a deeper, more holistic and scientific approach to design and planning. Evidence Based Design (EBD) approaches have been gaining renewed importance as data is increasingly available to designers and planners. However, access to evidence related to certain design needs and requirements does not lead to a linear translation of evidence into design solutions. EBD can, however, replace some of the assumptions made during design by grounded evidence. For instance, having an access to multimodal data on and analysis of user, usage, and perception information of public places in dense urban environments can provide designers with a lot of evidence. Rather than considering a typical user, evidence would reflect a whole number of users with their own preferences, desires and behavioural patterns such that a public space can be responsive to each and every one of these users, at the same time or over time.

Design is an open ended endeavour with many unrelated inputs and many preconceptions. Many different kinds of data are needed in order to gain an understanding of and produce proposals for the various aspects. Big urban data, open government data, social media data, other forms of user volunteered data, and real-time sensor data from urban infrastructure all help urban designers and planners to understand how people use urban spaces. These allow them to reason on and enhance socio-demographic as well as environmental aspects of cities, and at the same time, minimise potentially negative impacts. The research challenge lies in finding out which behavioural hypotheses can be drawn from specific urban data sets and their combination, and understanding the relationship of these hypotheses with spatial and organisational aspects of urban spaces: thus, design.

Tools can be developed to give designers and users of urban public spaces access to this evidence and to support the design process to create responsive spaces. To this end, the aim is to link professional design knowledge on urban space design and big data. These tools will be equipped with design analysis, recommendation, generation, and evaluation methods, tailored for specific design moments and conditions. In order to achieve this, techniques for extracting high-level information and presenting this extracted information to users and designers to inform the actual design decision making need to be further investigated. A design process needs to be developed that defines how to operationalise existing computational methods for analysing, clustering, and interpreting different data types together with dynamic visual representation, visualisation, and interaction techniques. This would be integrated seamlessly with urban design simulation and recommendation tools, as urban design and decision making elements. Urban design synthesis using data related approaches have already been developed in various contexts (Chaszar and Tunçer 2014; Koltsova et al. 2012).

Developed systems and tools will be offered to many various users of spaces, to collect feedback and inputs on various design directions and solutions. This framework could be applied in various scenarios to test how designers and users of spaces can use the tools to facilitate better informed design processes, in turn improving our future cities.

Building on the previous four research challenges in this chapter, the research questions that will be addressed are as follows: Can we integrate big data, user input and preferences, and designer knowledge for urban design recommendation? Which data sets can be used theoretically for which design moments and directions? Which useful hypotheses

Big Data-Informed Urban Design

can be found for specific cases or data sets? What are the most essential information sets needed for the design and planning of new urban areas?

Outlook: The Future Urban Design Laboratory

Urban design and management in the past were often based on principles, precedents, intentions, and anecdotal data. The increasing availability of big data offers an additional and important contribution to future urban design and management: the combination of successful previous design with Big Data-Informed Urban Design. This type of design is not exclusively data driven, because such an approach would exclude too many important design factors that cannot be covered by big data at the present time. And most of all, it would exclude the knowledge and experience of citizens.

Big Data-Informed Urban Design bridges the gaps between data sensing, data analytics, visualisation and the urban design process. It needs to recognise self-organisation, dynamics and emergence of various stocks and flows such as people, transport, materials and energy in the development of urban systems. It could provide a basis for the long-term coupling of urban planning and urban design with the management of the future city, because the same structures and data would be used.

For this, it is necessary to develop and employ the concepts of citizen design science and cognitive design computing to integrate expert design knowledge and exploit massive citizen feedback. Both promise to enable new creative designs that could drive promising solutions for future urban challenges, and at the same time assure and enable responsive urban environments that have the potential to trigger a continuous liveability improvement cycle.

Open issues have been identified that require further research: static policies need to be replaced by more dynamic and responsive ones; more insights about the human design process have to be revealed to support more complex design tasks; urban scaling laws and generic properties of cities have to be found to quantify emergent effects; more intuitive design tool interfaces and consent-making approaches have to be developed to empower citizens, and multi-modal data analysis approaches need to be developed that provide more holistic planning perspectives.

Big Data-Informed Urban Design will be successful if a positive outcome occurs on three levels: on the fundamental level, if the understanding and utilisation of urban data and thereby the formalisation of expert knowledge for the design process increases; on the research level, if the integration of cognitive design computing and complexity science methods is workable; and on the application level, if Big Data-Informed Urban Design contributes to the concept of the responsive city and is able to interactively explore the design scenarios it creates. Singapore and Zürich were chosen to be the first practical test sites for this approach.

Bibliography

Bar-Yam, Yaneer (2015). 'Complexity theory applied to policy worldwide', *Modelling Complex Systems for Public Policies*, eds. Bernardo Alves Furtado, Patrícia A M Sakowski, and Marina H Tóvolli. Brasília.

Batty, Michael (2013a). *The New Science of Cities*. Cambridge, Massachusetts: MIT Press.

Batty, Michael (2013b). 'Defining geodesign (= GIS + Design?)', *Environment and Planning B: Planning and Design* 40(1): 1–2.

Bettencourt, L M A (2013). 'The origins of scaling in cities', *Science* 340(6139): 1438–41.

Brandt, Robert M, Gordon H Chong and W Mike Martin (2010). *Design Informed: Driving Innovation with Evidenced-Based Design*. Hoboken: John Wiley & Sons.

Chaszar, Andre and Bige Tunçer (2014). 'Integrating user and usage information in a design environment', *Rethinking Comprehensive Design: Speculative Counterculture*, 45–54, paper presented at 19th *International Conference of the Association of Computer-Aided Architectural Design Research*, Kyoto, Japan.

Chaudhuri, Siddhartha, Evangelos Kalogerakis, Leonidas Guibas and Vladlen Koltun (2011). 'Probabilistic reasoning for assembly-based 3D modelling', *ACM Transactions on Graphics* 30(4): 35–43.

Derix, Christian and Prarthana Jagannath (2014). 'Digital intuition—Autonomous classifiers for spatial analysis and empirical design', *The Journal of Space Syntax* 5(2): 189–215.

Dillenburger, Benjamin (2010). 'A retrieval-system for building-plots', in *Future Cities*, 893–900, paper presented at 28th *Conference on Education in Computer Aided Architectural Design in Europe*, Zürich, Switzerland.

Ervin, Stephen (2011). 'A system for geodesign', paper presented in 12th *International Conference on Digital Landscape Architecture*, Dessau, Germany.

Faludi, Andreas and Bas Waterhout (2006). 'Introducing evidence-based planning', disP—*The Planning Review* 42(165): 4–13.
Bill Hillier and Hanson, Julienne (1984). *The Social Logic of Space*. Cambridge: Cambridge University Press.

Bill Hillier, Leaman, Adrian, Stansall, Paul and Bedford, Michael (1976). 'Space syntax', *Environment and Planning B: Planning and Design*, 3 (2) pp. 147–85.

Janssen, Patrick (2013). 'Evo-Devo in the Sky', in *Generation, Exploration and Optimisation—Computation and Performance*, 205–14, paper presented at *eCAADe Conference* 31.

Jones, Gavin W (2013). *The Population of Southeast Asia*, Working Paper Series No. 196, Global Asia Institute, National University of Singapore.

Khan, Zaheer and Saad Liaquat Kiani (2012). 'A cloud-based architecture for citizen services in smart cities', paper presented in *5th International Conference on Utility and Cloud Computing*, 315–20.

Kiran, Mariam, Peter Murphy, Inder Monga, Jon Dugan and Sartaj Singh Baveja (2015). 'Lambda architecture for cost-effective batch and speed big data process-ing', paper presented in *International Conference on Big Data*, 2785–92.

Koltsova, Anastasia, Bige Tunçer, Sofia Georga-kopoulou and Gerhard Schmitt (2012). 'Parametric tools for conceptual design support at the pedestrian urban scale: Towards inverse urban design', *Digital Physicality*, 279–87, paper presented at *eCAADe Conference*, Prague.

König, Reinhard (2015). 'CPlan: An open source library for computational analysis and synthesis', *Real Time*, eds. B Martens, G Wurzer, T Grasl, W E Lorenz and R Schaffranek, 245–50, paper presented at 33rd *eCAADe Conference*, Vienna, Austria.

König, Reinhard, Lukas Treyer and Gerhard Schmitt (2013). 'Graphical smalltalk with my optimization system for urban planning tasks', *Computation and Performance*, eds. Rudi Stouffs and S Sariyildiz, 195–203, paper presented at 31st *eCAADe Conference*, Delft, Netherlands.

Langenhan, Christoph, Markus Weber, Marcus Liwicki, Frank Petzold and Andreas Dengel (2011). 'Sketch-Based methods for researching building layouts through the semantic fingerprint of architecture', *Designing Together*, ed. P Leclercq, A Heylighen, and G Martin, 85–102, paper presented at *CAAD Futures*, Liège, Belgium.

Lensky I M and R Drori (2007). 'A satellite-based parameter to monitor the aerosol impact on convective clouds', *Journal of Applied Meteorology & Climatology*, 46(5): 660–6.

Martinez-Cesena, Eduardo Alejandro, Pierluigi Mancarella, Mamadou Ndiaye and Markus Schläpfer (2015). 'Using mobile phone data for electricity infrastructure planning', paper presented at *Analysis of Mobile Phone Networks* (NetMob), Cambridge, USA.

Naik, Nikhil, Jade Philipoom, Ramesh Raskar and Cesar Hidalgo (2014). 'Streetscore—predicting the perceived safety of one million streetscapes', paper presented in *Workshop on Web-Scale Vision and Social Media*, 793–9.

Nielsen, Jakob (2006). *Participation Inequality: Encouraging More Users to Contribute Webpage*. Available from <http://www.useit.com/alertbox/participation_ine-quality.html> Accessed on 15 November 2016.

Puppim de Oliveira, Jose A and Christopher N H Doll (2015). 'Urban governance and the systems approaches to health-environment co-benefits in cities', *Cad Saude Publica*, 25–38.

Schläpfer, Markus, Luis M A Bettencourt, Sebastian Grauwin, Matthias Raschke, Rob Claxton, Zbigniew Smoreda, Geoffrey B West and Carlo Ratti (2014). 'The scaling of human interactions with city size', *Journal of Royal Society Interface* 11(98).

Stiny, George and William John Mitchell (1978). 'The Palladian grammar', *Environment and Planning B: Planning and Design* 5(1): 5–18.

UN Human Settlements Programme (2010). *Solid Waste Management in the World's Cities, Water and Sanitation in the World's Cities*. ISBN 978-1-84971-169-2, 2010.

Surowiecki, James (2005). *The Wisdom of Crowds*. New York: Anchor Books.

Tollefson, Jeff (2012). 'Megacities move to track emissions', *Nature* 492, 20–1.

United Nations Human Settlements Programme (2013). *Planning and Design for Sustainable Urban Mobility*. New York: United Nations.

Wetz, Peter, Tuan-Dat Trinh, Ba-Lam Do, Amin Anjomshoaa, Elmar Kiesling and A Min Tjoa (2014). 'Towards an environmental information system for semantic stream data', *28th International Conference on Informatics for Environmental Protection*, 100–8, Germany.

Woetzel, Jonathan, Lenny Mendonca, Janamitra Devan, Stefano Negri, Yangmei Hu, Luke Jordan, Xiujun Li, Alexander Maasry, Geoff Tsen and Flora Yu (2009). *Preparing for China's Urban Billion*. McKinsey Global Institute.

Big Data-Informed Urban Design

Ian Smith, Chan Ghee Koh,
Didier Vernay

Cyber Civil Infrastructure

to ensure that massive investments are optimally managed, that infrastructure modifications are well engineered, and that future designs are improved. Savings due to more informed decisions can be up to hundreds of millions of dollars, particularly when replacement of important infrastructure, such as a bridge, is avoided (Sweeney 1990). Infrastructure managers can respond to information provided by sensors to optimise maintenance and management of civil infrastructure. Sensors may also provide useful information to assess the vulnerability of infrastructure. In this way, the resilience of infrastructure systems is assessed more accurately and more informed engineering measures can thus be taken to address vulnerability, ageing and other issues.

Worldwide, the need for strategic infrastructure requires an annual expenditure of more than US$3.7 trillion, or five per cent of global GDP. Since the current supply is only $2.7 trillion each year, there is an infrastructure spending gap that is currently US$1 trillion per year (World Economic Forum 2014). Figure 1 presents the three levers that could help to narrow the gap between global infrastructure demand and supply. One of these levers involves more informed decisions related to ageing infrastructure such as extension, improvement and repair.

The replacement of all ageing infrastructure is not sustainable, not cost effective, not convenient, not safe, and sometimes not possible. Fortunately, civil infrastructure often has much reserve capacity since behaviour models at the design stage, prior to construction, are necessarily conservative. More accurate estimates of real behaviour are needed once infrastructure is in service. We use sensor measurement data combined with site inspection results and engineering knowledge to improve behaviour models.

Improved knowledge of current performance leads to better predictions of performance when weighing decisions such as extension, improvement, repair and replacement. Current strategies for interpreting data are weak. Such strategies do not adequately account for the typically high levels of systematic modelling uncertainty and when uncertainty information is not complete, interpretation—and most critically, predictions—may be biased.

The case of Singapore is a good example of how cities can increase their attractiveness through wise investments in civil infrastructure. The implementation of cyber civil infrastructure has the potential

Challenges in Implementing Cyber Civil Infrastructure

The first research challenge concerns the development of sensor-data interpretation methodologies to improve predictions of behaviour models. The second research challenge is related to the development of measurement-system-design methodologies to define the number, the location and the types of sensors to be used for structural identification. Finally, the last research challenge concerns the impact of monitored structures on the responsiveness of infrastructure management systems, on the resilience of infrastructure assets as well as on future designs. The challenges are described in Figure 2. These challenges will be transformed into research projects performed through teamwork. Each challenge is described in the following sections.

Sensor Data Interpretation

Where sensors are able to measure directly parameters of interest (such as indoor temperature), data interpretation is usually straightforward and the necessary action to be taken is often clear (for example, a thermostat that triggers cooling action). However when direct measurement of key parameters is not possible, data interpretation becomes more complicated.

Low-cost approaches involve signal-analysis techniques such as correlation based methods SOM (Moosavi et al. 2015), PCA and wavelet analyses (Çatbaş et al. 2013; Posenato et al. 2010; Laory et al. 2013).

Rising infrastructure demand
~US$ 3.7 trillion/year

Levers to narrow the gap

↓ 1 Reduce demand

↑ 2 Build more new
         infrastructure

↑ 3 Extend, improve
         and repair existing   Scope of
         infrastructure   this project

New supply
~US$ 2.7 trillion/year

Gap

Existing aging
infrastructure supply

Global infrastructure demand / supply

Time

Challenges

1 **Sensor-data
   interpretation**

Model updating
& Reserve capacity
estimation

Data mining
& Outlier detection

Continuous Monitoring

Sampling the
parameter space
& Feature selection

Geotechnical
construction
monitoring

2 **Measurement
   system design**

3 **Impact
   of monitored
   structures**

Impact on future
designs

Impact on
responsiveness and
resilience of cities

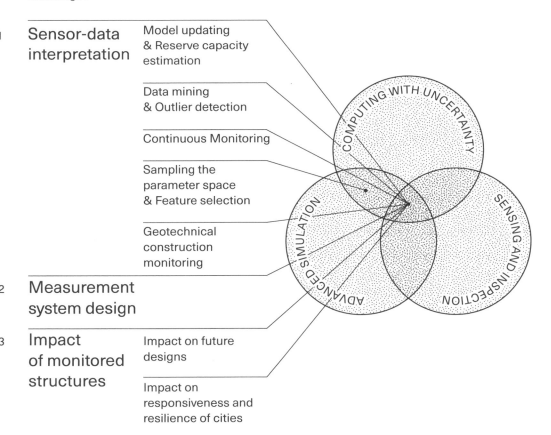

COMPUTING WITH UNCERTAINTY

ADVANCED SIMULATION

SENSING AND INSPECTION

Fig. 1   Schematic view of the three levers to narrow the gap between global infrastructure
           demand and supply. The third lever is the scope of this project. Adapted from
           World Economic Forum, Strategic Infrastructure, Technical Report, April 2014.
Fig. 2   Research challenges and topics.

Use of such strategies result in, for example, detection of system anomalies with only weak information related to location and cause, since there is no physical-principle-based model. Such approaches are thus not very useful for predictions and for guiding decisions related to repair, strengthening and replacement of infrastructure.

Greater decision support is possible through the application of behaviour model-based identification methodologies that are founded on the principles of structural mechanics. In this sense, the word identification involves finding either a set or sets of model-parameter values that lead to good explanations of measurement data. Identified models are thus useful for determining causes of measured effects (real behaviour) and then for predicting future performance. This is especially useful when studying aspects such as new geometries, modified geometries and changing environments. When dealing with civil infrastructure, such aspects are usually more important than damage detection, which is a typical research driver in other engineering fields such as aeronautics and electrical engineering.

The vast majority of model-based identification strategies involve minimising the difference between predictions and measurements using curve-fitting techniques of various levels of sophistication to obtain one calibrated model of behaviour (Çatbaş et al. 2013; Mottershead et al. 2011; Spencer Jr. and Cho 2011). Unfortunately, it is rare that this strategy results in a model that is useful for applications beyond the loading conditions and the range of data that were used for the calibration. Machine learning algorithms have also been used in identification tasks (Joshua and Varghese 2010; Saitta et al. 2010).

Model-based identification is essentially a diagnosis and as a result, it is intrinsically ambiguous (Smith and Raphael 2013). Indeed, there can be many explanations for measurements taken from complex systems. Therefore, population approaches (evaluation of many model instances) are most appropriate. Bayesian updating (Beck and Katafygiotis 1998) is the most widely studied population approach. Over the past 10 years, hundreds of papers have promoted the use of some form of Bayesian inference strategy. However, a recent article in Science warned of the dangers of using Bayesian approaches when key information (in this case, prior probabilities) is incorrect (Efron 2013). More importantly, Efron noted that when in doubt, results obtained from Bayesian updating should be checked using other approaches.

An alternative strategy to Bayesian updating is based on the recognition that measurements are more useful when they falsify models rather than validate them (Tarantola 2005, 2006). This has led to methodologies for model falsification in areas such as environmental science (Beven 2002) and civil engineering (Raphael and Smith 1998).

Currently, it is not clear which population approach is best for the context of civil infrastructure. While Bayesian updating is popular among many researchers, recent research by this PI has shown that typical assumptions of likelihood functions (for example Gaussian white noise) result in biased predictions when they are applied to measurements on civil infrastructure (Goulet and Smith 2013). Furthermore, systematic modelling uncertainties are unavoidable in civil engineering and they subtly induce additional correlations that, unless explicitly included, contribute further to prediction bias. Also, when little is known about uncertainty distributions, the model falsification approach is more robust than typical implementations of Bayesian methods. There is a need to compare population approaches on real cases so that negative effects such as prediction bias can be avoided for a range of situations.

The research questions that will be addressed are as follows:

- Are there sensor-data interpretation methodologies that are reliable and robust for a range of applications where civil infrastructure is monitored? For example, simple approaches, such as residual minimisation (curve fitting model predictions to measurement data) are known to have low levels of fidelity and robustness for predictions beyond the scope of measurement data. Are there methodologies that do better in typical contexts of civil infrastructure?
- What is the best use of sensor data from static load test and continuous monitoring for the purpose of estimating the reserve capacity and the remaining life of structures?
- What is the best use of sensor data for the purpose of improving predictions during geotechnical construction phases?

116

These questions lead to the following project objectives:

- Create a framework that combines physical-principle modelling, simulation and sensor data interpretation for civil engineering through appropriate adaptation of the science of measurement-based identification of behaviour models that are derived from the field of structural mechanics
- Compare Bayesian model updating with model falsification in terms of criteria such as fidelity, robustness in the presence of unrecognised errors and compatibility with heuristic engineering knowledge
- Study sampling efficiency in the parameter space and determine how to reduce the dimensionality of the parameter space.
- Employ data-mining techniques to support the next step of the identification (e.g. add sensors, additional inspection, etc.)
- Develop methods to detect outliers in measurement data.
- Evaluate several case studies in full-scale civil-engineering contexts in Singapore

Measurement System Design

In recent years, sensor technology has undergone important improvements in terms of accuracy and affordability. However, data acquisition systems still remain expensive. Moreover, the possible locations of sensors are often constrained due to accessibility limitations. For these reasons, it is often either impossible or not cost effective to deploy a dense network of sensors on infrastructure. This has motivated the development of measurement system design methodologies.

When sensors are used in civil engineering systems, their configuration is often solely based on engineering judgement. Measurement system design aims at defining sensor configuration in a more rational and systematic way. The objective of measurement system design is to define the number, the location and the types of sensors to be used in order to provide a maximum amount of information, given a set of system constraints, for the identification of the structural behaviour. The design of measurement systems has focused much attention in international research in recent years (Robert-Nicoud et al. 2005; Goulet and Smith 2012a). However, measurement

system design methodologies that fulfil the above objective are still challenging at present (Yi and Li 2012).

The performance of measurement system design methodologies depends on the knowledge of modelling uncertainties. Appropriate methodologies have to be developed and improved in situations where modelling uncertainties are seldom known such as civil engineering systems. Furthermore, challenges are also related to the selection of a sensor configuration when multiple conflicting criteria, such as cost, number of sensors, redundancy in sensor network and information gain, need to be evaluated and optimised simultaneously.

The research questions that will be addressed are as follows:

- Sensor-system design optimisation is known to be closely dependent on how data is interpreted. Is it possible to tailor sensor-system-design methodologies to those data interpretation methodologies that do well for the measurement of civil infrastructure behaviour?
- Is the methodology applicable to other contexts?

These questions lead to the following project objectives:

- Create appropriate methodologies for measurement system design. These methodologies need to be compatible with the best methodologies for measurement data interpretation.
- Evaluate several case studies in full-scale civil engineering contexts in Singapore

Impact of Monitored Structures

Enhanced understanding of behaviour supports decision making related to modification and extension of existing systems and in-service management. Most of the existing maintenance management systems rely solely on visual inspection to assess infrastructure performance (Frangopol and Liu 2007). Sensor data provides additional information for optimal management. Infrastructure managers can respond to information provided by sensor data to make more informed decisions related to infrastructure management. This contributes to improving the responsiveness of infrastructure management systems.

Furthermore, civil infrastructure systems of the future will be expected to perform in contexts and environments that today can only be partially defined. Sensors can be used to future proof existing infrastructure. Sensors might also provide useful information for assessing their vulnerability to changing conditions or natural disasters. In this way, the resilience of civil infrastructure systems is evaluated more accurately and appropriate engineering measures to improve resilience become apparent.

Implementation of cyber civil infrastructure has the potential to improve future designs. Current design procedures do not offer any advantage in terms of load and resistance factors when structures are measured. Monitoring structures could contribute to lowering the cost of new civil-infrastructure projects, particularly in situations where either serviceability or fatigue criteria govern designs through the use of less conservative design models.

The research questions that will be addressed are as follows:

- Does cyber civil infrastructure contribute significantly to increasing the knowledge of current performance and the future quality of civil infrastructure? More directly, is it worth making measurements of civil-infrastructure behaviour and if so, when and how?
- Is cyber civil infrastructure useful for improving the responsiveness of infrastructure management to changing neeeds and the resilience of infrastructure assets?
- How can cyber civil infrastructure be used to optimise management, guide infrastructure modifications and improve future designs?

These questions lead to the following project objectives:

- Evaluate success according to criteria such as enhanced decision-making capacity, robustness, cost and contribution to future design strategies
- Evaluate the impact of monitored structures on the responsiveness of infrastructure management to changing needs and the resilience of infrastructure assets.
- Identify case studies that demonstrate the usefulness of using advanced sensor-data interpretation methodologies to improve the synergies between science and design within the field of civil infrastructure

In meeting the objectives mentioned for each research challenge, there will be an increase in Singapore's ability to manage and extend lives of existing infrastructure while accounting for inherent reserve capacity that is typically introduced during design stages. It will also improve the responsiveness of infrastructure management to changing needs and the resilience of infrastructure assets in Singapore.

Current Research on Cyber Civil Infrastructure

An iterative structural identification framework has been developed in (Pasquier and Smith 2016). The following five tasks are included in this framework: monitoring, modelling, in situ inspection, structural identification, and prognosis. No task sequence is prescribed; engineers, placed at the centre of this framework, opportunistically selected the task that is the best at the time. Figure 3 provides a schematic.

A key task is the in-situ inspection activity. This is where the engineer is able to detect signs that the structure is not behaving as intended. Typical observations are presence of cracks in the concrete, deterioration of supports, corrosion damage, out-of-plane movements, evidence of differential settlement, excessive deflection and fatigue cracking in steel components. Usually, not all relevant observations indicate a reduction of capacity. This information is essential to the formulation of the initial model class(es) in the modelling activity. For example, it has to be decided if either the design-model parameterisation is sufficient or a completely new model class is needed. Also, in-situ inspection guides alternative choices of model classes in situations where complete model classes are falsified during structural identification (see below).

When uncertainties can be quantified, population approaches are possible, for example (Goulet et al. 2013). The model-falsification approach does not require complete knowledge of dependencies such as the correlations between errors (Goulet and Smith 2013). Figure 4 presents a static load test carried out on the Langesand Bridge at Lucern, Switzerland. Measurements were used to improve the knowledge of its current performance through model falsification.

Recent comparisons with Bayesian model updating have shown that while traditional applications using Bayesian methods are precise and accurate when all is known, they are not robust in the

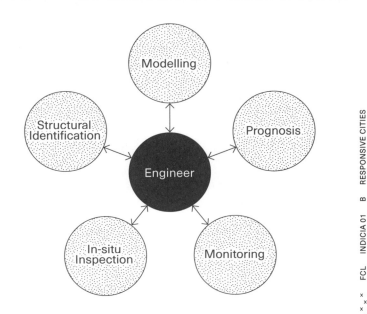

Fig. 3   A schematic of the framework for cyber civil infrastructure that was developed by R. Pasquier at EPFL (Simplified from Pasquier et al. 2016). Engineers opportunistically move from one activity to another according to a range of scenarios and contexts. No sequence is imposed.

presence of approximate models (Pasquier and Smith 2015). Management of discrete populations of behaviour models is an emerging engineering strategy for task such as diagnosis, control and design. Candidate models are used to provide ranges of predictions for prognosis.

Model falsification helps explore the space of possible model classes. The existence of thresholds means that all model instances could be falsified. This indicates that the model class is wrong. If all model instances are falsified, new hypotheses are formed regarding structural behaviour, additional site investigations may be carried out and this could include additional measurements. Such information is combined with engineering knowledge to create new model classes for model instance comparison with measurements. The framework described in Figure 3, with the engineer at the centre, is intended to support such iterations.

These methods often suffer computational challenges due to high execution times for multiple analyses and because of the exponential complexity of sampling in terms of the number of parameters. The team at the Future Cities Laboratory has much

experience working with many techniques that mitigate the negative effects of high computational requirements. Computation times are reduced with the use of surrogate models. Long execution times due to the exponential nature of sampling are avoided by careful sensitivity analysis, stochastic search and feature selection (Saitta et al. 2010).

Following recent successes over the past 15 years in applying model falsification to bridge diagnosis (Robert-Nicoud et al. 2005; Saitta et al. 2010; Goulet and Smith 2012b; Pasquier et al. 2014), to leak detection in water supply networks (Goulet and Smith 2013) and additionally to improving airflow simulations around buildings (Vernay et al. 2015; Papadopoulou et al. 2016), this methodology will be further developed and adapted to a range of case studies in civil engineering.

The model falsification approach also leads to a quantitative method for configuring measurement systems (Goulet and Smith 2012a). This method also reveals situations where the addition of sensors decreases the performance of the measurement system due to a reduction in the amount of useful information. Maximising entropy of prediction values for

Fig. 4   Static load test carried out on the Langesand Bridge, Lucern, Switzerland to increase
knowledge of its current performance.

sensor location is a powerful method that has been used for bridge diagnosis over a decade (Robert-Nicoud et al. 2005) and at Future Cities Laboratory for wind studies (Papadopoulou et al. 2016).

A quantitative indicator called identifiability has been developed to evaluate the usefulness of monitoring (Goulet and Smith 2012b). Low identifiability indicates that the measurement system design (choice of sensors as well as their locations) is not likely to result in information that will be useful to improving knowledge of real behaviour.

Conclusion

While strategic infrastructure supply is $2.5 trillion per year, the total world construction market is estimated to add approximately USD7.5 trillion worth of built environment each year and this number is expected to double in the next decade. Synergies involving sensing, computing and advanced modelling create opportunities for improved design,

engineering and management of huge investments in human, financial and material resources. Design will benefit through experiential return and this will contribute to knowledge of the interface between science and civil infrastructure design.

Specific outcomes are as follows:

- This research contributes to a growing body of work related to sensor data interpretation. As best practices move away from curve fitting single behaviour models, discrete population approaches are expected to emerge as useful, robust and general strategies for sensor data interpretation of civil infrastructure.
- Improved knowledge of real behaviour of the case study infrastructure is a certain short-term outcome. This will lead to more informed management decisions related to activities such as repair, modification and replacement. Generalisation to similar infrastructure elements through further measurement and interpretation might yield similar

120

advantages. In most cases, better knowledge of behaviour serves to quantify the extent of over-design and this leads to significant economies of infrastructure investment.
- Improved knowledge related to the impact of monitored structures on future designs, on the responsiveness of infrastructure management systems and on the resilience of infrastructure assets is a long-term outcome.

Bibliography

Beck, James L and Lambros S Katafygiotis (1998). 'Updating models and their uncertainties. I: Bayesian statistical framework', *Journal of Engineering Mechanics* 124(4): 455–61.

Beven, Keith (2002). 'Towards a coherent philosophy for modelling the environment', in *Proceedings of the Royal Society of London. Series A: Mathematical, Physical and Engineering Sciences*, 2465–84.

Çatbaş, Necati F, Tracy Kijewski-Correa and Emin A Aktan (2013). *Structural Identification of Constructed Systems*. Reston: American Society of Civil Engineers (ASCE).

Efron, Bradley (2013). 'Bayes' theorem in the 21st century', *Science* 340(6137): 1177–8.

Frangopol, Dan M and Min Liu (2007). 'Maintenance and management of civil infrastructure based on condition, safety, optimization, and life-cycle cost', *Structure and Infrastructure engineering* 3(1): 29–41.

Goulet, James-A and Ian F C Smith (2012a). 'Performance-driven measurement system design for structural identification', *Journal of Computing in Civil Engineering* 27(4): 427–36.

Goulet, James-A and Ian F C Smith (2012b). 'Predicting the usefulness of monitoring for identifying the behavior of structures', *Journal of Structural Engineering* 139(10): 1716–27.

Goulet, James-A and Ian F C Smith (2013). 'Structural identification with systematic errors and unknown uncertainty dependencies', *Computers & Structures* 128: 251–8.

Goulet, James-A, Marie Texier, Clotaire Michel, Ian F C Smith and Luc Chouinard (2013). 'Quantifying the effects of modeling simplifications for structural identification of bridges', *Journal of Bridge Engineering* 19(1): 59–71.

Joshua, Liju and Koshy Varghese (2010). 'Accelerometer-based activity recognition in construction', *Journal of Computing in Civil Engineering* 25(5): 370–9.

Laory, Irwanda, Thanh N Trinh, Daniele Posenato and Ian F C Smith (2013). 'Combined model-free data-interpretation methodologies for damage detection during continuous monitoring of structures', *Journal of Computing in Civil Engineering* 27(6): 657–66.

Moosavi, Vahid, Gideon Aschwanden and Erik Velasco (2015). 'Finding candidate locations for aerosol pollution monitoring at street level using a data-driven methodology', *Atmospheric Measurement Techniques* 8(9): 3321–56.

Mottershead, John E, Michael Link and Michael I Friswell (2011). 'The sensitivity method in finite element model updating: A tutorial', *Mechanical Systems and Signal Processing* 25(7): 2275–96.

Papadopoulou, Maria, Benny Raphael, Ian F C Smith and Chandra Sekhar (2016). 'Optimal sensor placement for time-dependent systems: Application to wind studies around buildings', *Journal of Computing in Civil Engineering* 30(2).

Pasquier, Romain, James-A Goulet, Claire Acevedo and Ian F C Smith (2014). 'Improving fatigue evaluations of structures using in-service behavior measurement data', *Journal of Bridge Engineering* 19(11): 1–10.

Pasquier, Romain and Ian F C Smith (2015). 'Robust system identification and model predictions in the presence of systematic uncertainty', *Advanced Engineering Informatics* 29(4): 1096–1109.

Pasquier, Romain and Ian F C Smith (2016). 'Iterative structural identification framework for evaluation of existing structures', *Engineering Structures* 106: 179–94.

Posenato, Daniele, Prakash Kripakaran, Daniele Inaudi and Ian F C Smith (2010). 'Methodologies for model-free data interpretation of civil engineering structures', *Computers & Structures* 88(7): 467–82.

Raphael, Benny and Ian F C Smith (1998). 'Finding the right model for bridge diagnosis', in *Artificial Intelligence in Structural Engineering*, 308–19. Springer.

Robert-Nicoud, Yvan, Benny Raphael and Ian F C Smith (2005). 'Configuration of measurement systems using Shannon's entropy function', *Computers & Structures* 83(8): 599–612.

Saitta, Sandro, Prakash Kripakaran, Benny Raphael and Ian F C Smith (2010). 'Feature selection using stochastic search: An application to system identification', *Journal of Computing in Civil Engineering* 24(1): 3–10.

Smith, Ian F C and Benny Raphael (2013). *Engineering Informatics: Fundamentals of Computer-Aided Engineering*. Hoboken: John Wiley & Sons.

Spencer Jr, Billie F and Soojin Cho (2011). 'Wireless smart sensor technology for monitoring civil infrastructure: Technological developments and full-scale applications', in *Proceedings of the World Congress on Advances in Structural Engineering and Mechanics (ASEM'11)*, paper presented at *The 2011 World Congress on Advances in Structural Engineering and Mechanics (ASEM'11)*, Seoul, South Korea.

Sweeney, Robert A P (1990). 'Update on fatigue issues at Canadian national railways', in *IABSE Workshop Lausanne (Zurich: International Association for Bridge and Structural Engineering)*, 111–6.

Tarantola, Albert (2005). *Inverse Problem Theory: Methods for Data Fitting and Parameter Estimation*. Philadelphia, PA: SIAM.

Tarantola, Albert (2006). 'Popper, Bayes and the inverse problem', *Nature Physics* 2(8): 492–4.

Vernay, Didier G, Benny Raphael and Ian F C Smith (2015). 'Improving simulation predictions of wind around buildings using measurements through system identification techniques', *Building and Environment* 94(2): 620–31.

World Economic Forum (2014). 'Strategic infrastructure'. *Technical Report*.

Yi, Ting-Hua and Hong-Nan Li (2012). 'Methodology developments in sensor placement for health monitoring of civil infrastructures', *International Journal of Distributed Sensor Networks* vol. 2012.

FCL INDICIA 01 B RESPONSIVE CITIES

Alexander Erath, Tanvi Maheshwari,
Pieter Fourie, Michael van Eggermond

New Ways to Understand Mobility in Cities

Cities are complex systems that combine relatively stable stocks of buildings, infrastructure and technology as well as fluctuating flows of air, water, energy, capital and people. The capacity of cities to combine such diverse stocks and flows enables them to function as rich places of exchange. All the good things we associate with urban life—chance encounters, lively public spaces, vigorous businesses, creative opportunities—rely on such places of exchange.

But designing effective, rich and equitable urban places of exchange is a complex process. It involves managing the relationship between stocks and flows to produce urban places that balance elements that are stable and unstable, fixed and fluid, durable yet ephemeral. How people, air, and water weave through a city's buildings, across its public places, along its streets is one of the great challenges of urban planning. Even if flows are increasingly virtual, such that communication between people and things is not place bound, managing the relationship between stocks and flows still matters.

Following the rise of motorised transport technologies, city planners have generally accepted the car as one of the primary technologies of flow. As a result many other modes of non-motorised transport such as walking and cycling have been marginalised or forgotten altogether. One of the great challenges of planning contemporary and future cities is how to revive, diversify and innovate new kinds of transport flows and recalibrate them to the urban fabric.

Practically speaking, many factors are involved. How urban density and land use are distributed has a significant effect on where people live, work, study, shop or spend leisure time—and hence when, where and how long people travel to these destinations. The structure of the road network, shape and size of land parcels, land use patterns and building morphologies all constitute urban form. Together they impact how people travel in cities. However, in addition to urban form, a key determinant is the design of the streets on which people walk, cycle and drive. The way streets are designed not only influences how safe and comfortable people feel when walking and cycling, but also how enjoyable it is, unleashing further potential for social interaction and commercial viability.

There is abundant literature describing these phenomena, proposing models to describe public travel behaviour, and a range of software tools available to simulate traffic flow on various spatial scales. However, recent and ongoing technological development in the field of Virtual Reality (VR) and the continuous generation of Big Data streams that document urban mobility could open new windows for scientific insights and practical applications for urban transport planning.

Studying public perception and behaviour in the real world is usually restricted by how existing environments are designed. Since adapting the urban built environment to better serve active mobility requires substantial efforts even for pilot interventions, VR offers an unprecedented opportunity to study and understand the interrelation between the built environment and mobility behaviour in an experimental setting. It allows a more nuanced understanding of how people perceive different street design options and to investigate how they would potentially adapt their travel behaviour without the need to actually reconfigure existing streets. Such pre-occupancy evaluation can help to understand user reactions triggered by different design options, and help to communicate design trade-offs to various stakeholders of a street design project.

Big Data streams that describe urban mobility flows are being continuously generated; people leave digital traces from their mobile phones when travelling, from swipe smart cards when using public transport and engage in social media activities or pay for goods and services using cashless payment transmissions. This data allows researchers and planners to understand today's travel patterns at an unprecedented level of detail. Before such Big Data sources became available, similar information could only be

Fig. 1   A human scale urban design with active frontages makes walking a comfortable,
         inspiring experience and invites people to linger and socialise.
Fig. 2   To enhance traffic flow, planners have installed a pedestrian overpass to connect
         two pedestrianised areas which has undesired separation effects.

Fig. 3   Streams of urban mobility data are generated as passengers use smart cards for payment of public transport services.

generated using transport simulation models that were based on traditional survey data such as population census and travel diaries which are usually only surveyed approximately every five years. However, while those models allow the adaptation of both demand and supply in what-if scenarios of different future plans, the application of Big Data on urban mobility is so far restricted mainly to data analytics.

To allow for prediction in what-if scenarios, it is important to understand and contextualise the information contained in such Big Data sources to enable the inference of socio-demographic profiles and activities. This will inform models of travel behaviour and help adapt the data for agent-based, large-scale transport simulation frameworks such as MATSim, which models the travel and activity patterns of a city's entire population over the course of a day. Given the granularity and continuous generation of the input data and standardisation of data formats, this will not only enable new applications for transport modelling such as operational planning, but also considerably lower the efforts required to implement and maintain agent-based transport simulation models.

Understanding How to Promote Active Mobility Using Virtual Reality

In a rapidly urbanising world that is threatened by the impacts of man-made global warming due to ever increasing CO_2 emissions, effective strategies to decarbonise urban mobility is an urgent need. While in developed economies urbanisation generally can lead to a reduction in transport energy consumption due to a general trend of spatial centralisation and the related expansion of public transport services (Creutzig et al. 2015), urbanisation in low-income countries usually leads to increased travel demand, expansion of motorisation and hence higher energy consumption and more CO_2 emissions (Jones 1991; Lefèvre 2009; Ribeiro et al. 2007).

Besides urbanisation, ageing is the second major demographic transition the world is currently experiencing. The way cities are designed and the range of options available for people to travel have a direct impact on public health, especially for the older cohorts (Yen et al. 2009). It has repeatedly been demonstrated that living in neighbourhoods with

Fig. 4   La Rambla in Barcelona is a tree-lined pedestrian mall served by public transport
               both by buses and underground mass rapid transit which encourages people to walk
               and mingle. It is a good example of how streets not only can serve mobility demands
               but also provide public space.

various retail options and streets designed to accommodate active mobility are associated with better public health outcomes (Beard and Petitot 2010). Low density, mono-functional sprawl has been found to be associated with obesity and lower levels of physical activity which both increase the risk for diabetes and cardiovascular disease (Fecht et al. 2016; Saelens et al. 2003). Good street design, convenient access to public transport and diverse retail outlets also encourage individuals to remain engaged with their local community and to maintain supportive social networks ultimately leading to lower rates of depression (Mair et al. 2008) and improved well-being (Eibich et al. 2016).

Walking and cycling allow for random encounters that lead to more social interactions, and those modes of transport also cost far less than private cars or public transportation in terms of direct user costs and public infrastructure investment. These transport modes are also socially equitable, as it is affordable to everyone and physically possible for most people. Finally, when cycling is a popular mode of transport, like in Copenhagen or Amsterdam where more than 30 per cent of the traffic movement is by bike, it also helps to alleviate road congestion and crowding on public transport. It saves space as bicycles require much less space for both use and parking.

At the same time, several studies show that the real and perceived danger or discomfort imposed by motor traffic discourages walking and cycling (Jacobsen et al. 2009) for a majority of the population (Furth 2008; Geller 2009). In most cities with a high share of active mobility, presence of dedicated infrastructure to separate bicyclists and pedestrians from fast and heavy motor traffic is widespread (Pucher and Dijkstra 2000; Pucher and Buehler 2008). In developed countries and cities that lack such infrastructure, the number of people who walk or cycle is low. Similarly, cities within the US with more dedicated bicycling infrastructure tend to have more bicycle use (Buehler and Pucher 2012; Dill and Carr 2003).

125   New Ways to Understand Mobility in Cities

In developing and emerging economies, walking and cycling is an important form of transport primarily for the urban poor. However, due to the lack of infrastructure to support active modes of transport, traffic safety is a key concern. In such conditions, investment in infrastructure to support active mobility can also help address transport equality issues.

The assessment of the impact of the built environment on mode choice, especially for non-commuting activities, has been also widely addressed in the literature. Several authors have tried to assess the impact of aggregate-built design variables such as block size and number of intersections on mobility and mode choice (Cervero and Kockelman 1997; Kitamura et al. 1997; Zhang et al. 2012). However, only very few studies assess the direct effect of the built environment on individual travel behaviour. For example, a recent ex-post study (Cascetta and Cartenì 2014) based on stated preference data demonstrated how the hedonic quality of remarkable metro station architecture affects route choice behaviour in Naples, Italy.

A central reason for this lack of a strong body of evidence documenting the direct impact of urban and street design variables on individual mobility choices may be the methodological challenges, including setting up experiment design that is suitable for generating valid results.

Improvements in walking and cycling infrastructure are usually rolled out gradually over long periods of time. At the same time, travel choice behaviour is characterised by habitual choices (Gärling and Axhausen 2004). While it is practical to test interventions such as distribution of free bus tickets or better awareness of alternative transport modes, it is usually unfeasible to change the physical environment in the context of a scientific study.

The opening of new infrastructure can open windows of opportunity, but studying the impact on individual travel behaviour requires a longitudinal experiment design which typically needs substantial research resources. In addition, the researcher typically has to deal with uncontrolled effects such as changing weather conditions or fuel price levels. So the experimental variation is limited to how the new infrastructure has been built, while other design options must remain untested.

Fig. 5   (a–b) Prototype renderings to illustrate different street designs from a cyclist's perspective.

Fig. 6   First prototype of a Cycling Simulator at NHTV University of Applied Sciences Breda, NL.

Identifying these limitations, researchers have used sketches in stated preference surveys to communicate design. For example, to understand how safe from crime people feel given different street design and levels of street lighting (Börjesson 2012) or how urban design variables impact pedestrian route choice (Erath 2015). Using a similar approach but employing simple 3D visualisations, (Martínez and Barros 2014) found that people strongly value a range of pedestrian infrastructure design such as presence of barriers and trees, while variables such as composition of traffic and land use are of lower importance. A key advantage of using computer-generated visualisations as compared to sketches is that it allows to easily collate design scenarios by selectively activating the relevant digital layers.

Recent advances in computer graphics and lowered barriers to entry into the field of video games have opened new opportunities for generating realistic 3D scenarios suitable for behavioural studies. Mostofi Darbani et al. (2014) demonstrated in a small pilot study the potential of using video game

environments for choice modelling. They used a 3D stated preference survey on choosing a neighbourhood by comparing it with a traditional, text-only stated preference approach. While they modelled various 3D scenarios manually—possibly time intensive—Procedural Modelling tools can generate parameterised 3D visualisation from a set of rules which perfectly support applications for stated preference surveys. It allows researchers to efficiently generate hundreds of different design configurations based on an experiment plan which then can be used for survey work.

Walking and cycling must be considered a multi-sensory experience which includes vision, auditory, somatic sensation, olfaction and vestibular stimulation. Conducting survey work to understand the perception of various street design options based on static pictures only can be restrictive. Therefore, we argue that to fundamentally understand the relationship between the built environment and its ability to make active transport modes a positive experience, one needs to study the cognitive processes used while walking and cycling. The availability and visual

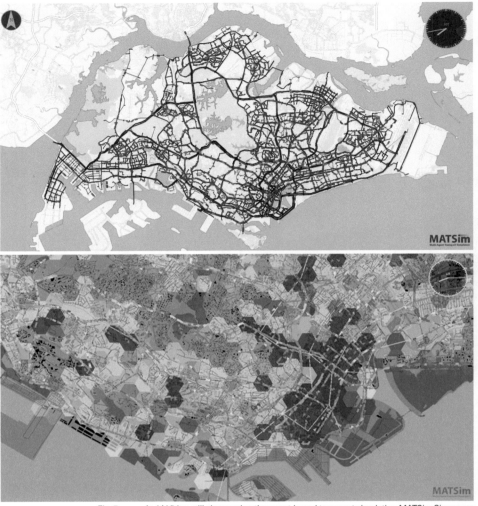

Fig. 7   (a–b) Video still showcasing the agent-based transport simulation MATSim Singapore
              which models transport flows based on individual vehicles and persons.

quality of consumer-grade head-mounted displays and progress in computer graphics offer new opportunities to use VR not only for computer games but also for research applications.

Driving simulators have been used in transport research since the 1960's (Schlesinger et al. 1964) to study driver behaviour and their interaction with the vehicle and the road environment. Simulators have been used as research aids in fields such as road safety, testing innovative road designs, usability of intelligent transport systems, impaired travel behaviour and vehicle layout (Blana 1996). Recently, a few research groups have also developed cycling simulators (Herpers et al. 2009; Mills 2012) for applications in the areas of road safety and traffic education.

These cycling simulators use a projected screen and three displays mounted side by side as visualisation system, a standard bicycle with sensors and actuators, and a surround sound system to create an immersive experience. It has been shown that visual cues significantly dominate the perception of visual depth in the majority of applications (Herpers et al. 2012). Using consumer-grade head-mounted displays as part of a cycling simulation setup may lead to a substantially enhanced visual immersion and new applications for research, for example to study the perception and measured physical reactions that different street design and traffic operation scenarios trigger.

Fig. 8   The combination of data on road networks and public transport schedules,
behavioural models and Big Data sources documenting travel demand will lead
to new types transport simulation models.

Given the novelty of these technologies, it is required to first demonstrate the validity of such approaches for research by answering questions such as:

- How are urban environments presented in VR perceived differently from the real world?
- Which are the limitations of studying street design reconfigurations using virtual reality?
- How do different people engage with Virtual Reality?
- How can measurements of physical sensors such as eye tracking, skin conductivity and heartbeat variability enhance qualitative survey approaches (such as a talking interview) in VR applications?
- Once satisfactory answers to those questions are found, VR will allow the addressing of a set of application-oriented research questions more directly than ever before:
- How do streets need to be designed so that a wider range of people choose to use active mobility?
- How does the physical ability and social context influence the individual's perception of, and engagement with, active transport modes?
- How do traffic levels and composition influence people's perception of traffic safety?
- In a city context such as in Singapore, how can we provide evidence-based design guidelines for retrofitting a modernist inspired, tropical town to better serve the needs of pedestrians and cyclists?

Addressing such research questions should help to inform urban design and transport planning towards healthy, happy and environmentally friendly cities. It will allow the investigation of how new technologies can be used for practical planning applications, pre-occupancy studies and citizen participation in urban planning and design.

Using Big Data for Transport Planning

While street design has a direct impact on active mobility, many trips stretch across distances that are best covered by motorised transport. Travel demand models have been applied since the 1960s to describe traffic flows on a city, region, or even country level, and to help evaluate future infrastructure and policy scenarios. Although the methodological frameworks have changed considerably, for example to describe travel demand based on individual agents rather than aggregated flows, the core input used to develop those models remained largely the same. They use data describing the spatial distribution of places of residence, jobs and education combined with models that describe the generation, distribution and mode choice of trips based on travel diary surveys. Since those surveys normally only can cover one to two per cent of the population living in the area of interest, the travel demand can only be described by generalising travel patterns as observed from this comparably small sample.

The availability of new Big Data sources such as mobile phone cell tower transaction logs or public transport smart card data that document mobility flow helps the understanding of travel patterns on a much bigger scale and level of detail. These data streams however are opportunistically collected and do not include all necessary information required for use in travel demand models. Therefore, pre-processing techniques are needed to extract information on individual travel patterns. Big data sources have to be fused with other data sources, such as travel diary survey and credit card transactions to infer further information that is important for predictive transport demand models such as the purpose of observed activities and socio-demographic information on the person travelling.

Given the amount of data to be processed, techniques from the fields of machine learning and computational statistics are required, which call for an interdisciplinary research setup. In the field of mobile phone data, earlier applications mainly focused on the extraction of mobility patterns (Reades et al. 2007; Calabrese et al. 2011), but only very recently have researchers made attempts to apply sophisticated machine learning techniques to contextualise the mobility information from call detail records. For example, Widhalm et al. (2015) constructed a Relational Markov Network and trained its parameters in an unsupervised manner using Expectation Maximisation, while (Paiement et al. 2015) designed a Neural Network representation of a Hidden Markov Model to infer the activity schedules of the agents of a MATSim implementation for the San Francisco Bay area.

While smart card data usually do not require any considerable pre-processing techniques to derive information on individual mobility patterns, they only cover trips made by public transport. Applied to regional or national scale, this allows for the direct use of such data as travel demand for agent-based transport simulation (Bouman et al. 2012). In the urban context, however, where service reliability and stop-to-stop travel times can be substantially affected by congestion, further modelling techniques are required. Fourie et al. (2016) introduced a stochastic model of the speed of buses between public transport stops and dwell time behaviour at stops, and applied it in a simplified MATSim implementation to the public transport of Singapore. This stochastic, data-driven approach not only improved the simulation time substantially, but enabled the model to predict the operational stability of alternative public transport schedules.

These two examples illustrate how well activity-based transport-demand modelling and agent-based simulations tie in with new Big Data sources, as both originate from the concept of individual travel patterns rather than aggregate traffic flows. The successful combination should open new fields of application. For example, agent-based transport simulations could be applied to what-if scenarios to support operational planning of public transport services and help adapt schedules for recurring special events, or planned deviations due to construction works.

The use of such Big Data streams would also dramatically reduce the time and effort required to implement agent-based transport simulation models, as mobile phone data is being generated in any city all the time, and is stored in standardised formats. This substantially lowers the barrier-to-entry for applying agent-based transport simulation as a transport planning tool. Furthermore, due to the nature of the opportunistic frequently collected data inputs, the model can easily be kept up-to-date.

However, the challenge of working with datasets that differ with regards to data granularity, collection period, spatial area covered, and sourced from different domains calls for an exploration of cross-domain data fusion methodologies, ideally specifically designed for the transport planning field. Dealing with privacy-sensitive data also calls an open debate about the ethics of using such Big Data sources. Such a debate could contribute to the development of data anonymisation approaches that optimally consider the trade-off between maintaining maximum data granularity for improved modelling, and addressing data privacy concerns by blurring and aggregating individual data points.

Transport Planning and the Future
of Urban Mobility

The way urban form developed, and how streets and roads have been designed has always been tightly connected with available vehicle technologies. Raised walkways, such as those used in ancient cities, experienced a revival in eighteenth century Europe to separate pedestrian traffic from carts and horse droppings.

Likewise, rail technology provided the mobility backbone for the Garden City concept (Howard 1902). But the emergence of garden suburbs served by a rapidly expanding commuter train network turned Howard's original idea of connected but relatively independent cities upside down. Mass motorisation further fueled urban sprawl and continues to do so worldwide, particularly in emerging economies, leading to ever increasing levels of congestion and environmental problems. Meanwhile cities with high quality of living continue to expand their public transport networks and redesign streets to better cater for the needs of pedestrians and cyclists.

With the rapid development of technologies like computer vision and artificial intelligence, widespread commercial launch of autonomous vehicles is expected within the next 10 to 30 years. Since autonomous vehicles liberate passengers from the task of driving, allowing them to pursue other tasks while travelling, the cost of driving will be perceived as substantially lower than today. Basic economic theory therefore suggests that more miles will be travelled. It is currently unclear whether such induced demand can be counterbalanced through road capacity gains due to platooned driving and higher efficiency from electric drive trains and lower vehicle weights.

Such projections underline the importance of rethinking conventional methods of transport planning and street design. The key challenge of travel demand modelling will shift from predicting mobility flows to developing tools to assess and communicate the likely impact of new vehicle technologies. These, once introduced to the market, could dynamically manage mobility demand on a daily basis and evaluate strategies how to improve operational planning such as dynamic vehicle repositioning and smart charging.

If autonomous vehicles will be mainly used as shared cars, the demand for parking will likely drop considerably, freeing up a tremendous amount of urban space. This would provide new opportunities to design and program streets to directly address the potential problems that autonomous vehicles can cause. Additionally, public health will become an ever important issue for ageing societies, ones that are more likely to prefer a self-driving car over any physical activity required to move from point to point.

Future streets must be designed to invite people of all ages and backgrounds to walk and cycle and offer opportunities for people to mingle and socialise. Only then can mobility support the sustainable development of urban societies.

Bibliography

Beard, John R and Charles Petitot (2010). 'Ageing and urbanization: Can cities be designed to foster active ageing?', *Public Health Reviews* 32(2): 1.

Blana, E. (1996). *Driving Simulator Validation Studies: A Literature Review*. Available from <http://www.its.leeds.ac.uk> Accessed on 12 June 2016.

Börjesson, M. (2012). 'Valuing perceived insecurity associated with use of and access to public transport', *Transport Policy* 22: 1–10.

Bouman P, Milan Lovric, T Li, E van der Hurk, L Kroon and P Vervest (2012). 'Recognizing demand patterns from smart card data for agent-based micro-simulation of public transport', in 11th *International Joint Conference on Autonomous Agents and Multiagent Systems* (AAMAS), ed. AAMAS, Valencia.

Buehler, Ralph and John Pucher (2012). 'Cycling to work in 90 large American cities: New evidence on the role of bike paths and lanes', *Transportation* 39(2): 409–32.

Calabrese F, G Di Lorenzo, L Liu and C Ratti (2011). 'Estimating origin-destination flows using mobile phone location data', *IEEE Pervasive Computing* 10(4): 36–44.

Cascetta, Ennio and Armando Cartenì (2014). 'The hedonic value of railways terminals. a quantitative analysis of the impact of stations quality on travellers behaviour', *Transportation Research Part A: Policy and Practice* 61: 41–52.

Cervero, Robert and Kara Kockelman (1997). 'Travel demand and the 3Ds: Density, diversity, and design', *Transportation Research Part D: Transport and Environment* 2(3): 199–219.

Creutzig, Felix, Giovanni Baiocchi, Robert Bierkandt, Peter-Paul Pichler and Karen C Seto (2015). 'Global typology of urban energy use and potentials for an urbanization mitigation wedge', *Proceedings of the National Academy of Sciences* 112(20): 6283–6288.

Dill, Jennifer and Theresa Carr (2003). 'Bicycle commuting and facilities in major us cities: If you build them, commuters will use them', *Transportation Research Record: Journal of the Transportation Research Board* 1828(1): 116–123.

Eibich, Peter, Christian Krekel, Ilja Demuth and Gert G Wagner (2016). 'Associations between neighborhood characteristics, well-being and health vary over the life course', *Gerontology* 62(3): 362–370.

Erath, Alexander (2015). 'Modelling for walkability: Understanding pedestrians' preferences in Singapore', 14th *International Conference on Travel Behavior Research*, Windsor, UK.

Fecht, Daniela, Lea Fortunato, David Morley, Anna L Hansell and John Gulliver (2016). 'Associations between urban metrics and mortality rates in England', *Environmental Health* 15(S1).

Furth, Peter G (2008). 'On-road bicycle facilities for children and other 'easy riders': Stress mechanisms and design criteria', paper presented at *Transportation Research Board 87th Annual Meeting*.

Gärling, Tommy and Kay Werner Axhausen (2004). 'Introduction: Habitual travel choice', *Transportation* 30(1): 1–11.

Geller, Peter (2009). *Four Types of Cyclists*. Working Paper. Portland: Portland Office of Transportation.

RESPONSIVE CITIES   B   INDICIA 01   FCL

Herpers R, D Scherfgen, M Kutz, J Bongartz, U Hartmann, O Schulzyk, S Boronas, T Saitov, H Steiner and D Reinert (2012). 'Multimedia sensory cue processing in the FIVIS simulation environment', in *Multiple Sensorial Media Advances and Applications: New Developments in MulSeMedia*, eds. George Ghinea, Frederic Andres, and Stephen R Gulliver. IGI Global.

Herpers R, D Scherfgen, M Kutz, U Hartmann, O Schulzyk, D Reinert and H Steiner (2009). 'FIVIS—A bicycle simulation system', in *World Congress on Medical Physics and Biomedical Engineering*, September 7–12, 2009, Munich, Germany, *IFMBE Proceedings*, eds. Olaf Dössel and Wolfgang C Schlegel, 2132–2135. Berlin, Heidelberg: Springer.

Howard, Sir Ebenezer (1902). *Garden Cities of Tomorrow*. Swan Sonnenschein & Company, Limited.

Jones, Donald W (1991). 'How urbanization affects energy-use in developing countries', *Energy Policy* 19(7): 621–30.

Kitamura, Ryuichi, Patricia L Mokhtarian and Laura Laidet (1997). 'A micro-analysis of land use and travel in five neighbourhoods in the San Francisco Bay Area', *Transportation* 24(2): 125–58.

Lefèvre, Benoit (2009). 'Long-term energy consumptions of urban transportation: A prospective simulation of 'transport–land uses' policies in Bangalore', *Energy Policy* 37(3): 940–53.

Mair C A, V Diez Roux and S Galea (2008). 'Are neighborhood characteristics associated with depressive symptoms? A critical review', *Journal of Epidemiology & Community Health*.

Martínez, Luis Miguel Garrido and Ana Paula Borba Gonçalves Barros (2014). 'Understanding factors that influence pedestrian environment quality', paper presented at *Transportation Research Board 93rd Annual Meeting*, Washington D.C.

Mills, Casey (2012). *Driving and Bicycling Simulator Facilities Webpage*. Available from <http://cce.oregonstate.edu/node/234> Accessed on 12 June 2016.

Paiement, Jean-Francois, Mogeng Yin, Jeff Pang, Colin Goodall, Ann Skudlark, Chris Volinsky and Alexei Pozdnoukhov (2015). 'Data analytics for urban mobility modeling', paper presented at *Bloomberg Data for Good Exchange Conference*, New York City.

Pucher, John and Ralph Buehler (2008). 'Making cycling irresistible: Lessons from the Netherlands, Denmark and Germany', *Transport Reviews* 28(4): 495–528.

Pucher, John and Lewis Dijkstra (2000). 'Making walking and cycling safer: Lessons from Europe', *Transportation Quarterly* 54(3): 25–50.

Reades, Jonathan, Francesco Calabrese, Andres Sevtsuk and Carlo Ratti (2007). 'Cellular census: Explorations in urban data collection', *IEEE Pervasive Computing* 6(3): 30–8.

Ribeiro, Suzana K, Shigeki Kobayashi, Michel Beuthe, Jorge Gasca, David Greene, David S Lee, Yasunori Muromachi, Peter J Newton, Steven Plotkin, Daniel Sperling and others (2007). '*Transportation and its Infrastructure*'. Institute of Transportation Studies.

Saelens, Brian E, James F Sallis and Lawrence D Frank (2003). 'Environmental correlates of walking and cycling: Findings from the transportation, urban design, and planning literatures', *Annals of Behavioral Medicine: A Publication of the Society of Behavioral Medicine* 25(2): 80–91.

Schlesinger, Lawrence E, Bernard Karmel and Stanley Cohen (1964). 'Systems analysis of driving simulation', *Human Factors: The Journal of the Human Factors and Ergonomics Society* 6(4): 383–92.

Widhalm, Peter, Yingxiang Yang, Michael Ulm, Shounak Athavale and Marta C González (2015). 'Discovering urban activity patterns in cell phone data', *Transportation* 42(4): 597–623.

Yen, Irene H, Yvonne L Michael and Leslie Perdue (2009). 'Neighborhood environment in studies of health of older adults: A systematic review', *American Journal of Preventive Medicine* 37(5): 455–63.

Zhang, Lei, Jin Hyun Hong, Arefeh Nasri and Qing Shen (2012). 'How built environment affects travel behavior: A comparative analysis of the connections between land use and vehicle miles traveled in US cities', *Journal of Transport and Land Use* 5(3).

Christoph Hoelscher, Victor R. Schinazi,
Tyler Thrash, John Zacharias

Theoretical and Methodological Challenges for Cognitive Research in the Built Environment

The Challenges of Understanding Urban Cognition

One significant feature of urbanisation in the twenty-first century is the increase in large, complex and densely populated city quarters. Airports, shopping precincts, sports venues and cultural facilities increasingly combine with generic function buildings such as hotels, housing, businesses and offices to produce horizontal and vertical nodes in a city. The capacity of such city quarters to bring large numbers of people into proximity produces crowds of unprecedented complexity. The manner in which such crowds 'behave' in space by aggregating, disaggregating, flowing or stalling generate new kinds of urban experience that can be thrilling, bewildering, stressful or even threatening. In turn, this creates a set of complex challenges for architectural design and its capacity to understand human behaviour and crowd dynamics.

Many physical criteria for such measures as air quality, thermal comfort or the carbon footprint of a building have been developed to a mature level for the design and construction of dense city quarters. However, our understanding of how human needs and capabilities interact in such contexts is less well understood. Cognitive science and behavioural research can help develop the necessary theories and methods to inform this aspect of urban design. This is important as more and more urban designers, planners and policy makers recognise that sustainability is linked to human well-being and that both are necessarily at the centre of progressive city making efforts.

Disorientation and congestion can contribute to psychological stress in urban environments and influence the desire to engage with public spaces. Pedestrian stress can also have implications on the commercial and social viability of buildings such as shopping centres, cultural amenities or sports venues. This raises the question of how the modern city as well as large-scale buildings can be designed to be beneficial for the mental health and well-being of users, whether they are residents or visitors. Contemporary urban planning emphasises the need for high-density mixed-use city quarters that can accommodate living, work and play in densely populated neighbourhoods; support a viable local economy; provide high standards of accessibility; and ensure the personal well-being of its inhabitants.

This chapter's approach is to describe how to investigate the manner in which people perceive and mentally process their urban environments. Specifically, we are interested in densely populated urban quarters that are characterised by the presence and movement of large numbers of pedestrians. In this context, the research identifies and models spatial information processes such as pedestrian orientation in complex surroundings and navigation choices within and between connected building structures. Understanding such patterns is not only relevant for predicting occupancy patterns, congestion and capacity limitations—and thus the correct sizing of places, spaces and hallways—but also links to other cognitive, perceptual and affective or emotional factors of city life.

Cognitive science and architectural and environmental psychology research have developed a rich canon of methods to measure human behaviour and interaction with the built environment. Such measures provide the basis for incorporating a human-centred perspective into the design process. In this process, design decisions are informed by scientific theories and observations in existing, already-built settings using the technique commonly known as post-occupancy evaluation. In principle, these decisions can also be empirically tested by simulation and experimentation techniques before a building project is physically implemented.

The capacity to conduct such simulations in advance of construction allows for pre-occupancy evaluation. This technique represents a new approach to translating research methods into practical applications. Based on behaviour observations in existing settings, design variations are generated as digital models, and these models are then tested with real people in a Virtual Reality (VR) environment. This allows simulated viewing and moving through a building. This technique can be further enhanced by populating the building or urban scene with virtual characters (avatars) to convey a realistic sense of a highly active, densely populated environment. Such an approach can yield unique insights into how people experience various design options and allows for the calibration of the design process to human needs.

At the same time, such an effort requires a strong collaboration between designers and cognitive researchers. Two core aims of our research are, first, to link spatial analysis, design ideation, design development and the empirical validation of design options and, second, to address the technological, scientific and theoretical challenges involved. To do this, we elaborate on the relevant theoretical and methodological elements and introduce a case study from Singapore.

Scientifically Addressing Urban Cognition

Our research agenda is an integrative element of the *Responsive Cities* approach that aims to address the previously identified shortcomings of most smart cities efforts (see Challenges for Responsive Cities). In a world increasingly filled with digital sensors and networks, more and more data sets are becoming available. The dominant challenge now is to identify the most useful data that can appropriately inform design interventions. This requires a scientifically reliable selection of behavioural and cognitive measures to provide a valid basis of observations and their integration into a feedback loop involving designers, planners and governance. Together, these will help generate meaningful solutions via small and large scale design interventions.

Ultimately, this goal requires that research in architectural cognition understands the cognitive and behavioural requirements of designers and patrons of urban space. Here, we need to address the cognitive, behavioural and affective needs of the inhabitants that live, work and travel or 'use' the city. We also need to consider the cognitive abilities and limitations of the designers and decision-makers that design the city to *anticipate* human behaviour and experience (see Figure 1).

Towards this end, we need to address high-level challenges both with respect to design actions and user behaviours. These challenges include how to convince stakeholders and decision-makers of the value of evidence-based design. We also need to identify what design decisions and options have a significant impact on behaviour and cognition of urban dwellers and to define what aspects of human behaviour should be impacted by design interventions. Corresponding questions will be asked about building user perceptions, attitudes and well-being. Researchers should also identify how to reliably measure these human qualities and how to establish a causal link between environmental design choices and human-centred outcomes. Finally, it is critical to determine how to make empirical data relevant for different design stages such as formative and confirmatory evaluations, pre-occupancy and post-occupancy.

We adopt the following integrative approach: we will complement behavioural experiments and observations in real-world settings with the testing of design alternatives using VR models. We will also calibrate and develop existing methods of spatial analysis and simulation to predict human cognition and behaviour. We will characterise users in terms of competencies and expectations by means of psychological testing, questionnaires and interviews. In addition, we will measure users' preferences and reactions to environmental design features using eye-tracking and physiological measures of stress and well-being.

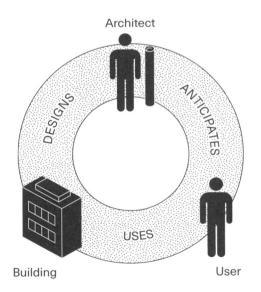

Architect

DESIGNS

ANTICIPATES

USES

Building   User

Fig. 1   The roles of architectural designer and building user.

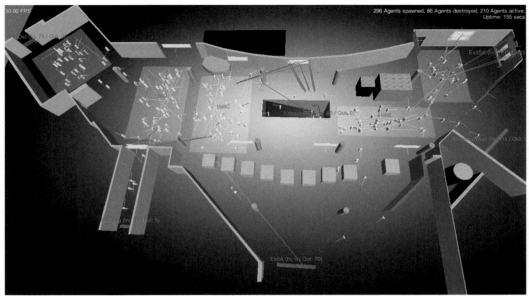

30.00 FPS

296 Agents spawned, 86 Agents destroyed, 210 Agents active.
Uptime: 155 secs

Fig. 2   A prototype of multi-agent simulation of passenger behaviour in Frankfurt Airport transit hub with cognitively plausible agent behaviours for wayfinding, signage reading and decision-making.

Capturing Human Behaviour
and Experience in Urban Space

Spatial orientation and wayfinding rely on core elements of human cognition, such as perception, memory, learning, reasoning and emotional appraisal (Montello 2005; Wiener et al. 2009). Hölscher, Tenbrink and Wiener (2011) stress that wayfinding is a decision-making process that is strongly influenced by a person's familiarity with the environment, general expectations regarding urban and indoor layouts, heuristics and navigation strategies (see also Passini 1996; Hölscher et al. 2006). Human movement is only partly guided by conscious route planning and is largely guided by what is perceived from the environment (Hölscher, Tenbrink and Wiener 2011). This highlights the role of visual attention to environmental structure (e.g., the layout of corridors and streets) and objects that can serve as landmarks for orientation and place identity (Wiener et al. 2012). Carlson and colleagues (2010) suggest that the complexity of wayfinding is the result of the interaction between the individual, the building setting and the mental representations of that setting, such as cognitive maps. The difficulty of wayfinding is further shaped by environmental features such as quality of signage, the complexity of layouts and local intersections, visibility and vertical

connections along a route (Giannopoulus, Kiefer, Raubal, Richter and Thrash 2014; Hölscher et al. 2006).

Collecting behavioural data in real environments such as shopping malls and city streets allows researchers to draw inferences regarding the current state of those environments and to predict future states. For example, understanding the cause of congestion in a busy city centre may allow researchers to prevent such congestion in the future. Systematic variation—that is, changing one or two aspects of the environment and observing the effects of these changes on people's behaviours—is critical for drawing such inferences. Such studies can also be enriched using a variety of technologies including eye tracking and physiological measurement devices, such as EDA (electrodermal activity or skin conductivity) and ECG (electrocardiogram) plots. Eye tracking methods can be used to measure the direction of a person's gaze and the way in which it corresponds to specific aspects of the built environment such as signage and maps. One challenge with eye tracking in real environments is that it is difficult to determine the objects towards which gaze is directed. To do this, researchers can employ computer vision algorithms or code the data with human judges. Coupled with questionnaires, physiological data can be used in order to measure affective responses such as stress and

Theoretical and Methodological Challenges
135   for Cognitive Research in the Built Environment

engagement to the built environment. One challenge of physiological data, however, is that they are difficult to interpret without other converging methods.

Real-world data collection allows for the post-occupancy evaluation of behaviours in building projects that are already complete (Preiser, Rabonowitz and White 1998) but is not feasible during the critical design stages. Therefore, the establishment of a VR laboratory within Future Cities Laboratory will allow for the systematic variation of building geometries, materials, textures and signage systems. Scholars such as Shen, Zhang, Shen, and Fernando (2013) have used 3D digital building models and agent-based modelling of occupant behaviours as input during stakeholder meetings.

These models have not yet been empirically validated with human users. One promising approach for validation is to visually render a building design in a Cave Automatic Virtual Environment (CAVE). A CAVE typically consists of between three and six wall-sized projection surfaces, which users stand or sit inside to experience a simulation. We will implement both CAVE and Head-Mounted Display (HMD) setups to address various research questions. This technology will allow us to pinpoint the impact of various spatial variables on human behaviour and to systematically compare layout alternatives. The design of these alternatives will provide opportunities for cooperation with local design teams for specific public sites in Singapore.

Nonetheless, VR is no panacea for the realistic prediction of user reactions (Donato and Moser 2016). As such, we are tasked with finding a scientifically and pragmatically appropriate balance of real-world measurement, VR experimentation and computational simulation of human wayfinding that is both methodologically rigorous and can be generalised across scenarios.

A key feature of public areas in a city such as Singapore is the high density of pedestrian movement. The degree of crowding can have a significant impact on navigation decision-making, for example, the presence of other people blocking the visual field and occluding environmental cues and signage. This requires that any reliable predictive computer simulation of human wayfinding behaviour links collective movement models such as emergency egress models (Helbing et al. 2001) with visual perception, decision-making and other higher-level cognitive functions (Moussaid et al. 2011; Robin et al. 2009; Becker-Asano et al. 2014). To date, almost all commercial simulation tools make relatively simplistic assumptions about human wayfinding. For example, the CAST airport simulation platform (Airport Research Centre 2016) assumes perfect knowledge and error-free behaviour from navigating passengers. Within the current project, we will develop a novel multi-agent simulation of pedestrian navigation that encompasses typical navigation errors, the misinterpretation of signage and various individual differences of spatial thinking (Figure 2). This model will be used to populate the VR environments employed for comparing design interventions at both building and neighbourhood scales.

The current revival of environmental and architectural psychology is driven by an increased uptake of evidence-based design in architecture and urban planning, and by technological advances that enable better data collection and processing. Computational models of human spatial cognition have previously been hampered by a need for a more comprehensive theory of navigation decision-making and by limitations in computing power such as multi-agent modelling with realistic cognitive features. At the same time, mobile sensors, mobile data collection devices such as smartphones, VR tools (especially HMDs) and the underlying digital modelling tools such as Building Information Modelling (BIM) have now become feasible for architectural and psychological research. As sketched above, this project will bring together these technological advances in a unique cycle of observation, analysis, design modelling and evaluation.

The targeted experiments and observations in the project directly complement and will be equally informed by the emerging Big Data work in Singapore and within the Future Cities Laboratory. However, in contrast to these projects, we focus on *targeted* data. We will develop controlled and detailed observation studies with theory-driven experimental variations. These studies work with fairly small samples of participants, while collecting data at a high resolution such as observing details regarding movement and the stationary use of locations. These data are highly interpretable as they are elicited based on explicit spatial tasks, for example finding a destination or choosing a pastime, together with verbal and survey data. Our targeted data are linked with large-scale observations regarding group-level transport, both with respect to the choice of public transport mode and work and leisure travel activities.

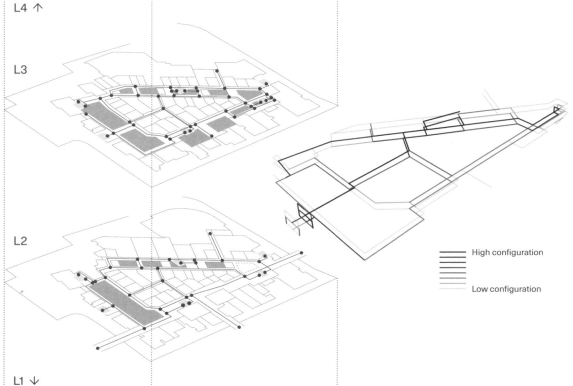

L4 ↑

L3

L2

L1 ↓

High configuration

Low configuration

Fig. 3   Rush-hour pedestrian traffic at the connection between MRT station and shopping facilities.

Fig. 4   3D spatial analysis of a multi-level shopping centre environment.

Why Look at Cognition and Behaviour to Improve Urban Design?

The rapid development of Asian cities has introduced many challenges to the maturing urban environment. A legacy of the twentieth century planning practices that embraced technological advances raises questions regarding compatibilities with contemporary trends as evidenced by the healthy cities movement (Lafond 2015) and low-carbon planning. The adaptation of cities conceived for motor transport but now in the throes of demotorisation is a challenge for the adaptation of infrastructure, as well as the core research focus of humans and their activities.

The interface of human domains with the dominant infrastructure calls for better public space environments. In particular, the collectivisation of movement calls for more comfort in public space and the integration of public space with myriad private purposes. Planning in the last decades has emphasised utility and technological advance but has given relatively little consideration to how people perceive and navigate urban space.

High-density environments characterise Asian cities and have particular challenges with respect to cognitive processes. For example, a more three-dimensional urban environment is cognitively more complex and requires more careful attention to the way the environment is connected (Hölscher et al. 2006). Over the past few decades, mobility has been advanced and the environment is more networked and represented, but movement at the human scale has been thwarted and channelled into the more limited urban space of sidewalks and corridors. The consequences for a more sedentary population that travels less on foot and uses less of the urban environment warn that certain dimensions of the urban environment need to be redressed.

A more compact and necessarily vertical city is a particular challenge for the aging populations of the most developed Asian countries. Children and the disabled are other major vulnerable groups for whom current mobility technologies are poorly adapted. As a consequence, new forms of urban segmentation are arising in the city, in addition to the socioeconomic challenges (Jones et al. 2003).

Public space remains important, not only because of its great importance for civic identity and urban culture, but also because an increasing proportion of accessible space is privately owned or controlled. Although many social researchers have critiqued the privatisation of public space in the contemporary world (Dovey 2014), few have gone further to probe the possibilities inherent under a largely private regime. Shopping environments are of particular interest because they play an important role in the leisure activities of urbanites and are currently undergoing rapid change in the context of e-commerce. How people visit, what they do on their visits and what they look for in their 'shopping' trips is not well understood, but we continue to create places purely devoted to the consumption of goods.

A future shopping environment is likely to harbour many more possibilities than those suggested by conventional shopping centres; that is, more possibilities than simply those of retailing. However, the making of such environments can best be supported by conceiving them first as a sensory experience and then as places of utility and exchange. In general, it is reasonable to suggest that the seminal places of public culture in the future will be hybridised, multifunctional, as well as highly networked with other significant locations in the city. Researchers and the public sector need to tackle these issues of cultural transition because it is less likely that the private sector, with its legitimate but narrow agenda, can do so on its own.

So far in the professions of urban planning, architecture and landscape architecture, we have concentrated on designing places by relying on experiences from similar cases to guide the present. Relatively little has been done to build environments by taking inspiration from the study of perception and behaviour. In addition, contemporary efforts in these domains have emphasised a narrowly defined geography without anticipating the effects of linking these places within their larger urban setting (Dovey 2014). It is one thing to experience and use a place, but humans experience a continuum of places and times with indeterminate limits. Several studies on European public spaces, perhaps beginning as early as Camillo Sitte (Collins and Crasemann-Collins 2006), have pointed to the position of public place in an experiential network of the city. This is not necessarily the city of lines and territories conventionalised by urban planning practice but a city that involves both the physical and the felt. Ultimately, the city of the future is a city of experience accommodated by a hopefully supportive physical environment.

Human-centred future cities will involve considerable efforts for increasing reliance on technology and technocratic solutions. The history of twentieth century urbanism reminds us that relying on intuition and theories to accommodate hypothetical human needs is not sufficient. Any important changes wrought in the future urban environment should be tested against human experience. Not only do we require a thorough understanding of the dynamics of the urban environment and the perceptions of local people, but this knowledge must also serve as a foundation for the exploration of alternative futures. To the extent possible, we must use humans' experiences of those alternatives to guide our decisions.

Case study—Integrating Transport and Shopping in Singapore

Our work in Singapore concentrates on public and semi-public areas with a focus on high-traffic pedestrian environments: primarily multi-level buildings that often have a number of underground levels and connections without direct sunlight. Functionally, these buildings tend to be mixed-use transport hubs, cultural amenities, and shopping centres. While such buildings and building ensembles are typically characterised by complex vertical circulation networks, we will also extend our efforts to better understand the usage and pedestrian orientation in covered walkways at street level, raised crosswalks and underground connection networks.

Singapore offers an excellent platform to study multi-level and mixed-use urban complexes with ground level and underground Mass Rapid Transit (MRT) stations (see Figure 3). The site chosen for the pilot study is at a mixed-use shopping centre, Westgate, located inside a newly developed local hub in the Jurong East area. The hub combines various urban functions, such as shopping, dining, leisure activities, offices, apartments, and a hospital. This case study within a complex built environment allows us to investigate spatial decision making in a high density and vertical environment.

This pilot study represents the application of new technological developments in applied psychological research. The main research questions are how different levels of pedestrian density or *crowdedness* in the building affect path choices and how perceptual processes modulate these choices. The geometric structure of the building, especially its layout and vertical connections, are expected to have a strong impact on such movement choices as well

as on visual attention patterns. The project uses a combination of multi-level spatial measures, pedestrian tracking and the quantification of the level of crowdedness. A multi-level spatial analysis is needed to provide standardised and comparable spatial measures of configurational features. In contrast to standard space syntax tools working in the two-dimensional analysis of space, the new tools describe the multi-level, complex built environment of the site. Here, we will apply new techniques, such as three-dimensional space syntax and 3D visibility graph analysis (see Figure 4).

Navigation destinations are chosen based on the results of the 3D spatial analysis. The destinations are characterised by different degrees of complexity and thus the difficulty with which they are located during a search task. This performance data can be related to the location and type of vertical transportation mode (stairs, elevator or escalator), location of entrance, and the complexity of corridor geometry. The time of day, level of crowdedness, and an individual's prior familiarity with the building are also expected to impact navigation behaviour. We will also capture psychological and physiological data. This includes the tracking of route choices and hesitations, the recording of verbal comments, as well as eye tracking and EDA/ECG. Through the combination of different data sources, we can generate a more integrated understanding of navigation in this setting.

The most immediate output will be a test of the validity and reliability of the novel tools and analyses developed for public spaces in the context of Singapore. The analysis will allow us to observe the impact of spatial features and vertical movement on participants' choices and wayfinding performance. Furthermore, such a study will shed light on the influence of different levels of crowdedness on navigation. We will test whether the expected differences suggested by the 3D spatial analysis do indeed result in behavioural variations. Particularly, crowdedness is expected to serve both as a source of guidance by providing cues for other patrons, but also as a hindrance by blocking views or obstructing access for navigation. At a later stage, physiological measurements should allow us to see how different numbers of people affect participants' arousal, stress and decisions.

In subsequent studies, we intend to investigate a central hub area, such as Marina Bay or Orchard Road. Particularly interesting are the underground

Theoretical and Methodological Challenges
139 for Cognitive Research in the Built Environment

MRT connections and vertical conjunctions, as well as underground and covered walkways. Measurements will include route preferences and the use of these spaces by different groups of people. We expect to establish indices regarding design aspects such as the width, height and lighting of spaces, both above ground and underground. Another focus of attention will be on the existing mapping and signage.

By applying the behavioural analysis to wayfinding tasks and eye-tracking data, we intend to develop new design guidelines that take the vertical movement into consideration and formulate recommendations for the adjustment of existing systems.

Bibliography

Airport Research Centre (2016) *CAST Simulation Website*. Available from <http://www.airport-consultants.com/cast-simulation> Accessed on 1 August 2016.

Becker-Asano C, F Ruzzoli, C Hölscher and B Nebel (2014). 'A multi-agent system based on Unity 4 for virtual perception and wayfinding', in *Pedestrian and Evacuation Dynamics 2014 (PED2014). Transportation Research Procedia Volume 2*: 452–5.

Carlson L, C Hölscher, T Shipley and R Conroy Dalton (2010). 'Getting lost in buildings', *Current Directions in Psychological Science 19*(5): 284–9.

Collins G and C C Collins (2006). *Camillo Sitte: The Birth of Modern City Planning*. Mineola, NY: Dover Publications.

Donato F and E I Moser (2016). 'A world away from reality', *Nature* 533: 325.

Dovey K (2014). *Framing Places—Mediating Power in Built Form*. London UK: Routledge.

Gaigné C, S Riou and J F Thisse (2010). 'Are compact cities environmentally friendly? Lyon-St-Etienne, France: Groupe d'analyse et de théorie économique'. Available from <http://ssrn.com/abstract=1553776> Accessed on 12 October 2016.

Giannopoulos I, P Kiefer, M Raubal, K F Richter and T Thrash (2014). 'Wayfinding decision situations: A conceptual model and evaluation', *Proceedings of the Eight International Conference on Geographic Information Science*.

Helbing D, P Molnar, I J Farkas and K Bolay (2001). 'Self-organizing pedestrian movement', *Environment and Planning B: Planning and Design 28*(3): 361–84.

Hölscher C, T Meilinger, G Vrachliotis, M Brösamle and M Knauff, M (2006). 'Up the down staircase: Wayfinding strategies and multi-level buildings', *Journal of Environmental Psychology* 26(4): 284–99.

Hölscher C, T Tenbrink and J Wiener (2011). 'Would you follow your own route description?', *Cognition 121:* 228–47.

Jones C, C Leishman and C Watkins (2003). 'Structural change in a local urban housing market', *Environment and Planning A* 35(7): 1315–26.

Lafond L J (2015). *National Healthy Cities Networks in the WHO European Region. Promoting Health and Well-Being throughout Europe*. Available from <http://www.euro.who.int/en/health-topics/environment-and-health/urban-health/publications/2015/national-healthy-cities-networks-in-the-who-european-region.-promoting-health-and-well-being-throughout-europe-2015> Accessed on 12 October 2016.

Montello D R (2005). 'Navigation', in *The Cambridge Handbook of Visuospatial Thinking* (pp. 257–94), eds. P Shah and A Miyake. Cambridge: Cambridge University Press.

Moussaïd M, D Helbing and G Theraulaza (2011). 'How simple rules determine pedestrian behavior and crowd disasters', *Proceedings of the National Academy of Sciences* 108(17): 6884–8.

Passini R (1996). 'Wayfinding design: Logic, application and some thoughts on universality', *Design Studies 17*: 319–31.

Preiser W F E, H Z Rabonowitz and E T White (1988). *Post-Occupancy Evaluation*. New York: Van Nostrand Reinhold Company.

Robin T, G Antonini, M Bierlaire and J Cruz (2009). 'Specification, estimation and validation of a pedestrian walking behavior model', *Transportation Research Part B 43*: 36–56.

Shen W, X Zhang, G Qiping Shen and T Fernando (2013). 'The user pre-occupancy evaluation method in designer–client communication in early design stage: A case study', *Automation in Construction 32*: 112–24.

Wiener J M, S J Büchner and C Hölscher (2009). 'Taxonomy of human wayfinding tasks: A knowledge-based approach', *Spatial Cognition and Computation 9:* 152–65.

Wiener J M, C Hölscher, S Büchner and L Konieczny (2012). 'Gaze behaviour during space perception and spatial decision making', *Psychological Research 76*(6): 713–29.

Theoretical and Methodological Challenges for Cognitive Research in the Built Environment

Simon Schubiger,
Stefan Mueller Arisona, Chen Zhong,
Zeng Wei, Remo Burkhard

Advanced Tools and Workflows for Urban Designers

Architectural, urban planning and design mediums have been enhanced by powerful digital technologies since the last decades of the twentieth century. But the more recent rise of predictive modelling, big data and urban science could profoundly restructure these mediums. Procedural- and agent-based modelling software have particularly important roles in such a restructuring. Beyond expansion of the representational palette, these kinds of software have the potential to change the relationship between design, planning and everyday urban experience.

Allied with newly abundant geospatial and socio-economic data—from such sources as real-time sensors, smart phones, intelligent buildings and smart city systems—procedural- and agent-based modelling can take their place in representing hybrid cyber-physical cities. In this scenario, representations are not merely materialised, but are in a constant and circular exchange with the physical stocks and flows of the city.

Both procedural- and agent-based modelling substantially expand what can be represented in urban planning and design, supplementing conventional form- and material-based information with information on ecology, land-use, land-value, property ownership, and the mobility patterns of people, goods and traffic.

Despite the far-reaching possibilities of this emergent medium for city making, the contemporary situation is fractured and cluttered. Different software, platforms and computer-aided design tools are promoted by different manufacturers. This chapter examines the possibilities for this new medium for city making by proposing pathways through this shifting software environment for the urban design process. The investigation focuses on procedural modelling, as distinct from mere three-dimensional (3D) modelling, its effects on urban design practice, and how it can effectively support the work of architects, planners and engineers.

We first look at how newly available data can be organised and managed at the scale of a city and in 3D (Section 2). Described as *City Information Models (CIMs),* these data sources are developing quickly and increasingly being used as data back ends in administration and planning offices. We will highlight a prominent example and show how it integrates with Geograpical Information System (GIS) and provide a general overview of the most important properties of a 3D CIM. This paper will provide a brief introduction

The medium of formal city making is both physical and representational. That is, the physical stuff of cities—brick, stone, mortar, steel, rubber, glass and asphalt—is represented in drawings, models and specifications before it is put in place. This disciplinary common sense has long since underpinned the work of architects, urban designers, planners and engineers. As Robin Evans famously pointed out, 'architects do not make buildings, they make drawings of buildings' (Evans 1989). We need drawings—maps, plans, sketches, designs, models and blueprints—to study the possible arrangements of materials in advance of the usually expensive, time-consuming and often dangerous concerted act of building.

The relationship between the physical stuff of buildings and their representations is never fixed nor stable. Materials and drawings can be misaligned.

This is due to many factors, including inadequate drawings, lack of data, the inherent resistance of the materials, bad workmanship, or simple error. There are many different ways to manage such misalignments. Some contributors aspire to make representations ever more accurate and construction systems ever more controlled to better determine the physical outcome. Others accept the misalignment for pragmatic reasons, or exploit it for aesthetic and social ones. Those in engineering disciplines manage the inevitability of such misalignments through the concepts of tolerance and structural redundancy.

to procedural modelling in Section 3, based on the CGA (Computer Generated Architecture) Shape Grammar, as implemented in Esri's CityEngine, ArcGIS 10.x, ArcGIS Pro and also available as a library for third party applications. It will show how a procedural model can be used to integrate urban design knowledge. Finally, it will present how the techniques can be used to work with land use and building function planning in 3D, and how to work with street networks and block subdivisions. The chapter concludes with an outlook and final remarks.

The 3D City Information Model

An urban planning project takes place within an existing context of built structures, legal requirements and its natural surroundings. In contrast to traditional 2D GISs, these environments are inherently 3D especially within a city where the third dimension is often the only option for growth. There are, therefore, increasing needs to model the planning context with rich 3D information.

Whereas earlier 3D city models were almost exclusively used for visualisation and had in turn relaxed requirements regarding accuracy and semantics, today's applications ask for spatial information models that are general enough to serve a wide range of use cases beyond visualisation. Several standardisation efforts are under the way such as CityGML (Kolbe et al. 2005), INSPIRE (Perego et al. 2012), FG-DC-STD-003 (Halfawy et al. 2006) or Esri's 3DCIM which specify semantic-rich information models. They not only cover the 3D representation of constructions and their spatial attributes but also the natural environment and sub-surface structures.

A closer look at Esri's 3DCIM as an example of such an information model reveals that the 3DCIM is complementary to Esri's well-established Local Government Information Model (Crothers 2011) and the Building Information Model BISDM (McCabe and Young 2011).

A 3D-mapped city is a vast a collection of features, networks and surfaces, and there are many approaches to modelling it for processing, analysis and visualisation. A design goal of the 3DCIM is to be compact and simple in its structure, making the core of the model easy to understand and to populate with data. Content-wise, the 3DCIM is organised into three basic themes: the built environment, the legal environment, and the natural environment. Each of these themes shares some common attributes and traits, as described below.

The Built Environment
The built environment comprises features and networks that are created or actively managed by humans. These features include: structures (buildings, bridges, tunnels), utility networks, multimodal transportation networks (interior and exterior), installations (street furniture and sensors), and street trees.

The Legal Environment
Features in the legal environment represent land use plans and regulations, and property ownership boundaries. These include land use zones, which can have a nested structure (zones that are within and override the regulations of larger zones), and may have both 2D and 3D dimensional attributes such as maximum buildable heights. These regulations are typically stored as tables and may also apply to parcel or ownership boundaries.

The Natural Environment
The natural environment comprises all naturally occurring features on, above or below the earth's surface. This can include land cover such as wilderness areas, biomes and water bodies, but can also include surface and subsurface geologic structure as well as above-earth atmosphere, climate, and weather.

3D City Information Model Structure
A set of 'Feature Classes' (FC) and 'Object Classes' (OC) describe the 3DCIM model in detail, as summarised in Figure 4. In order to considerably shorten design iterations and evaluation, a 3DCIM is typically combined with a rule based system such as Computer Generated Architecture (CGA) which is presented in the next sections. The utilisation of off-the-shelf rule libraries can shorten the design cycle even more, since they directly integrate with the underlying information model and need little or no customisation.

Procedural City Modelling Workflows

Rule Based Systems
The design and modelling of urban structures using classical, polygon-based methodologies

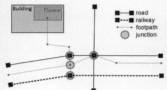

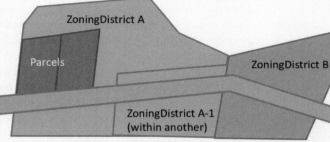

ZoningDistrict A

Parcels

ZoningDistrict B

ZoningDistrict A-1
(within another)

ZoningDistrict O
(overlay=true)

Built Environment
Buildings Model
- FC Building
- FC BuildingShell
- FC BuildingShellPart
- FC BuildingEntrancePoint
- FC BuildingRidgeLine (in v2.0)
Interiors Model
- FC Floor
- FC InteriorSpace
- FC InteriorStructure
- FC InteriorInstallation
Installations Model
- FC StreetFurniture
- FC Sign
- FC Sensor
Transport Networks (Multimodal, combined Interior/Exterior)
Trees (with Analytical/Realistic Representations)
Utility Networks (v2.0)

Legal Environment
Land Ownership
- FC Parcel (with Minimum/Maximum Zoning Shell Representations)
- OC ParcelBorderInfo
Land Use Zoning and Constraints
- FC LandUseZone
- OC LandUseConstraint

Natural Environment
Land Cover
Geology (v2.0)
Atmosphere (v2.0)

Basemap
Terrain
Orthoimagery
Topographical Map

Fig. 1   Examples of built environment: interiors (left); transportation networks (middle);
            structures (right).
Fig. 2   Example of overlapping zoning regulations in the legal environment.
Fig. 3   Example of the natural environment in a city scape.
Fig. 4   Data models for built environment data, legal and the natural environments
            as related to the GIS basemap.

can be very time consuming. Large-scale planning projects can highlight the limits of 3D tools in terms of scalability and maintainability. Furthermore, adapting and modifying a planning project to changing constraints can be difficult due to a high number of edit operations required on a polygonal model. Design iterations can thus be very expensive, leading to restrictions on changes which can limit a systematic exploration of the design space.

Rule based or procedural modelling approaches the time and quality challenge with a completely different modelling perspective generated from spatial rules. A prominent example of such a rule system is CGA as implemented in Esri's CityEngine, ArcGIS 10.x and ArcGIS Pro software. Procedural models are descriptions of spatial structures—for example an architectural style—encoded with parameterised CGA rules. These rules can be easily applied to large areas, with the corresponding 3D models generated by the software instead of being hand-modelled by architects or designers. Because of the rule-based nature, every design change immediately results in a newly generated 3D representation. This shortens iterations from days or weeks to seconds or minutes and enables new workflows where hundreds of design variants can be explored, analysed and optimised by stakeholders while respecting all rule-based regulatory and other constraints.

A Simple Procedural Model

The following CGA example will show how procedural modelling is different from the classical polygon based modelling such as that used by CAD software. The goal is to model a simple multi-story building and extract Gross Floor Area (GFA) for different floor usages within an urban planning project.

The first step in producing a procedural model is the translation of the spatial structure of the building into a set of rules. Although this example focuses on a building, the same principles can be applied for other purposes, such as street networks or vegetation.

A CGA rule tells the system how an input *shape* is transformed through *operations* into a number of resulting *shapes*. In this example the building footprint is taken as the input shape for the rule, it is extruded vertically along the y-axis and the result of this extrusion is the building massing as per:

```
attr height = 30
Footprint --> extrude(height) Massing
```

This rule reads as 'take the input shape *Footprint*, extrude it by *Height* and apply the *Massing* rule'. In this case, the *Massing* rule is undefined. Undefined rules automatically result in the creation of a 3D shape so *Massing* actually stands for the result of the extrusion of the input shape. This very simple rule already shows two advantages of the procedural model over a fixed CAD model. First, the rule can be controlled geometrically depending on the input shape (in this case the building footprint) and a massing will be generated which follows the outline of the footprint.

Furthermore, the rule is parameterised by the *height* attribute, which controls the extent of the extrusion. This means the *height* attribute as well as the footprint geometry can be interactively changed by the designer or linked to GIS data, which enables it to be driven by an external data source.

The next step is the subdivision of massing into multiple floors. For that purpose, the massing is split along the y-axis into a ground floor, intermediate floors and a roof as per:

```
attr roofHeight = 1
attr floorHeight = 3
attr groundFloorHeight = 4
Massing-->split(y){
    groundFloorHeight: Floor |
    {~floorHeight: Floor}* |
roofHeight: Floor}
```

This massing rule reads as: 'Take the input shape and split it upwards along the y-axis. For splitting, apply the following pattern: create a ground floor with height *groundFloorHeight*, create as many floors as possible with approximately *floorHeight* height and finally add a roof with *roofHeight*.' Again, the attributes *groundFloorHeight*, *floorHeight*, and *roofHeight* allow easy parameterisation of the resulting 3D model and enable the rapid evaluation of different designs.

The last step in this example is the calculation of the GFA for the use types "retail", "office", and "apartment". For visualisation purposes, the use types will be colour coded by a simple mapping function between use types and RGB colours thus:

```
col(useType) =
    case useType == "retail":"#ff0000"
    case useType == "office":"#00ff00"
    case useType == "apartment":
                                "#0000ff"
    else:       "#888888"
```

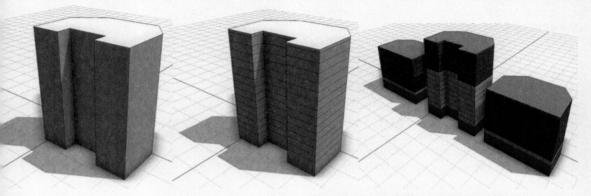

Name	Value					
floorHeight	3					
groundFloorHeight	4					
height	30					
ratio	0.5					
roofHeight	1					

⌄ Reports

Report	N	%	Sum	%	Avg
GFA.appartment	4	40.00	3160.73	40.00	790.18
GFA.office	4	40.00	3160.73	40.00	790.18
GFA.retail	1	10.00	790.18	10.00	790.18
GFA.roof	1	10.00	790.18	10.00	790.18
GFA	10	100.00	7901.83	100.00	790.18

Fig. 5   An example of procedural model showing an extruded massing (left), the massing subdivided into floors (middle), and a planning proposal with colour-coded use types (right).

Fig. 6   Interactive control of the rule attributes and rule-based GFA calculations.

For this GFA calculation, the Massing rule is replaced by a slightly more complex rule. Its main purpose is to take into account the ratio between office and apartment space. This is expressed in the *Floors* rule consisting of the subdivision into the two use types by a *split* operation and a *ratio* attribute. The *ratio* attribute allows the designer to explore different floor space distributions concurrently with an immediate visual as well as analytical feedback as per:

```
attr ratio = 0.5
Massing-->split(y) {
    groundFloorHeight:Floor("retail")|
Floors |
    roofHeight:Floor("roof")}

Floors-->split(y){
    'ratio:{~floorHeight:Floor
                    ("office")}*|
    '(1-ratio):{~floorHeight:Floor
                    ("apartment")}*}
```

```
Floor(useType)-->
    colour(col(useType))
    report("GFA." + useType,
                    geometry.area(bottom))
```

In this *Floor* rule, the *colour* operation sets the *colour* of the shape and *report* evaluates an expression (in this case the bottom area of the shape) and stores the result under the given key "GFA." + *useType* where *useType* is replaced with the actual use type value such as ("retail", "office"or "apartment"). This reporting capability is the source for all analytical processes that follow, and its results can be stored directly in a geodatabase.

Obviously, this example is a very crude approximation because some space will be needed for service structures such as elevators, stairways, ventilation, utilities and so on. But the basic principle is described and the powerful visual representation-generating mechanism allows a visual representation simultaneously with an analytical result.

Advanced Tools and Workflows
for Urban Designers

Figure 6 shows the interactive controls for the attributes defined in the rule file as well as the results of the GFA calculations.

Procedural modelling can be successfully applied in large-scale urban environments ranging from complex zoning and planning scenarios (Singapore Urban Redevelopment Authority 2014) to fictional cityscapes for Hollywood movies such as 'Cars 2', 'Total Recall', or 'Man of Steel'. Besides Esri, other companies provide ready-to-use CGA rule libraries, thereby considerably reducing the time required for rule writing.

Once a parametric model is created for a given area of interest, it will be available to specific design workflows, such as dealing with land use, street network design and analysis, or specific evaluation as highlighted in the coming sections.

Case Studies

Land Use

Land use is about the human use of space which defines planned functions in urban areas. It involves the management and modification of a natural environment or wilderness into a built environment such as fields, pastures, and settlements (Watson et al. 2000). Land use planning is considered one of the most crucial subjects in urban planning, and an indispensable aspect in all kinds of urban simulation application (Waddell 2002).

This section presents a possible workflow that illustrates the transformation of 2D GIS data into smart 3D city models. The workflow was realised using ArcGIS and CityEngine 3D geometry modelling and visualisation capabilities.

Shapefiles, which are used to store land-use information, can be imported directly. Based on the attributes in a planning map, CGA rules can be derived to constrain the layout and functions of building environments. CGA is used as a medium to transform these attributes and rules into a procedural modelling process to produce an intuitive 3D scenario. Moreover, empirical knowledge can be used to enrich the 3D scenario and bring it one step closer to the reality—another advantage of procedural modelling techniques.

Figure 7 shows an example of a simplified 3D scenario generated from a 2D land-use map. This example demonstrates mixed-use urban space, which has been addressed in related work such as (Zhong

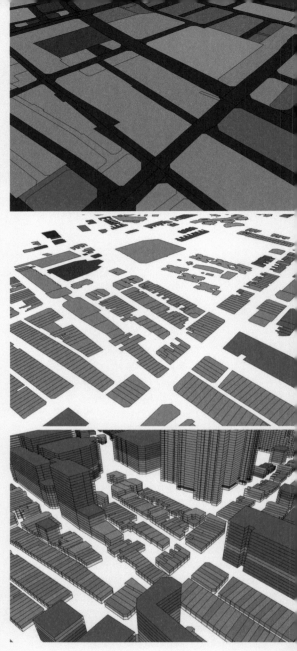

146   Fig. 7   (a–c) Generating a 3D mixed-used scenario from a 2D land-use map.

Fig. 8   Visualisation of street analysis results, automatic street width calculation and constraint-based block subdivision.

et al. 2014). The land use plan provides the constraints to dominating functions in one specified area. However, not specified in the land use plan are specific building functions which define how a building is actually used.

Thus, building function refers to information from a smaller spatial scale and includes specifications for multiple floors such as building volumes, and is thus not fully compliant with land use. Therefore, a 3D scenario is required to give full details of building functions and to accurately depict urban space. Figure 7(a) refers to the original land use plan, while Figure 7(b) shows 2D building footprints that strictly follow the land use plan.

Figure 7(c) shows a 3D scenario generated by procedural modelling, which takes the land use planning as a base but adds more local/contextual information about the real usage of buildings. In this scenario, two simple rules were applied: First the number of floors is proportional to the area of a building footprint; second, that the buildings might have multiple use types on different floors. Based on investigated information, the possible combinations could be "commercial + residential" or "commercial +

storage + office", which are demonstrated in Figure 7(c) with different colour codes.

Street Networks and Block Subdivision

Street networks represent the arteries of a city and define the formal shape and structure through enclosed blocks, building lots and spaces in between. Creating and manipulating street networks has seen increasing tool support over the past years. Software like Autodesk's Civil 3D (Autodesk 2012) extend parametric design beyond street networks and can be applied to almost any network-like structure. This even includes related civil engineering tasks such as cut and fill of existing terrain. Esri's CityEngine gives the urban designer tools that allow interactive changing of network structures while maintaining block subdivision constraints such as minimal or maximal areas, and street access. Furthermore, space syntax based integration (Hillier et al. 1976) and centrality calculations on a street network can be directly translated to street attributes such as providing necessary transport capacity.

Thanks to the parametric nature of these software products, the urban designer can concentrate on high level network layout tasks, and rely on the software to create the dependent spaces, shapes and structures. These tools work hand in hand with procedural building and street models to result in a fully integrated and interactive workflow—one where network changes are immediately reflected in the block subdivision and in turn affect the footprints of procedural buildings.

For analysis and visualisation, CGA rules can be applied equally to streets to result in a seamless procedural modelling environment for buildings, streets, and vegetation across a wide range of the urban designer's needs while transforming the way they work within the urban space (Jeffries 2014).

Conclusion

Although modern software tools enable new workflows and a completely new way in which urban designer can interact with planning proposals, they also come at a price. Learning and deploying new tools and the demands of a completely different approach to 3D modelling such as CGA calls for a major investment in software licenses, infrastructure and training.

Despite all the efforts of the different vendors to provide interoperability of tools and common exchange standards, small mismatches in the data can still require careful manual adjustments as part of the workflow.

This means every urban designer has to decide, on a project-by-project basis, if the investment in training and changes to processes outweigh a closer interaction with stakeholders and the design space flexibility. Designers that take the first approach praise the increase in flexibility, rapidity of design changes, reduction in tedious calculation tasks and the management of the legal environment that it can bring. As Elliot Hartley (Garsdale Design) noted, 'It used to take ages to change one parameter. Now you can do it at the click of a mouse' (Jeffries 2014).

This paper asserts that mouse-clicks implemented by great designers, empowered with new tools, will shape a better urban future.

Bibliography

Autodesk (2012). *Road Design with AutoCAD® Civil 3D®*. Available from <http://www.ideateinc.com/whitepapers/civil/Road%20Design%20with%20AutoCAD%20Civil%203D%20whitepaper.pdf> Accessed on 18 December 2016.

Crothers H (2011). 'What is the local government information model?', *ArcGIS Blog*. Available from <https://blogs.esri.com/esri/arcgis/2011/09/28/what-is-the-local-government-information-model/> Accessed on 18 December 2016.

Evans R (1989). 'Architectural projection'. In *Architecture and its Image: Four Centuries of Architectural Representation,* eds. E Blau and E Kaufman. Montreal: Canadian Centre for Architecture.

Halfawy M R, D J Vanier and T M Froese (2006). 'Standard Data models for interoperability of municipal infrastructure asset management systems', *Can. J. Civ. Eng.* 33: 1459–69.

Hillier B, A Leaman, P Stansall and M Bedford (1976). 'Space syntax', *Environment and Planning B* 3: 147–85.

Jeffries S (2014). *The Yorkshire Dales Family Who are Designing Entire Cities in Iraq.* Available from <https://www.theguardian.com/cities/2014/aug/26/yorkshire-dales-family-designing-cities-in-iraq> Accessed on 28 September 2016.

Kolbe T H, G Gröger and L Plümer (2005). 'CityGML: Interoperable access to 3D city models', in *Geo-Information for Disaster Managment*, eds. P D P van Oosterom, D S Zlatanova, and E M Fendel, 883–99. Springer: Berlin Heidelberg.

McCabe C and J Young (2011). *GIS for Federal Buildings: BISDM Version 3—Esri*, Proceedings of the 2011 Esri Fed. Users Conf., Washington.

Perego A, C Fugazza, L Vaccari, M Lutz, P Smits, I Kanellopoulos and S Schade (2012). 'Harmonization and interoperability of EU environmental information and services', *IEEE Intell. Syst.* 27: 33–9.

Singapore Urban Redevelopment Authority (2014). *Esri User Conference Webpage*.

Waddell P (2002). 'UrbanSim: Modeling urban development for land use, transportation, and environmental planning', *Journal of the American Planning Association* 68: 297–314.

Watson R T, I R Noble, B Bolin, N Ravindranath, D J Verardo and D J Dokken (2000). *Land Use, Land-Use Change, and Forestry: A Special Report of the Intergovernmental Panel on Climate Change.*

Zhong, Chen, Xianfeng Huang, Stefan Müller Arisona, Gerhard Schmitt and Michael Batty (2014). 'Inferring building functions from a probabilistic model using public transportation data', *Computers, Environment and Urban Systems* 48: 124–37.

Advanced Tools and Workflows
for Urban Designers

Timothy Morton

Where are All the Megacities?

Like many people on this planet I live in a megacity that is Houston. What's strange is, these entities are very difficult to point to, in pretty much any way. In particular, theories of urban development seem to have trouble coping with megacities, what their boundaries are, where they start and stop.

I've given the name *hyperobject* to any entity that is so massively distributed that it becomes hard to access or even point out, with or without recourse to huge datasets and equipment to enhance our capacity to perceive and calculate. Megacities are definitely hyperobjects.

Hyperobjects have a very special property, which is that they show how *the whole is always less than the sum of its parts*. This surprising concept sounds deeply counter-intuitive, but is paradoxically very easy to think once you get used to it, a fact that I hypothesise has to do with the very long history of the fantasy underpinnings of the neoliberal economic system (also known as 'reality'). This system is simply the current version of a logistical programme that has been running in the background of 'civilization' since its inception. According to the underlying logic of the programme, the whole is always greater than the sum of its parts. To say the least, this idea has now reached its use-by date. Indeed, it is directly complicit in all kinds of violence (social, psychic and philosophical).

Moreover, this radical new set-theoretical concept is very helpful for thinking about how all kinds of human domain—art, culture, politics for instance —can proceed in what I call the time of hyperobjects. This time is characterised by planetary and ecological awareness on a bewildering number and variety of scales. We urgently require new ways of perceiving, imagining and thinking, in particular ways that are not contaminated by the very logistics that gave rise to our era in the first place.

Megacities demand new ways of thinking that could be of huge benefit across a whole host of humanistic and social science domains.

So, in my day job, I'm an ontologist. What does that mean? I think about the structure of how things are. Ontology is not exactly about *what exists*, but rather about *how things exist*. If something exists, how does it exist?

Well, I'm in the region of ontological thought that we called object-oriented ontology, or OOO. There are various features of the way OOO talks about how things exist. For example, OOO holds that things exist in such a way that they're not constantly present in any sense.

Another thing that we hold about how things exist is that if a thing exists, it exists in the same way as something else.

This is what they call *flat ontology*—existing in the same way. Now before we get any further let's pause here and make an important statement, which is that a *flat ontology* is a very, very different animal indeed to *flat ethics*. Very, very different—that's four verys, and I'm using four because this issue keeps coming up when we think about this stuff. It's very important in particular because there's a branch of ecological ethics, the deep ecological, that is indeed a flat ethics, and which says some quite bad things, I feel.

According to flat ethics, if a thing exists it has *as much right to exist* as another thing. That's strikingly different from saying that a thing exists *in the same way* as another thing. The classic, and to my ears amazing and horrifying, deep ecological example of flat ethics is that the AIDS virus has as much right to exist as a patient with AIDS.

Now this ethics, which is often associated with such concepts as the Gaia hypothesis—kinds of holism, in other words—is in fact deeply relevant to our discussion of megacities. This is because the ethical equality derives from an implied model of holism that I call *explosive holism,* according to which things end up being components of a machine. In other words, they are replaceable. If a part in a car malfunctions you can replace it. According to the explosive holism that underwrites flat ethics, if polar bears go extinct, for example, that's okay because nature will evolve something to take the polar bear's place. Polar bears don't matter. Nature matters, or what Aldo Leopold calls *the biotic community*. By *community* he means a whole that is ontologically more important than its parts. The machine needs to be maintained. The parts are expendable. Gaia and biotic communities and nature don't sound like machines, but they are, in a sort of squishy green disguise.

Now according to OOO a thing exists in the same way as another thing, so a biotic community or Gaia or nature *cannot* in fact be more important than its parts or components, because those parts, such as polar bears, exist in the same way. There are wholes—a football team exists in the same way as a football player—but these wholes are *weaker* or *slighter* or to use that nice English term *weedier* than you once thought. This is holism rather than reductionism—society *does* exist; it's not just a collection of individuals, despite what Margaret Thatcher insisted on. But it's a strange holism in which the whole doesn't transcend the parts.

Why strange? It's because we keep saying this thing to ourselves. We keep saying *the whole is always greater than the sum of its parts*. It sounds true but it only sounds true because you keep saying it to yourself, assured of the fascinating cleverness and rightness of this concept. The more I think about it the more I think this is some kind of retweet of an axiom that underwrites agricultural age religion, also known as religion as such. It's not that this is too old a resource for us cool kids. It's that it isn't. It's that the logistics of this agricultural age have been continuing to play out, like a computer programme in the background, all the way up to the present moment, such that they now have succeeded in covering the entire surface of Earth with so-called 'civilization' and its discontents, which is to say global warming and the Sixth Mass Extinction Event in the history of life on Earth.

We can begin to detect evidence of this agricultural or as they say Axial Age ideology in such statements as *my god is bigger than yours*, a thought that structures a whole lot more than explicitly theistic statements. Take, for example, the fashionable habit of referring to Cthulhu, H.P. Lovecraft's insane horror god. Cthulhu is going to kill you as soon as he wakes up—it just happens like that. He's clearly bigger and badder than the average god, and more a product of cynical reason too, hence his attractiveness with a certain strand of speculative realism that cleaves to nihilism. Since some philosophy is caught in patriarchal threat display, let's put it that way, Cthulhu is very popular as an upside-down, masochistic version of the already-masochistic sense that my invisible old guy with a beard who wants to kill you is bigger and more sadistic than yours.

So, as we can see, there are distinct ethical, not to say political, advantages in disbelieving this form of holism, the kind of holism that says that the whole is always greater than the sum of its parts. Has it ever been proved? Not really. The trouble is, we don't want to be reductionists either, at least I don't. If you are, then there's no problem at all with megacities, for one. They just don't exist at all: they are reducible, like all wholes, to their parts.

Take for example the popular concept of emergence. Emergence is also a Tinkerbell sort of concept that doesn't really work without some form of belief. It's also anthropocentrically scaled in many cases. A boiling kettle, for example, is a good example of what physicists call a phase transition in this case between liquid and gas. It seems that all the electron-jumps that humans call boiling liquid suddenly 'emerges' as steam coming out of the kettle, but this is just from our human point of view. It emerges for someone. It's not an inherent property of liquid molecules. It gets into everything, this bug. Capitalism is theorised as an emergent property of industrial machines—when you have enough of them joined together in a network making other machines, pop! Suddenly you have capitalism proper, according to Marx. But this means that capitalism is like God, always greater than the sum of its parts. Concepts such as distributed agency and actor-networks also suffer from a kind of emergentism that suggests that the whole is greater than the sum of its parts. They're sort of low-volume, ambient retweets of notions of active versus passive—you can't get to active from passive, without some theistic concept of emergence happening. And the concepts of active and passive are rigid products of Neoplatonic Christianity, which most people when questioned wouldn't want to be retweeting consciously.

So, basically, and I'm just going to break it to you here so as not to cause too much suspense, *the whole is always less than the sum of its parts*.

What?

We're so familiar with the opposite that this sounds absolutely ridiculous. We're so used to saying that the whole is always *greater* than the sum of it parts. But can we be so sure? Prove it.

According to explosive holism, everything is a component in a gigantic machine that transcends its parts. The machine might have lots of green soft decorations on it, as in the concept of Gaia. But it's still a machine. The components are fully replaceable. Someone dies of AIDS? Doesn't matter, Gaia will fill in the gap if necessary. Polar bears go extinct? Doesn't matter. Gaia will just evolve some new critters to take their place.

What we need instead is the inverse of explosive holism, something I call *implosive holism*. According to explosive holism, the whole is always bigger than the sum of its parts. Explosive holism contaminates everything that uses it, like a bug in software, from Marxism to systems theory to the Gaia hypothesis. According to Marxism when you have enough machines making other machines in a gigantic network of factories, poof! Suddenly industrial capitalism, capitalism for real, has emerged. Emergence is a fantastic example of explosive holism. Cybernetic biology proposes that when you have enough physical subsystems whirring away, poof! Life emerges, or consciousness emerges. Dead matter is logically and chronologically prior.

This is all a theistic magic trick. It stems from the idea of an omnipresent creator being who is always ontologically greater than the universe. Everywhere we look, we find this deity added to what we are looking at, in such a way that this being is added consistently everywhere at the same time, with no loss of signal, as it were, so the deity is bigger than the sum of his or her or its parts, namely the universe. Explosive holism is behind the impulse to claim that my god is bigger than yours. He's so wide you can't get around him, he's so high you can't get over him.

Now the nice thing about OOO is that it doesn't allow you to contaminate your thought with this irritating, toxic and ultimately violent explosive holist bug. This is because, as I just pointed out, if a thing exists then it exists in the same way as something else. Wholes exist. Parts exist. Wholes exist the same way as their parts. The whole is one, by definition. The parts are many. Therefore the whole is always less than the sum of its parts! The logic is so beautifully straightforward that the reason for our puzzlement at this idea, this implosive holism, must come from somewhere that isn't logical.

What we know to be the case, the existence of interconnected beings, is something I now call *the symbiotic real*. The symbiotic real is always implosively holist, at every level. A single word I use for implosive holism is *subscendence*, which is like transcendence but sort of upside down. Subscendence isn't leaping into a beyond. Subscendence is leaking out of a whole. Precisely because everything exists equally, in an implosive whole you simply *can't* have a flat ethics. For example, if you are going to be nice to bunny rabbits it means you're not going to be nice to bunny rabbit parasites. Interconnectedness means that there's weirdly less of everything. This is rather beautifully and hilariously encapsulated in the US tax code, where a married couple count as one and a half people. Effectively, when you get married you become three-quarters of a person.

And implosive holism or subscendence is why wholes are *fragile*. It doesn't make any sense to call an omnipresent god fragile. (Let alone an omniscient or omnipotent one.) If we're going to say that things such as 'the balance of nature is fragile,' like we used to say in the 1970s, subscendence gives you the real ontological reason why, the reason that has to do with the structure of how things are. That's what ontology is: it's an account of how things exist, not of what exists. A lichen exists such that it is one, while its fungal and algal parts are two. A lichen is fragile.

Nature as a concept is for sure explosively holist. There is more to it than the sum of its parts. When we try to look for it, there's some kind of excess that gestures beyond where we are looking. Now this kind of thing, this nature thing, is most definitely hierarchal, unlike symbiosis. It's easy to determine who is the top and who is the bottom.

Nature is a concept. But nature isn't just a concept. Nature is a whole set of psychic, social and philosophical protocols, gestures, algorithms and movements.

What we want instead is an implosive, weak holism, and it's just exactly this holism that enables us to describe megacities.

Okay so let's go there again, because implosive holism, or as I'm calling it *subscendence*, is tricky because we've been telling ourselves it is not correct in various ways, some of them nonverbal, for quite some time. Remember that OOO says that if a thing exists, it exists in the same way as something else. OOO allows for wholes—there are not just football players but also football teams, and football teams exist in the same way as football players.

Okay, so the football team is one. Ontologically one. While the football players are eleven. Eleven is greater than one. The whole exists in the same way as the parts. So the whole is always less than the sum of its parts!

Now this is so childishly logical that one shouldn't spend any time worrying about it. But what interests me is precisely the reaction that we all have, that I had at first, that this is an unthinkable idea. It tells us something about the force of the explosive holist concept that the whole is always greater than its parts—ontologically greater—and thus about where it comes from. It tells you why materialists who are atheists prefer reductionism to holism. Richard Dawkins takes one look at James Lovelock and Lyn Margulis and freaks out. A less freaked out holist would make a strong distinction between a Lovelockian explosive holism and a Margulian implosive holism.

Implosive holism has a marvelous effect on identity. It means that there are beings and that these beings are themselves, but in such a way that they never quite coincide with themselves. Beings are leaky. Being authentic doesn't really mean being totally and utterly something that transcends its parts, like everything has an Intel-inside stamp on it. Funnily enough being an author and being authentic in that sense aren't things we need to get rid of at all or feel bad about or reduce to something else, because that kind of authorship already contains all kinds of other beings. There is no point in getting rid of it, like the poststructuralist tactic of thumbing your nose at the political father or moving from work to text or from author to reader (these are all Barthes). Such a tactic leaves explosive holism intact for someone else to appropriate. What needs to happen instead is that we go inside the HAL 9000 of holism and take it apart from the inside, removing some of its cassette tapes to make it a bit less of itself than once it was.

Take the concept of world, which doesn't mean the physical planet, but the totality of projects and motivations and so on in which we're involved. In this sense saving the world could mean repairing a badly damaged spacecraft in another galaxy just as much as it could mean quantitative easing. Wholes such as worlds are always ontologically less, which is one way of thinking about how they are necessarily perforated. Yet pervasive. The good news is that everything gets to have a world, not just humans and not just conscious beings and not just sentient beings and not just animate beings. This is because worlding can't be confined simply to cognitive activities, and cognition can't be the top or only access mode, the only 'correct' way beings relate to things.

And the other good news is that these worlds are perforated, ragged and tattered. Four thousand holes in Blackburn Lancashire ... It's not like how Heidegger says, that humans are rich in world while the beings he calls animals are poor in world while beings such as rocks have no world at all. It's that everything has a world, and that these worlds can be shared. Worlds necessarily contain gaps because they are less than the sum of their parts. This is inherent in Heidegger's concept of world which depends on the Slinky-like, lopsided or as he says ecstatic quality of the beings that assemble world. But everything is like that, in order for his own theory to work, a fact that Heidegger himself is keen to paper over with a nervous anthropocentrism that is nowhere justifiable according to his very own view. This anthropocentrism underwrites the even less tenable Nazism that seduced him. But unlike Adorno, I think that Heidegger only works when these sorts of bug are removed from his thought. It's not that we have to get rid of the notion of world. It's that we have to take some of the wind out of its sales.

Worlds are perforated. Just ask Houston. Hibiscus flowers burst through the concrete. The lack of zoning laws means that I can start Tim Morton's autobody and tattoo parlor on my front lawn. Electric cables sag into the street. Huge pools of storm water are ponds for frogs. Thought is only one access mode among many and it's not the top access mode, better than say brushing against or flying into or ignoring. So nonhumans live in cities just as much as humans. So we should design cities with this in mind.

There actually isn't this rigid firewall separation between reality or and the real, like some very strict Kantian and Hegelian psychoanalytic theory is saying. The real is a whole that is less than the parts that access it: there is a weird excess of reality over the real (just ask someone playing Pokémon Go). Boundaries are permeable and worlds are perforated, so you can have new ideas and so you can share this world with tigers, and tigers can share their world with you, up to a certain shade of grey point.

And social systems and political formations must also be wholes that are less than the sum of these parts. Which means that there can be no top level, one size fits all political solution to anything. And that we are free to make them, knowing that they won't fit everything. Consider ecological action, action that is with relation to what I'm now calling the symbiotic real. This real is most definitely a whole that is less than the sum of its parts. Ecological action always excludes at least one being. If you are going to be nice to bunny rabbits it means you can't be nice to bunny rabbit parasites. I find this idea profoundly relaxing, and indicative of a certain humour. There's no way to stretch the net to fit over everything. Worlds aren't shrink wrapped or vacuum sealed.

We don't have to choose between incremental little rearranging of deck chairs on the Titanic of whatever this political and economic system this is, and some massive apocalyptic change of everything.

Mentioning the apocalypse is important. That's the point—this way of thinking really is agricultural age religion version 2.0, philosophy edition, where truth is white not black.

We don't have to choose between life and death with a gun to our head, like hardcore pro-life arguments try to force us into accepting. We don't have to cling for dear life to the idea that we should cling to things for dear life, or just like our normal belief about belief, the one that Richard Dawkins shares with fundamentalists, and just like our normal idea of what the word *survive* means. Since about 10,000 BC that concept of survival has very successfully almost totally killed off the planet, to the point where in the name of survival we have started the Sixth Mass Extinction Event, which ends up with us going extinct, because our world just collapsed since we were trying to put an Intel inside label on everything, or rather a *This is a human being decision thing*, otherwise known as anthropocentrism. We would have gotten away with it if it hadn't been for those pesky life forms!

We don't have to agree that the Buddhist idea of no-self means that you're just a bunch of atoms. What it really means is that you are open. You are a whole that is less than the sum of its parts. Which means that you can do stuff, and in particular, you can do new stuff.

And in the end, there are no shrink wrapped, vacuum sealed cities either, despite city centres and cathedrals on hills and so on. Megacities tell us something true about all cities. Things have boundaries but these boundaries are neither thin nor rigid. Everything sort of sprawls like a megacity. Things don't really have centers, then, even if they have mathematical centers because they have a definite shape. The mathematical model might have a center, but the concept of center doesn't apply in the *physical* world, for example.

It's funny how, as I was saying earlier, the US tax code talks about the property of subscendence. Recall that subscendence is the inverse of transcendence, sort of transcendence downwards rather than upwards. The US tax codes specifies that a married couple count

as one and a half people. When you get married, according to the code, you become three quarters of a person—which is also quite accurate. Indeed you figure out that you never were one hundred percent yourself. You were never self-contained. The whole subscends its parts.

Which also means that gigantic things such as megacities or neoliberal capitalism or global warming may be physically colossal, but ontologically they are quite tiny, and their parts do so much more than being part of them. Weather is always a symptom of climate. Rain is now a symptom of global warming. But rain subscends global warming. It's so much more than that, equally so. It's a lovely ersatz pond for these toads in my street. It's this soft warm thing that falls on my arm. It's the way rocks smell after a shower.

Hyperobjects are gigantic entities that cannot be pointed at directly, such as global warming or indeed megacities, multi-functioning, multi-dimensional beings that are hard even to compute, namely to map or analyse using computational power—it takes terahertz of processing speed to map global warming. As modernity has developed hyperobjects have become visible—perhaps the first one in the modern period was El Niño, the Pacific weather phenomenon. But hyperobjects have been around since as they say the quote unquote dawn of civilization. The very first was probably the kind of epidemic that the ancient Greeks called miasma. When you are settled in a city state, you may notice that all your cows are dying mysteriously. Humans are also affected. Something is wrong, but it is hard to locate exactly where or what this wrongness is. The hyperobject comes in and out of phase with human temporalities.

But these things shouldn't intimidate us. There is ontologically less of them weirdly than we have learned to believe. Oedipus believed, along with the rest of his culture, that the epidemic was a miasma, an ambient pervasive expression of some kind of deeply ingrained blood guilt. With the noir logic of ecological awareness that Oedipus is the first in Greek literature to exemplify, the detective realises that he is the criminal, in a way that obliquely computes the ways in which humans, operating under the aegis of a certain agricultural logistics that began in Mesopotamia and in other parts of the world at the start of the Holocene, are indeed responsible for creating the conditions in which epidemics can arise.

However, the languages of guilt, shame and punishment that underwrite this recognition—in Greek tragedy it is formalised as *anagnorisis*—scale the hyperobject in such a way as to make it seem ontologically greater than the sum of its parts. The languages of apocalypse and guilt that underwrite our contemporary global warming discourses perform much the same function, ensuring that aesthetics, ethics and politics, not to mention ontology, remain within a theistic framework, the framework devised within the operation of the agricultural programme (which I call agrilogistics). But you can't use a framework designed to justify the programme to figure out how to transcend that programme.

What instead needs to happen is to face up to the radical finitude and contingency of the hyperobject, its non-ominipotence, non-omnipresence and non-omniscience. We are not sinners in the hands of an angry god or made scientists writhing in the tentacles of a Cthulhu. The current fascination with Lovecraft as a touchstone for our era and for its speculative realist philosophy is in fact the latest iteration of a theistic inhibitor on understanding what is happening and acting on it. Cthulhu doesn't mean that everything is interconnected—he's got the whole world in his tentacles, sort of thing. Cthulhu means that *nothing matters at all*. Cthulhu is eliminative materialism with its atheist fig-leaf stripped off. Eliminative materialism is a profoundly nervous reaction to the gap between phenomena or data and things or the real, the gap discovered by Kant as the reason for explaining modern, which is to say, Humean causality theory, which is statistical, not theological. According to eliminative materialism, if you can explain the mind in terms of the brain entirely, there is no mind at all. Not even an emergent mind, the sort of deist compromise between reductionist materialism and holism. Eliminative materialism, like a bullet wound in a foot or for that matter the nail that fixed Oedipus to the mountainside, hobbles our ability to cope with hyperobjects at all. Something like a fatalist nihilism is its ethical upshot.

Set theories that have no place for paradoxical sets that contain contradictory members are artifacts of explosive holism. The Pac-Man Hegelianism that swallows everything in its path is an artifact of explosive holism. The search for that one size fits all social solution is most definitely an artifact of explosive holism. In their different ways all these phenomena are retweets of agricultural age religion that inhibit the future, namely a moment at which the *symbiotic real* is more truthfully encountered in social psychic and philosophical *realities*.

We do need a holism, but a weak holism along the lines I have been suggesting. The symbiotic real is a whole, but one that is less than the sum of its parts. 'Nature' is how we have been talking to ourselves about what is in fact the case, the symbiotic real. There is a sharp difference between the real and 'reality,' or our sense of realness. Our human, agricultural and neoliberal (and so on) reality is now violently impeding less coercive relationships with nonhuman beings. Less coercive relations with nonhumans would also give rise to less coercive ones between humans. In order to bring these about, one key tactic is completely to drop the concept of nature.

Now the thing about symbiosis is that it's actually impossible to decide which being is the host and which is the parasite. Consider lichen, that beautiful entity, leathery, papery, delicate green and so many other colors, growing on trees, rocks and other surfaces, and an indicator of good air. Lichen is a symbiotic community. Lichen consists of algae cooperating symbiotically with fungus. Who is the most important, the fungus or the algae? It's impossible to tell. Some parasites are utterly essential for remaining alive. Others are toxic. But some cross back and forth between these poles. There's no way to determine in advance whether some symbionts are going to be helpful or harmful.

When you scale it up enough you see the whole of the biosphere as symbiosis. That's the beauty and the power of the concept. And the lack of hierarchy holds at this level too. The whole idea of the food pyramid is an ideological ruse. If we lose our stomach bacteria we wouldn't be able to eat any of the food, to say the least, the eating of which enables us to put ourselves at the top of the eating charts (where else would we put our anthropocentric selves?).

What is the cognitive state and social fact of collectively inhabiting a subscendent, imposive whole? It is called *solidarity*. Solidarity is an interesting word. It describes a state of physical and political organisation, and it describes a feeling. This itself it interesting, because it cuts against a dominant, default ontological trend, default since the basic social, psychic and philosophical foreclosure of the human–nonhuman symbiotic real that we call the Neolithic. Let's think up a dramatic Game of Thrones sounding name for it. Let's call it *The Severing*.

Why this dramatic name? Well, I really do think that it's some kind of trauma, a trauma that we keep reenacting on and among ourselves (and obviously on and among other life forms). It creates a basic, in itself traumatic fissure between, to put it in those starkly cut and dried Lacanian terms, reality (the human–correlated world) and the real (ecological symbiosis of human and nonhuman parts of the biosphere).

Naturally, the cut and driedness of the Lacanian model is itself an artifact of The Severing, derived in large part from Hegel's defensive reaction against the shockwave sent by Kant's correlationist ontology. for Hegel, the difference between what a thing is and how it appears is internal to the subject, which in the largest sense for him is Geist, that magical slinky that can go upstairs all the way to the top, where the Prussian state hangs out. The thing in itself is totally foreclosed, thought only as an artifact of the strong correlationist thought space; strong correlationist as opposed to weak correlationist, which is Kant and OOO, where there is a gap but it's not inside the subject, it's in the thing or things, however many there are.

I'm fonder of Lyotard's way of thinking about all this. For Lyotard, the real-reality boundary must be perforated, like a sponge. Stuff leaks through. (It makes better Freudian sense too.) There is a loose, thick, wavy line between things and their phenomena, expressed in the dialectical tension between what Lyotard calls *discourse* and what he calls *figure*. Figure can bleed into discourse, by which Lyotard means something physical, nonrepresentational, 'silent' perhaps in the sense that Freud describes the drives as silent.

So solidarity in this light means human psychic, social and philosophical being resisting The Severing. This is not as hard as it seems, because the basic symbiotic real requires no maintaining by human thought or psychic activity—we have been telling ourselves that humans, in particular human thought, makes things real for so long that this sounds absurd or impossible. Solidarity, a thought and a feeling and a physical and political state, seems in its pleasant confusion of feeling-with and being-with, appearing and being, phenomena and thing, to be not just gesturing to this non-severed real, but to emerge from it, since in a way it is just the noise that symbiosis is already making. In this way, solidarity is not only the nicest feeling and political state (and so on), it is also the cheapest and most readily available because it relies on the basic, default symbiotic real.

Solidarity is a word used for the 'fact' (as the OED puts it) of 'being perfectly united or at one.' And solidarity is also used for the constitution of a group as such, the example given being the notorious notion of 'the human race,' or species, such as the dreaded Anthropos of the dreaded Anthropocene, which we all need to be thinking in all kinds of ways rather than wishing this embarrassing seeming generalisation seeming race, class and gender specificity-stripping Enlightenment horror, and lurking behind this, another transparent monster, the concept of *species* as such. And *solidarity* can mean *community*. In other words, solidarity presses all the wrong buttons for us post-68 New Left educated people. No wonder Hardt and Negri spend so much time finessing it into a diffuse deterritorial feeling of rhizomatic something or other, at the end of their magnum opus *Empire*.

We want something like solidarity to be as un-solid and as un-together as possible. We want something perhaps like the community of those who have nothing in common (Lingis), a community of unworking or inoperation (Nancy). On the other hand, we are obsessed with systems and how they emerge magically from simple differences that, in the Batesonian lingo, make a difference. In other words, we are either resisting an agricultural-age religion or we are promoting it by other means. In either case we are operating with reference to agricultural religion, which is the experiential, social and thought mode 1.0 (if you like) of The Severing. Houston, we have a problem.

What is the default characteristic of this thought mode? It is what I am now calling *explosive holism*. Explosive holism is a belief, never formally proved but retweeted everywhere all the time, that the whole is always greater than the sum of its parts. Either you are down with that—because you are a traditional theist or you are into cybernetics (or any number of deployments of this concept)—or you are the kind who shows their behind to the political father, as Roland Barthes put it. You are in church or you are thumbing your nose at church. In either case, there is a church. And this is the problem.

Truly getting over Neolithic theism and its various upgrades would be equivalent to achieving ecological awareness in social, psychic and philosophical space. That is because these modes of coexisting and thinking and feeling are artifacts of The Severing. It would be tantamount to allowing at least some of the symbiotic real to bleed through into human thought space, let alone human social and psychic space. So it sounds quite important. And I claim that what is blocking our ability to do so is in part a deep and therefore structural set theory that thinks wholes as greater than the sum of their parts. Such a theory turns wholes—community, biosphere (referring to nature in this case), the universe, the God in whose angry hands we are sinners—into a being radically different from us, radically bigger (transcendentally bigger), some kind of gigantic invisible being that is inherently hostile to little us. We are about to be subsumed, the drop is going to be absorbed into the ocean—Western prejudices about Buddhism perhaps are negative thoughts about explosive holism leaking into the thought space conditioned by that very holism, projected onto a so-called Eastern religion. It isn't very difficult to discern within this fear of absorption into the whole (along with its ecstatic shadow) the traditional patriarchal horror of the simple fact that (with full respect to Levi Strauss) we came from others. The way contemporary Hegelian psychoanalytic prose seems to juice itself on the uncanny over and over again is an in some ways quite embarrassing Stockholm Syndrome-like constant reassertion (needing to be reasserted to maintain the strong real-reality boundary) that we came out of vaginas. I mean, it shouldn't be that big of a deal. The moment at which it isn't a big deal, and so no longer uncanny in the sense of horrifying—though perhaps uncanny in the softer sense of being irreducibly strange, because it involves undecideable host-parasite symbiotic logics—is the moment at which imperial neoliberal 'Western' patriarchal thought space will have collapsed.

Megacities are great things to think with. They show you how much wiggle room there is 'underneath' these massive entities that seem to oppress us so much and put so many strains on our ability to comprehend them. Megacities are a way to think future cities, because if the future really is the future, which is to say if it no longer operates according to the agrilogistical programme, then future cities will be wholes that are less than the sum of their parts, which means that non-humans have just as much a place in them as humans. Now that's a thought to ponder while you water your vertical garden.

A lecture delivered at the Future Cities Laboratory annual conference in Singapore in September 2016.

C

Archipelago Cities

The process of industrial and urban reorganisation of former rural and natural areas, as in the case of palm oil production, has completely transformed the meaning that notions of the rural and the countryside used to hold. The rural has disappeared: it has become a conceptual black box and an unfamiliar geography, quietly transformed through less familiar, centripetal forces of urbanisation working away from the large centres.

Stephen Cairns

All cities have their hinterlands of one kind or another. The hinterlands of cities in monsoon Asia have very specific ecological, economic and demographic characteristics, which mean they interact with nearby urban growth in distinctive ways. In sheer quantitative terms, these regions already represent one of the world's dominant forms of settlement. Despite this, we have little up-to-date information on their extents or current characteristics.

FCL INDICIA 01 C ARCHIPELAGO CITIES

159   Archipelago Cities

Society will see 'a shift towards cultivating, breeding, raising, farming, or growing future resources, hand in hand with a reorientation of biological production'. Resources can be cultivated within the conventional soil-based agricultural framework, or micro-organisms that so far have not been considered useful for the energy or building industry could be bred in soil-less farms. A third approach is the industrialisation of natural and bio-chemical processes to rebuild bio-materials synthetically within a controlled environment.

The grand narrative of the urban has replaced the grand narrative of progress that dominated twentieth century thought. Simultaneously, nature is stepping back into our line of vision. With its negative connotation, that can be traced back to industrialisation, nature takes the form of climate change and natural catastrophes such as floods or desertification. With its positive connotation, nature takes the form of a rapidly growing demand for the beauty of landscapes and for domesticated areas for retreat and recuperation.

C   Archipelago Cities:
     Planning Beyond Urban Boundaries

A city cannot be viewed in isolation, be it from the immediate suburban surroundings, metropolitan region, hinterlands or larger national context in which it is located. Throughout history, cities have been characterised as places of economic and social exchange (Weber 1958). The flows of labour, natural resources, construction materials, food, financial capital, information and technology that these exchanges facilitated used to be conceived within a city-hinterland logic. Increasingly, as such flows reach across larger and larger distances, they appear to have very few territorial boundaries and seem to be unrestricted by this logic (Brenner and Schmid 2015). Flows are defined by an interdependence between economic principles of exchange and their enabling infrastructures. Their extended reach has important repercussions on political, social and cultural life and heavily influence urban spatial development (Harvey 1989; Lefebvre 1991).

Research on the sustainability and resilience of cities implies understanding how they are embedded in this wider interdependency. We need to critically study the nature of this interdependency if we are to intervene in and propose alternative ways to structure cities and their territorial relationships. For cities that have limited resources, such as Singapore, it is even more critical to explore long-term sustainable strategies for managing flows.

The importance of territorial setting for future cities is aptly recognised in the New Urban Agenda proposed in Habitat III in Quito 2016 (United Nations Conference on Housing and Sustainable Urban Development 2016). The agenda envisions cities that 'fulfil their territorial functions across administrative boundaries, and act as hubs and drivers for balanced, sustainable and integrated urban and territorial development' through a multilevel integrated approach. A workable framework that can support such vision is therefore needed.

We have adopted the term 'Archipelago Cities' for a set of research projects that tackle the role of cities in this territorial sense. The term metaphorically captures the structure of urbanised systems spread across large territories. Seemingly isolated cities and towns in such a system are actually connected by complex networks that facilitate resource exchanges between them. These archipelagos can be defined by a number of different elements such as the built-up area, population density, productive landscapes, and geological landscape and prominent features such as waterbodies, mountains and, in the case of many parts of Southeast Asia, volcanoes. We hypothesise that to plan and design for sustainable future of cities in Asia, we must appreciate how cities relate to their archipelagic context.

The archipelago metaphor resonates with the regions in Asia which are undergoing rapid and intense urbanisation—an area which includes South East Asia, Southern India and Southern China, and which is often called ASEAN+. Urbanisation in these regions has delivered quite novel and unprecedented urban forms, most of which cannot be easily understood in terms of existing European or North American urban models. In those areas urban growth has slowed, and many cities are even 'shrinking'. In this sense, we precisely invert Ungers' (Koolhaas and Ungers 2012) use of the term 'archipelago city' in his discussion of postwar Berlin. In contrast, cities in that area are growing rapidly and through unfamiliar and novel logics that are producing hybrid typologies as well as different kinds of 'city-hinterland' connectivity. The use of the term archipelago cities, therefore, takes a

Archipelago Cities:
Planning Beyond Urban Boundaries

critical stand in the debate on world urbanisation, by recognising the different nuances in defining the urban.

Emphasis will be placed on better understanding these interactions and their repercussions from economic, social, and environmental perspectives. Researchers hope to rethink the future scope and responsibility of urban planning and development in such a context, and to better grasp the infrastructural needs and development potentials of these urban constellations within their archipelagic setting.

Archipelago Cities consists of four projects that focus on future cities research at the national, regional and metropolitan scales.

The first, aims to better understand the metropolis-hinterland relationship in the context of longer-term policies for urban sustainability. New research then can offer new paradigms of urban design, urban planning and land use strategies for the planning of the intra-national region as necessary.

The second, examines the potential of existing urban-rural or *desakota* landscapes to inform future urban planning policy in Asia. Demographically speaking, such landscapes 'already represent one of the world's dominant forms of settlement'. As such, better understanding of how they grow and change will help inform development of planning tools that will support their future development as economically and environmentally viable settlement forms.

The third project aims to radically rethink the material aspects of how future cities in Asia are built. Urbanisation demands more building stock to accommodate growing urban populations. Building materials are sourced from greater and greater distances to meet the demand. The resulting flows are unsustainable. There is a need to explore sources of materials that are closer to hand, and new attitudes to deploying them. This also means developing

Fig. 1   Seamless border between volcano and coffee plantation as a productive landscape and town in Ungaran, Indonesia.

new commitment to moving laboratory research to pilot projects to full-scaled implementation of alternative construction materials in Asian cities.

The fourth research project, considers the wilderness landscape as an integrated part of the urban archipelago. Geological features in many Asian regions, such as volcanoes and rivers, hold an important role in shaping urban environments. Sometimes they function as a distant and picturesque presence, other times as sources of fertile soil and water, and still other times as an all too close disastrous presence in the case of floods and volcanic eruptions. Being both a productive and destructive force, the wilderness landscape needs to be included in planning future Asian cities.

These four research projects can shape a wider research emphasis in its own right, as part of the collective, transdisciplinary

Archipelago Cities:
Planning Beyond Urban Boundaries

research effort of FCL. This collective aim is to understand and support the sustainable development of future cities in the ASEAN+ region. Concepts such as 'extended urbanisation', *desakota*, 'landscape urbanism', 'decentralised urbanism', 'splintered urbanism' as well as 'urban metabolism' and 'urban mining' are important for the idea of the archipelago cities.

The collective project we have developed is for a strategic development framework on the island of Java. Titled, *Archipelago City Java: 1850–2050*, this framework would underpin the development of a sustainable extended urban region in Java. It would aim to support high population densities and a vibrant economy whilst enhancing existing productive landscapes, cultural heritage, and ecological diversity. The framework would serve as a credible foundation for realising existing urban development plans, developing new regional plans, and co-ordinating a set of concrete demonstration projects that would underpin capacity building in Java.

Java was chosen for a number of considerations. The island is one of the most rapidly urbanising, densely populated, agriculturally productive and geologically active regions in the world. Java's population will reach 240 million by 2020 (BPS 2014). By that time, 70 per cent of Java's population will live in urban areas, equating to a population of 170 million.

A megalopolis of this size would occupy the same area as the Tokaido Corridor in Japan (stretching from Mito in the Kanto region, via Tokyo through Osaka and Fukuoka), or the Northeastern megalopolis in the US (the Boswash Corridor), but with double and triple the population respectively (Cairns 2016). What will the cities, towns and landscape of Java look like with this kind of urban growth? How will the growing aspirations of urbanites, the ecological diversity, cultural heritage and agricultural productivity of this island be reconciled?

Archipelago Cities:
Planning Beyond Urban Boundaries

Fig. 2   An aerial view of contemporary Javanese urban-rural landscape.

The infrastructure backbone of Java spans from West to East in the form of a northern coastal roadway (along the former colonial *Grote Postweg*) and a regional railway, including a planned high speed railway. Cities, towns and villages in Java have urbanised along those transport infrastructure networks through a combination of megacity development (such as Jabodetabekpunjur, Gerbangkertosusila, Kedungsepur); secondary and tertiary town growth; urban sprawl and in-situ urbanisation of the countryside. Java has a very mobile population that migrates to and from hometowns and places of work, daily, weekly, monthly, and even seasonally.

These transport infrastructures not only crucially accommodate the flow of people but also the materials and goods across the island. They overlay a constellation of productive landscape, and a network of geological features such as volcanoes and rivers that shape the economic logic of the urban settlements in the surrounds and define their cultural narrative. Together they connect and shape the Javanese archipelago of cities. However unplanned development along these lines threatens to produce a vast entropic carpet settlement that engulfs the whole island and suffocates all of its ecological, cultural and environmental richness.

The macro figures in Java are comparable to other regions in Asia. The Bengal region at the delta of the Ganges River and the Sichuan Basin in Western China, for example, already have populations of well over 200 million at densities over 1,000 people per square kilometre. They are rapidly emerging as closely networked conurbations that interpenetrate high population densities with hybrid agricultural, manufacturing and service economies. Such regions will dominate the urban landscape of Asia in the coming decades.

The current models of urbanisation, city making, urban design, and regional planning are not fully adequate to address the complexity of conditions found in Java, Bengal and Sichuan —particularly with respect to the extent and density of settlement. New ways of thinking are needed for urbanisation in the tropics, on such large scales in such short timeframes. Without integrated and long-term planning, these regions are potentially threatened by ecological, social and economic disasters, for themselves and for the Southeast Asian region as a whole (Cairns 2016).

This framework is being developed collectively. The research teams within the Archipelago Cities scenario contributed their respective disciplinary expertise to the initial project outline. They will be joined by a wider coalition of architects, planners, engineers, social scientists, NGOs and government agencies, collaborating across disciplinary lines.

Bibliography

BPS (2014). *Statistik Indonesia 2014*. Badan Pusat Statistik.

Brenner, Neil and Christian Schmid (2015). 'Towards a new epistemology of the urban', *City* 19: 2–3: 151–82.

Cairns, Stephen (2016). 'Archipelago City Java: 1850–2050', *Future Cities Challenges* conference, 14–16 September, Singapore-ETH Centre, Singapore.

Harvey, David (1989). *The Condition of Postmodernity*. Oxford: Blackwell.

Koolhaas, Rem and O M Ungers (2012). *The City in the City-Berlin: A Green Archipelago*. Muller.

Lefebvre, Henri (1991). *The Production of Space*. Oxford: Blackwell.

Pollalis, Spiro (ed.) (2016). *Planning Sustainable Cities: An Infrastructure-Based Approach*. New York and London: Routledge.

United Nations Conference on Housing and Sustainable Urban Development (2016). 'Habitat III: New Urban Agenda, draft outcome document for adoption in Quito, October 2016'.

Weber M (1958). *The City*. Glencoe IL: Free Press.

Archipelago Cities:
Planning Beyond Urban Boundaries

Milica Topalovic

Palm Oil: Territories of Extended Urbanisation

The notion that urbanisation has become a planetary process, reaching every corner of the globe, is not new. At least since the early 1960s, many authors have understood urbanisation not as discrete instances of socio-spatial change in cities, but as a universalising condition of linked transformation of the natural and social world. Throughout the twentieth century, scholars have analysed the dissolving boundaries of the 'urban' and the 'city': French geographer Jean Gottmann was one of the first to document in 1961 the emerging geography of urbanisation of cities, coalescing together into an interconnected *Megalopolis* of the northeastern seaboard of the United States (Gottmann 1995). Planetary imagination of interconnected urban society and its ramifications marked much of the intellectual work in the following years.

In 1969, Buckminster Fuller published *Operating Manual for Spaceship Earth*, a vision for comprehensive planetary planning that intended to enable all of humanity to live with freedom and dignity, without negatively impacting the earth's ecosystems (Fuller 2017 [1969]). In the early 1960s, Marshall McLuhan wrote of the electronic media as base for a new social organisation, a 'global village' (McLuhan 1962), and in 1967–8 Greek urbanist Constantinos Doxiadis declared the arrival of *Ecumenopolis*—an inevitable, not-too-distant future destination of urbanisation process in which the totality of human settlements on the planet will evolve together into a single, earth-spanning, city (Doxiadis 1974). During and after the 1968 revolutions, critical theories on urbanisation began to shape up. Many pointed out the deeply conflictual character of urbanisation as it enables the expansion of capitalist relations. In 1972, the system thinkers of The Club of Rome posed the question of 'the limits to growth', accompanied by a dramatic illustration of the finitude of the earth's resources (Meadows et al. 1972). At the same time Henri Lefebvre wrote Urban Revolution, first published in 1970, predicting that urbanisation is central to the survival of capitalism, and therefore bound to become crucial terrain of political and class struggle (Lefebvre 2003 [1970]).

Indeed, urbanisation has become 'planetary'. But, the urbanisation concept, though highly popular and regularly cited by both the scientific world and institutions of territorial governance around the world, still lacks theoretical underpinning and epistemological framing in urban theory. Many anachronisms and misconceptions continue to be associated with urbanisation concept. Already Lefebvre in *Urban Revolution* wrote of 'blind fields', in which the true character of the urban and urbanisation remains relatively misunderstood, partly due to various ideologies, and partly as a product of disciplinary boundaries and academic departments that build conceptual blinders (Lefebvre 1970). Among the most important misconstructions of urbanisation, as Brenner and Schmid have pointed out (Brenner and Schmid 2015), are the conception of the 'urban' as a bounded settlement type, and the understanding of urbanisation as a process pertaining exclusively to cities. Linked to that is an anachronistic perception of 'rural-urban dichotomy', which continues to powerfully shape territorial politics from local levels to transnational institutional bodies including the UN and the World Bank (Brenner and Schmid 2014).

In contrast, the research project presented in this volume through this essay, proposes that 'the historical and contemporary geographies of urbanisation encompass much broader, if massively uneven, territories and landscapes, including many that may contain relatively small or dispersed populations, but where major socioeconomic, infrastructural and socio-metabolic metamorphoses have occurred precisely in support of, and as a consequence of, the growth imperatives of often-distant agglomerations' (Brenner and Schmid 2015). These broader territories and processes are subsumed under the term *extended urbanisation*.

This 'extended' character of urbanisation has been partially illuminated in classic accounts of city-hinterland relations, such as the study by William

Fig. 1   Luigi Ghirri, *Modena*, from the series Atlante, 1973
Ghirri shows the palm tree as a universal (cartographic) symbol. The grouping
of palm trees universally stands for an oasis—the first sign of water and shade,
a promise of human presence and urbanity.

Cronon of urbanisation of Chicago and its agricultural hinterland, the Great West (Cronon 1991). 'More recently, accounts of extended urbanization have emphasized the progressive enclosure, operationalization and industrialization of landscapes around the world —including rainforests, tundra, alpine zones, oceans, deserts and even the atmosphere itself—to fuel the metropolitan growth in recent decades' (Brenner and Schmid 2015). The relevant authors include Monte-Mór (2014), Schmid and Brenner (2011), Soja and Kanai (2014 [2006]) and others.

As a previous scarcely explored field of urban research, extended urbanisation needs urgent empirical and theoretical foundational work. The project presented here collects, analyses and compares examples of extended urbanisation in the Singapore region and other parts of the world. It comprises eight case studies, including territories of urbanisation of agro-industrial hinterlands (palm-oil) in Malaysia and Indonesia, the urbanisation of the Amazon through resource extraction, the expansion of green energy networks in the North Sea, the emergence of transnational urban regions along infrastructure corridors in West Africa, the territories and processes of circular migration in Bengal, and others.

What follows is an outline for an ongoing and paradigmatic case study of territories of extended urbanisation, the agro-industrial hinterlands of palm oil production.

Palm Oil—A New Ethics of Visibility for the Production Landscape

The palm tree is a powerful symbol: a synonym for desirable cities with favourable climates and a waterfront, the key ingredients of urban wealth and leisure landscapes. But it is also a symbol of remote wilderness, of countryside and of agricultural production that has been virtually forgotten. It now starts to represent the crucial, if less visible, dynamic reshaping of the rural realm—the growth and globalisation of agro-industrial production that is increasingly consuming land and landscapes around the globe and redefining the traditional meanings of rural or countryside areas.

Palm Oil: Territories of Extended Urbanisation

Moving beyond the notion of the rural in the traditional sense will be necessary for understanding the agro-industrial production landscapes: the expanding agro-industrial hinterlands such as palm oil plantations need to be subsumed into our conception of the urban as essential support territories providing vital resources to the cities in which we live.

Architecture and the visual arts also have an important role to play in researching, describing and making visible to the urban dweller the ongoing industrial reorganisation of the rural realm. These territories can no longer be seen as remote, residual or anachronistic: they are crucial territories of global capitalism and of urbanisation processes. A new ethics of visibility that extends from urban to rural is required.

Geography of Paradise

Though the palm family is extensive and diverse, comprising more than 2,500 known species (Virtual Palm Encyclopaedia), only a few types fit the ideals of blue sky and sea as tirelessly replicated by American conceptual artist John Baldessari in works such as *Palmtree Seascape* (2010), those Edward Ruscha photographed for *A Few Palm Trees* (1971) or the ones David Hockney painted in his *mise-en-scène* of *A Bigger Splash* (1967).

As a pictorial motif and a cultural symbol, the palm tree has always occupied the Western imagination. In the Book of Genesis it was the Tree of Life, the sacred tree of fertility and longevity, a symbol of spiritual victory over flesh and of peace in the aftermath of conflict. In the Age of Discovery and the colonial era, the palm arrived in the North as a symbol of the exotic and control over remote territories. In mid nineteenth century, the popular Palm Houses in Victorian Britain and elsewhere in Europe, such as the one designed by Decimus Burton and Richard Turner at Kew Gardens (1844–48), staged miniature palm jungles for European city dwellers in recognition of the ambitions and prestige of prosperous collectors and colonial elites. But soon after, the palm escaped the glass and iron conservatories to conquer coastal holiday resorts anywhere from the English Channel to the Mediterranean, from Torquay to Nice.

The palm has been a modern archetype ever since, one that stands at the intersection of wealth and leisure, marking our increasingly universal desire for tropicality. Urban palm trees grace images of desirable urbanity—residing by poolsides in condominiums and resorts. Synonymous of wealth and power, they are embroidered on both bathrobes and military uniforms. And drawings of palm islands cast an artificial emblem for satellite photography, transforming specific geographies into a common imaginary.

Palms are an ingredient of better cities, a sign of permanent leisure, of early retirement and the Sun Belt—of LAs, Miamis and Dubais everywhere. They provide identity to generic cities, which in the words of Rem Koolhaas, depend on the 'Edenic residue' and its 'immoral lushness' to supply the myth of the organic to the generic urbanism (Koolhaas 1995). Palms are the markers of the contemporary geography of Paradise. But there are other types of palm trees.

Geography of Production

If classified not according to the principles of botany, but to their place in the geography of urbanisation, then next to the city palm, a wide variety of other types can be distinguished. Among them are the palm species found 'in the wild', the palms of the rural areas, as well as the species of the production forests—the worker palms such as *Elaeis guineensis*, the oil palm.

According to the United Nations (UN) and other sources, the oil palm territory has more than doubled since 1990, and continues to grow at the same pace (UNEP GEAS 2011). Palm oil production currently covers an area the size of England and Wales, and most of it located in Malaysia and Indonesia (FAOSTAT 2013). Major expansion is ongoing in South Asia (Papua New Guinea and Thailand) and in West African countries (Nigeria and the Congo basin), where it will replace rainforest and rural smallholdings, facilitated by local governments, and predictably, the military (UNEP GEAS 2011). Palm oil's exceptional 'cleanliness'—a high yield with very little waste— makes it an ideal generic commodity, together with corn syrup, sugar or soy, a universal ingredient found in a myriad of food products, soaps, detergents and biofuels. Consequently, 90 per cent of its global production is controlled by multinational corporations and traded on financial markets (UNEP GEAS 2011).

The available data add that the production of a single tree typically averages 30 litres per year, and that per capita annual consumption of palm oil in the European Union is nearly 60 litres. One might imagine the statistically average EU citizen as a patron of two oil palms in Southeast Asia, and the entire EU controlling a palm oil hinterland roughly twice the size of Switzerland.

The issues of individual as well as institutional, public and corporate responsibility for the explosion of palm oil cultivation are frequently invoked.

At the level of corporate responsibility, instruments such as the Roundtable on Sustainable Palm Oil (RSPO) and the 'certified sustainable palm oil' label have been developed since 2004 (almost simultaneously with the EU carbon emissions trading system) to create a common framework of commitment for producers and traders. The criticism of such measures by Greenpeace and other organisations points at the jargon of corporate promises, which though it maintains the appearance of corporate responsibility, in reality has an indefinite execution date. For example, in the most optimistic estimates presented by the producing companies and members of the RSPO, only 20 per cent of actual palm oil production is certified 'sustainable' (RSPO); however, according to stricter social and environmental criteria, a 'sustainable palm oil' substance has never been produced.

At the level of governmental responsibility, the solutions are not readily available either. The sustainability agenda of public institutions is often simplified and narrowed to the 'clean and green' message for cities and their proximate environment, without having the interest or the instruments to reduce the massive, albeit remote ecological consequences of one's consumption patterns.

With corporations and institutions failing to tackle the issue, the responsibility falls to the individual. Critics of capitalism, including Marxist scholar Slavoj Zizek, have pointed that our culture tends to lay responsibility for the environmental mishaps of the late capitalist economy on the individual citizen-consumer. This, according to Zizek, leads to the symbolic but ultimately futile practices of 'ethical consumption'. Individual symbolic acts such as purchasing 'sustainable palm oil' only amount to 'the delusion of green capitalism' (Zizek 2011).

While the remote consequences of palm oil cultivation are framed in the West in relation to rainforest and biodiversity loss and carbon emissions, the lived realities of the palm oil plantations are nearly invisible, and are inevitably blurred through press reporting and other available information. Only an occasional disaster might bring them into view: 'Your cooking oil may be contributing to the haze', reads a billboard in Singapore, hinting at the annual burning of jungle and plantations due for replanting some two hundreds kilometres eastward on Sumatra. Each year the plantation fires may generate a cloud of toxic haze of geopolitical proportions: the haze may cover the region from Singapore to Kuala Lumpur and from Medan to Brunei in hazardous fumes, triggering the international diplomatic blame game, and contributing staggering amounts of carbon emissions to climate change arithmetic. The reliable yearly recurrence of the haze disaster has shown the difficult entanglement of capitalist production, geopolitics and environment: instead of working toward a solution, governments and the financial sector incentivise palm oil companies and turn a blind eye on the practices on the ground. In other words, only through fundamental structural change of the entire industry, change will be possible.

Investigations at ETH Zürich Architecture of Territory of palm oil plantations in Malaysia have shown that the establishment of the palm oil industry in the country since the mid-1950s—through the so-called Federal Land Development Authority (FELDA) schemes meant to alleviate rural poverty—has involved massive resettlement programmes that to date have affected more than 110,000 'settlers' (Topalovic et al. 2013). Industrial palm oil cultivation and processing is less labour intensive than any type of traditional fruit cultivation, requiring only about 25 workers per square kilometre. The land has therefore been gradually cleared of its former keepers, usually indigenous populations, who have been forced to migrate to cities such as Johor and Kuala Lumpur, catalysing rural-to-urban migration, and directly contributing to the omnipresent patterns of (uncontrollable) urban growth in the region. Though initially the local population was replaced with 'settlers' from other parts of the country who worked on the plantations, palm oil production today relies mainly on the more affordable, transnational migrant labour from other Southern and Southeast Asian countries, especially Bangladesh.

Palm Oil: Territories of Extended
Urbanisation

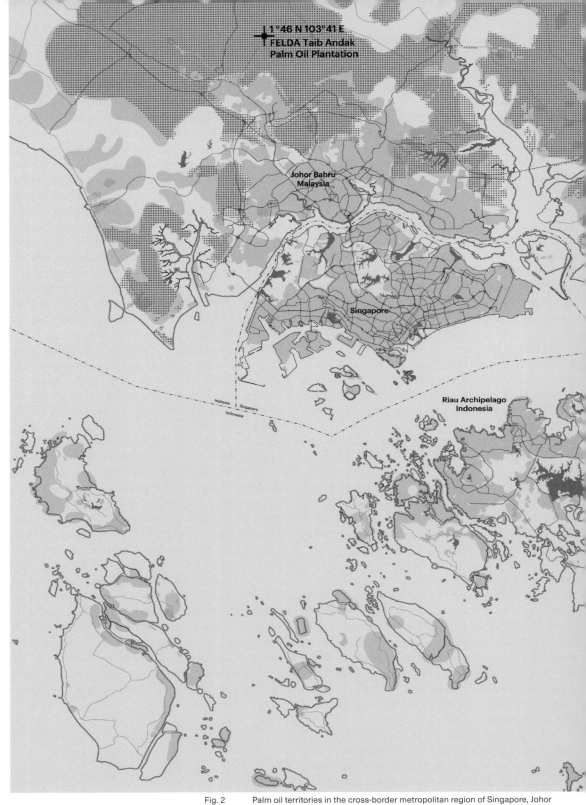

1°46 N 103°41 E
FELDA Taib Andak
Palm Oil Plantation

Johor Bahru
Malaysia

Singapore

Malaysia | Singapore
Indonesia

Riau Archipelago
Indonesia

Fig. 2   Palm oil territories in the cross-border metropolitan region of Singapore, Johor
and Riau Archipelago.
Singapore is located on the epicenter of the largest palm oil producing region in the
world, encompassing the Malay Peninsula, Sumatra and Borneo. Several multinationals
involved in palm oil production and trade have their headquarters in Singapore.

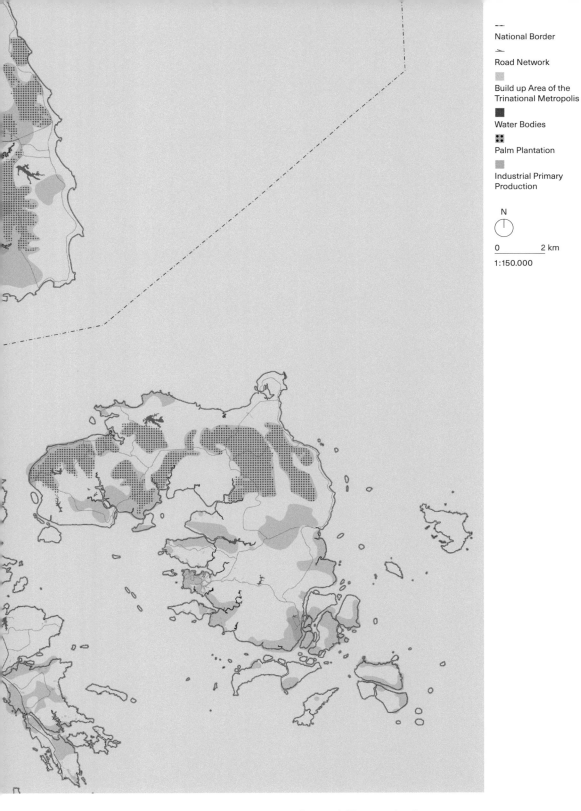

National Border

Road Network

Build up Area of the
Trinational Metropolis

Water Bodies

Palm Plantation

Industrial Primary
Production

N

0   2 km

1:150.000

Palm Oil: Territories of Extended
Urbanisation

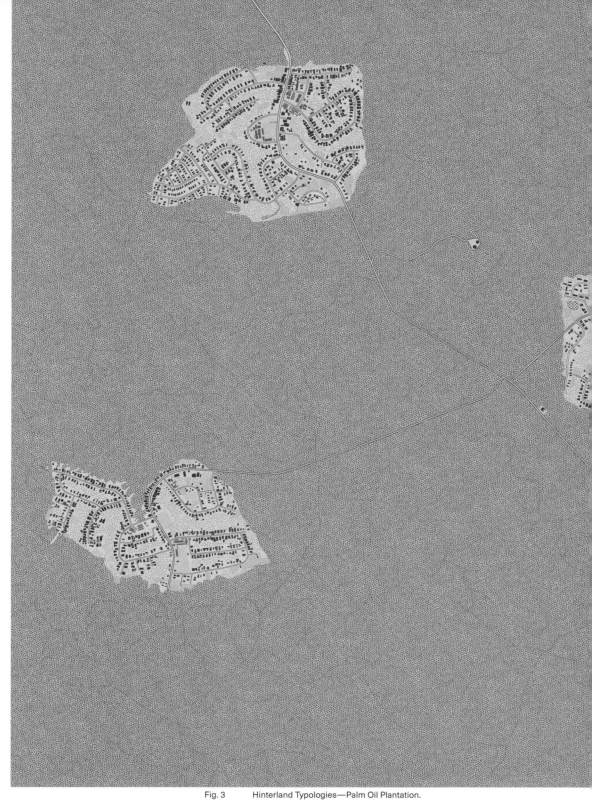

Fig. 3   Hinterland Typologies—Palm Oil Plantation.
A cluster of palm oil plantation village cooperatives, so called FELDA schemes, in Johor, Malaysia, around 50km northeast of Singapore (cluster Gugusan Taib Andak with villages FELDA Sungai Sayong, FELDA Bukit Besar, FELDA Pasir Raja and FELDA Bukit Ramun).

Palm Plantation

FELDA Coorperative Village

Palm Oil Processing Facility

Community Building

Mosque

Construction Site

Vegetation

Palm Tree Nursery

N

0   100 m

1:4.000

FCL   INDICIA 01   C   ARCHIPELAGO CITIES

Palm Oil: Territories of Extended Urbanisation

Palm Oil: Territories of Extended
Urbanisation

Fig. 4   (Left page, top) Palm oil mill # 2, (FELDA Taib Andak, Malaysia).
Fig. 5   (Left page, bottom) Burnt palm oil plantation # 9, (Pulai River, Johor, Malaysia).
Fig. 6   Oil palm production forest, (FELDA Taib Andak, Malaysia).
            An image of the oil palm should not be mistaken for the icon of tropicality and leisure,
            neither should it be dismissed as a symbol of indifference and hypertrophy of global
            consumption. Instead, it should be seen as the marker of the underrepresented and
            the unfamiliar hinterland geographies that need to be remapped.

The palm oil hinterlands and other industrial production landscapes that seem to be spreading rapidly and without apparent resistance are still an unfamiliar type of urbanisation that requires closer scrutiny. This is the modern-day *terra incognita* of industrial primary production, hidden from view in areas away from big cities and in clandestine spaces of exception, such as free-trade or export-processing zones, operated under 'special rules' and 'flexible labour' regimes. Seen from a distance, from our self-declared 'post-industrial' and 'post-working-class' societies in the cities of the West (or the North), and mediated through the lenses of popular techno-scientific representations, these production territories seem homogenised and undifferentiated, lacking both social and natural characteristics. They appear as Cartesian, technical landscapes without geographic aberrations, without specificities: a uniform pattern on a map, a grainy texture on Google Earth.

However, it is precisely this ostensibly unspecific geography that is the crucial terrain of the global economy. Tied in to the infrastructures of processing, logistics and trade, its economic utilisation seems to be helped by its abstraction from the concrete realities on the ground. It is easily mystified as a space of 'de-territorialised' and 're-territorialised' production, a part of the technological 'space of flows' and 'weightless economy' of trade. Through such elaborately distorted representations, production spaces are conceptually neutralised from the meanings of locality, place and ground. They become spaces reduced to economic transactions.

The palm oil plantations can no longer be understood as 'rural' in the traditional sense—these territories display neither the continuity of settlement and land ownership with the rural areas they came to replace, and nor do they provide any degree of social and economic autonomy (or self-sufficiency) for their residents and workers. They are territories where traditional rural socioeconomic relations have been reorganised in the form of industrial exploitation of the land, whose management and production is positioned within global supply chains. Palm oil territories should be understood as global agro-industrial hinterlands, a concomitant of the global capitalist economy and urbanisation processes. The rural is becoming completely industrialised and urbanised.

Ultimately, how should we perceive and conceptualise the territories of the palm oil production forests? More broadly, how can we understand the spaces of the world's agro-industrial hinterlands? What are the possibilities in these landscapes for critical (policy) interventions and for design? How might design become a tool for rethinking issues raised by palm oil production?

A precondition for any design—and for change through design—is the cultural visibility and clear conceptualisation of a given issue. However, the case here is not only that palm oil landscapes are remote and unknown to the West, but that (industrial) labour and production in the West itself are also generally removed and hidden from view. In fact, the 'disappearance of labour and production from the broader social imaginary' constitutes a widespread cultural symptom of the 'post-industrial' world (Roberts 2012).

Despite the diverse traditions of depicting labour and production in modern art—ranging from photography documenting the transformation of the American frontier during the second half of the nineteenth century, to social-realist art centred on the worker as the New Soviet man in the 1920s and 1930s, and the conceptual and minimal works of Bernd and Hilla Becher that record the disappearance of industrial architecture in the 1960s and 1970s, the later twentieth century marked a shift in cultural production. Mirroring the traumatic deindustrialisation of the West starting already in the 1960s, production and labour as categories of artistic engagement progressively diminished. Especially during the 1980s and early 1990s, in the post-industrial society, and within Postmodernist preoccupations with popular culture, commodity aesthetics, identity, gender and so on, 'large segments of labour and production were in fact concealed from common view since they were exported to the geo-political "margins"' (Roberts 2012).

Only in the late 1990s, a renewed interest in the economic subject, this time globalised commodity production and distribution, starts to return sporadically to North American and Western European art. Photographic works as distinct from each other as Allan Sekula's text-image essays on the global shipping industry (*Fish Story*, 1995) and later Andreas Gursky's monumental scenes of manufacturing (*Nha Trang, Vietnam*, 2004), share the same objective of seeking an image for the ostensibly endless, volatile and un-mappable subject of global capitalism. It could be argued that such efforts continue today and are critical, as production landscapes in particular remain abstract, distant and hidden from view. The scale, specificities and lived realities of territories such as the palm oil production forests are still largely incomprehensible or unknown. How, then, could the ethics of visibility be extended from cities to these territories? How can one create an 'index of the hidden and the unfamiliar' for the production forests (Simon et al. 2008)?

There is no doubt that production landscapes are no longer the 'absolute spaces' of nature they once were. They are socially produced spaces, a 'second nature' shaped by human activity, conceptualised and inscribed into contemporary forms of representation. This may seem to render any exploration dubious, and curiosity itself superfluous. In 1973, the Italian artist and photographer Luigi Ghirri pointed at this lack of curiosity for exploring the second nature when he wrote: 'By now, all the paradise islands dear to literature and to our hopes have already been described, and the only possible discovery or journey seems to be that of discovering the discovery already made' (Ghirri 2000). However, he also clarified that this perception is incomplete, and actually the opposite is true: 'Even within the most codified world' of the 'already-lived and seemingly totalising experience', 'infinite readings ... are always possible' (Ghirri 2000). The production landscapes should therefore be seen as a new frontier for launching the second Age of Discovery (Karen 2013), provoking a new kind of urge to explore the landscapes of our planet.

Furthermore, there is a need 'to resist a perception ... that neither the self nor the group has any real power to effect change (of global capitalism), that someone else far away is always preventing it ... in the larger network of seemingly inhuman, cybernetic global social relations' (Jameson and Miyoshi 1998). Global capitalism is not a Cartesian space nor the infinity of Spinoza. And though it sometimes feels that way, this can only be grounds for greater curiosity rather than inertia.

The process of industrial and urban reorganisation of former rural and natural areas, as in the case of palm oil production, has completely transformed the meaning that notions of the rural and the countryside used to hold. The rural has disappeared: it has become a conceptual black box and an unfamiliar geography, quietly transformed through less familiar, centripetal forces of urbanisation working away from the large centres. The characteristics of these territories—social, cultural, morphological and typological—are yet to be discovered, described and named. The new concepts and representations that will substitute the exhausted notion of the rural will have to show that industrial landscapes such as palm oil plantations are essential parts of our cities—they are the city. This will require thinking, imagining, designing and governing at a larger, transnational and planetary scale, which will be reflected in the locality.

Note

Older versions of this essay have appeared in *Trans 24—Normed*, 2014 and *AD: Designing The Rural: A Global Countryside in Flux*, July 2016.

Bibliography

Brenner, Neil and Christian Schmid (2014). 'The 'urban age' in question', *International Journal of Urban and Regional Research*, 38(3): 731–755.

Brenner, Neil and Christian Schmid (2015). 'Towards a new epistemology of the urban?', *City* 19: 151–82.

Brenner, Neil and Christian Schmid (2011). 'Planetary urbanization', in M Gandy (ed.) *Urban Constellations*, page 10–3. Berlin: Jovis.

Cronon, William (1991). *Nature's Metropolis: Chicago and the Great West*. New York: Norton.

Doxiadis, C A and J G Papaioannou (1974). *Ecumenopolis: The Inevitable City of the Future*. New York: Norton.

Food and Agriculture Organization of the United Nations (FAOSTAT) webpage. Online statistical service 2013. Available from <http://faostat.fao.org/site/567/default.aspx#ancor/> Accessed on 23 January 2017.

Fuller, Buckminster (2017 [1969]). *Operating Manual for Spaceship Earth*. Zürich: Lars Müller.

Gottmann, Jean (1995). *Megalopolis: The Urbanized Northeastern Seabord of the United States*. New York: Twentieth Century Fund.

Koolhaas, Rem (1995). 'Generic city' in *S,M,L,XL*, page 1248–68. Rotterdam: 010 Publishers.

Lefebvre, Henri (2003 [1970]). *The Urban Revolution*. Minneapolis: University of Minnesota Press.

Palm Oil: Territories of Extended Urbanisation

McLuhan, Marshal (1962). *The Gutenberg Galaxy: The Making of Typographic Man*. Toronto: University of Toronto Press.

Meadows, D H, D L Meadows, J Randers and W W Behrens III (1972). *The Limits to Growth*. New York: Universe Books.

Monte-Mór, Roberto Luis (2014). 'What is the urban in the contemporary world?' in N Brenner (ed.) *Implosions/Explosions: Towards a Study of Planetary Urbanization*, page: 260–7. Berlin: Jovis.

Roundtable on Sustainable Palm Oil (RSPO) webpage. Available from <http:www. rspo.org/about> Accessed on 23 January 2017.

Simon, Taryn et al. (2008). *An American Index of the Hidden and the Unfamiliar*. Stuttgart: Hatje Cantz.

Ghirri, Luigi (2000). *Atlante*, back cover. Milan: Charta. (Note: This book is based on Ghirri's photographic artwork *Atlante* produced in 1973).

Karen, Martha (2013). 'The master interviewer: introduction', an interview with Hans Ulrich Obrist, in *Surface Magazine*, 104: 124–33.

Jameson, Fredric and Masao Miyoshi (eds.) (1998). *The Cultures of Globalization,* page 352. Durham, NC and London: Duke University Press.

Soja, Edward and Miguel Kanai (2014 [2006]). 'The urbanization of the world', in N Brenner (ed.) *Implosions/Explosions: Towards a Study of Planetary Urbanization*, page 142–159. Berlin: Jovis.

Topalovic, Milica, Martin Knüsel and Marcel Jäggi (eds.) (2013). *Architecture of Territory: Hinterland— Singapore, Johor, Riau Archipelago*, a studio report, ETH Zürich (Singapore), page 64–77.

Roberts, Bill Roberts (2012). 'Production in view: Allan Sekula's fish story and the thawing of postmodernism', in *Tate Papers* 18, Autumn 2012. Available from <http:// www.tate.org.uk/research/ publications/tate-papers/ production-view-allan- sekulas-fish-story-and- thawing-postmodernism/> Accessed on 23 January 2017.

UNEP Global Environmental Alert Service (GEAS) (2011). *Oil Palm Plantations: Threats and Opportunities for Tropical Ecosystems*, December 2011 issue. Available from <http:// www.unep.org/geas/> Accessed on 23 January 2017.

Virtual Palm Encyclopaedia webpage. Available from <http://www. plantapalm.com/vpe/ introduction/vpe_ introduction.htm/> Accessed on 23 January 2017.

World Rainforest Movement (2006) *Oil Palm: From Cosmetics to Biodiesel—Colonization Lives On*. Available from <http://wrm.org.uy/ books-and-briefings/ oil-palm-from-cosmetics- to-biodiesel-colonization- lives-on/> Accessed on 23 January 2017.

Zizek, Slavoj (2011) 'The delusion of green capitalism', a lecture at the Graduate Center, City University of New York (CUNY) on 4 April 2011. Available from <http:// www.youtube.com/ watch?v=yzcfsq1_bt8/> Accessed on 23 January 2017.

Palm Oil: Territories of Extended Urbanisation

Stephen Cairns, Chen Ting,
Miya Irawati, Jennifer Lee

Urban-Rural Systems in Monsoon Asia

Provocation

When approaching any city from the air the first visible signs of settlement are usually rural in character. As the aircraft dips below the clouds a window seat view will reveal a landscape that is structured by geological forms and water systems, patterned by forests, plantations, and fields, defined by hedges, shelter belts, fences, serviced by lanes, roads, freeways, and railways, punctuated by villages, towns and industrial buildings. We take these impressions as signs of a productive hinterland serving our intended destination: the city.

If our flight is destined for an Asian city, particularly in the region known as 'monsoon Asia', the hinterland will look quite different to those surrounding European or American cites. Asian cities are typically larger, both in terms of their populations and spatial extents. Cities and hinterlands in many parts of monsoon Asia are also interpenetrated, so that it is often hard to distinguish the point where urban ends and rural begins. Furthermore, rural hinterlands are likely to be dominated by wet rice, a small holder, labour intensive form of agriculture distinct from the more mechanised wheat and maize agriculture typical of the hinterlands of many other parts of the world. The window seat view when approaching Trivandrum, Kolkata, Dhaka, Yangon, Hanoi, Bangkok, Chengdu, Shanghai, Jakarta, or Surabaya will reveal a landscape where urban and rural forms of settlement are mixed together. Traditional villages, rice fields, fish ponds, irrigation systems, and orchards, are interposed with industrial plants, office blocks, middle class gated housing estates, malls, golf courses, and toll roads.

The aerial view, of course, is a privileged one. It smooths out sharp differences in the landscape and offers pleasing patterns to the eye, conferring on the viewer a sense of 'rational intelligence' (Vidler 2000, 39). On the ground, the urban-rural textures of most of monsoon Asia press more forcefully on the senses. Routines of terrestrial everyday life unfold in a viscous medium consisting of rich sound- and smellscapes, intense social networks (virtual and face-to-face), slow moving traffic, hot and humid air, sweat, particulate matter, and, at certain times of the year, heavy rain. Without the depth of field of the aerial perspective, we visitors are inevitably implicated in this medium. The binary distinctions we depend upon for orientation in European or American cities—figure and ground, permanent and temporary, static and kinetic, organic and inorganic, formal and informal— become convoluted and unreliable in the cities and hinterlands of monsoon Asia.

Both aerial and terrestrial views serve as dual provocations for our research. In themselves, they tell us little about the way urban hinterlands in monsoon Asia developed, how they are structured, how they might develop, and what the fortunes of those who conduct their daily lives there could be. But taken seriously, they give pause for thought. They disrupt the conventions we rely on to understand cities, settlements and urbanisation. They prompt us to consider what it would mean to experience, represent, describe, analyse, let alone design or plan for such conditions.

All cities have their hinterlands of one kind or another. The hinterlands of cities in monsoon Asia have very specific ecological, economic and demographic characteristics, which mean they interact with nearby urban growth in distinctive ways. Sometimes dubbed *desakota* regions (Indonesian for 'village' and 'city') (McGee 1991), scholars have suggested this is a distinctly Asian settlement type that is anomalous compared to cities elsewhere. In sheer quantitative terms, these regions already represent one of the world's dominant forms of settlement. Despite this, we have little up-to-date information on the extent of this settlement type in Asia or its current characteristics. Furthermore, it is unclear what planning approaches, urban design strategies, and material and technological interventions might effectively support and enhance such rapidly changing, urban-rural settlement types. Even more speculatively, what might such hybrid urban-rural formations suggest for alternative visions of settlement elsewhere?

Our research is interested in the hinterlands of cities in monsoon Asia, and how they might be represented, theorised, and positioned within credible urbanisation pathways for Asia and beyond. To this end, we have articulated a set of three primary challenges.

The first challenge is ontological. It concerns defining urban-rural regions in monsoon Asia, understanding their characteristics, features and limits. Although not yet systematically described, we deduce that urban-rural regions represent a demographically and geographically significant form of settlement. A cursory review of population density distributions in monsoon Asia—particularly in the watersheds of the major rivers such as the Ganges, Mekong and Yangtze—show vast carpets of settlements with city-like densities. Research in the field (Xie, Batty and Zhao 2005; DST 2008; McGee 2009; Jones and Douglass 2008) confirms that new kinds of settlement are emerging in these regions, which rarely conform to conventional definitions of cities, be they based on administrative jurisdiction, population density or size. This ontological challenge has serious consequences. For example, the favoured categories that underpin UN urbanisation reports, upon which a host of government, industry, academic and civil society organisations rely for their own research, policy and planning initiatives, do not align to the empirical realities on the ground in monsoon Asia, where over 50 percent of the world's population already resides.

Second, there has been a notable lack of attention given to urban-rural regions in scholarship on cities, urban design, and the development of sustainable technologies and infrastructures for cities. The complexity and fluidity of urban-rural regions means that they present particular difficulties for the conventional understanding of the city and urban planning. For example, such areas of the city are rarely well documented. The *Desakota* Study Team (DST) point out that 'the fundamental role of economic diversification and other processes driving the *desakota* phenomena have remained hidden because the criteria for data collection are shaped by static distinctions between "rural" and "urban" areas' (DST 2008, 10). Existing cartographic conventions, while suited to recording hard urban infrastructures, such as suburban housing, industrial complexes, and freeways, tend not to register the more ephemeral, adaptive, kinetic, and incremental qualities of urban-rural areas. As a consequence, existing planning maps of such areas often leave them simply blank. In many respects, such urban-rural areas have, to date, benefited from their illegibility to the visual regime of state planning. They have spawned a wide range of systems of local self-organisation, in which areas of the landscape are managed, negotiated and developed. This relative illegibility, has allowed local innovations to develop, but also renders agricultural land vulnerable to speculation. The longer-term viability of urban-rural zones requires them to become legible enough to claim a stake in formal planning processes, without losing the bottom up qualities that have supported their development to date.

The third challenge concerns the mismatch between the long-term, one time aspiration of many urban technologies and infrastructures and the fluid and incrementally changing nature of urban-rural regions. We hypothesise that urban-rural regions could offer a pathway to a distinctive sustainable urban development by integrating high populations, diverse land uses, robust economies, rich natural ecologies, and vital sites of food production. These are land uses that are, in the dense and concentrated model of urbanism, typically separated. In this respect, we are interested in understanding different possible development trajectories, rather than assuming a singular urban teleology that terminates with an existing—usually European or North American—urban paradigm (see Webster 1995 on *desakota* as a 'transition phase' to Los Angeles). Realising this potential will require new approaches to urban planning and new attitudes to urban technology and infrastructure.

Desakota, Garden City, Meta-City

A small group of geographers and planners, including Terry McGee, Mike Douglass, Douglas Webster and Ira Robinson, were the first to look closely at such urban-rural regions, often under such headings as 'extended metropolitan region', 'mega-urban region', or 'peri-urban zone'. As McGee conducted much of his fieldwork in Indonesia, he coined the term *desakota* (from 'village' and 'city' in Indonesian) to acknowledge the 'indigeneity' of this phenomenon. Such urban-rural regions are characterised by a unique combination of features including: a tropical monsoonal ecology; the predominance of wet-rice agriculture; and relatively high populations. These primary features, amongst others, meant that urbanisation

Fig. 1   Aerial image of *desakota* landscape, West of Jakarta.
Fig. 2   Along Daan Mogot street, Tanggerang, Banten, Java.

unfolded in urban-rural regions in a distinctive way. This saw a radical mixing of land uses, infrastructures, once rural villages, gated suburbs, cottage industries, malls, golf courses, and industrial complexes. As rice agriculture is relatively labour intensive, the rice-growing regions usually supported quite large and dense populations. This factor means that most of the urban effects of urban-rural regions emerge locally to form a kind of in-situ urbanism, rather than one resulting from centrifugal sprawl from a defined urban centre.

The *desakota* idea has been a fertile way of conceptualising the ways in which distinctive rural territories have been urbanised. This shift of focus away from its origins in Indonesia has seen scholars in geography foregrounding the effects of distinctive governance systems and political economies on the shape of urban-rural regions. McGee et al. (2007), for example, looked at such regions in the context of centralised systems of government in China as an alternative lens on city-focused forms of urbanisation. This work was supplemented by a range of work that focused on the methodological aspects of studying urban-rural regions in China (Shi 1998; Sui and Zeng 2001; Xie, Batty and Zhao 2007; Zhao, and Zhang 2007). Other *desakota* studies were conducted in India (Casinader 1992), and Japan (Shapira, Masser and Edgington 1994).

Architecture, urban design and planning have a long-standing tradition of debate on horizontal cities, agricultural cities, decentralised cities and landscape urbanism. Key moments in this tradition include: Ebenezer Howard's 'Garden Cities of Tomorrow' (1898), Frank Lloyd Wright's 'Broadacre City' (1932; 1945; 1952); Ludwig Hilberseimer's 'City in a Landscape' (1949); Kisho Kurokawa's 'Agricultural City' (1960), Andrea Branzi's 'Agronica' (1995), Lars Lerup's 'Stim and Dross' (1995), Alan Berger's 'Drosscape' (2006) and Richard Ingersoll's reflections on 'sprawl-town (2006). Cedric Price's famous 'egg' diagrams of medieval, modern and extended cities, neatly captures the overall thrust of this disciplinary thread. Together they represent a rich exploration of the possibilities of a horizontal and 'weak' urbanism, as Andrea Branzi (1995) put it (see Waldheim 2010 for discussion on this tradition). The horizontalism of landscape urbanism offered important ways of revisiting the older traditions of decentralised urbanism that had been cast aside as mere car-driven, gasoline-fueled suburbanism. This extended suburbanism was later lamented and celebrated by Joel Garreau (1991)

in *Edge City,* and Deyan Sudjic and Philip Sayer (1992) in *The 100 Mile City,* and subsequently critiqued by New Urbanist architects and planners (for example, Duany, Plater-Zyberk and Speck 2000). Interest in horizontal urbanisation continued in the work of the Los Angeles School, with Edward Soja's (2000) *Postmetropolis* (see also Mostafavi 2010). This view resonated with the work of John Friedmann (1996) and Mike Douglass (1978) and their idea of 'agropolitan' districts. Friedmann and Douglass argued that 'town-centred, self-governing agropolitan districts could be developed in high-density rural or peri-urban areas to raise living standards and increase employment opportunities there' (Friedman 1996, 129). In Europe, geographer and planner Thomas Sieverts thematised the idea of the *zwischenstadt* (in-between city) in his book *Cities Without Cities* (2003 [1997]). Grahame Shane and Brian McGrath (2012) have elaborated this theme under the heading of 'meta-city'.

Of all of these analytical accounts of decentralised urbanisation, Kurokawa's is the only one that explicitly addressed conditions in monsoon Asia, and, in particular, acknowledged the formative role of rice agricultural in Asian urbanisation processes. Kurokawa sought to overcome the urban-rural dichotomy in Japan by declaring that 'rural communities are cities whose means of production is agriculture'. He proposed that 'agricultural cities, industrial cities, consumption cities, recreation cities should each form an integral part of a compact community', that would form '[a] distinct urban system'. Kurokawa's vision was no romantic valorisation of the vernacular countryside, but a search for new possibilities for the urban-rural landscapes of Asia based on rejuvenating existing agricultural communities with new transportation infrastructures combined with lightweight local technologies for managing the production of food and energy, and the treatment of waste. 'Agricultural cities have a potential as future cities', he insisted (Kurokawa 1960).

Three Contextual Clues

The provocations, research questions and overarching challenges that we have outlined so far become more precise and nuanced (and demanding) when we consider them in the context of different national jurisdictions in the monsoon Asia area. Our research intends to focus on five or six urban-rural

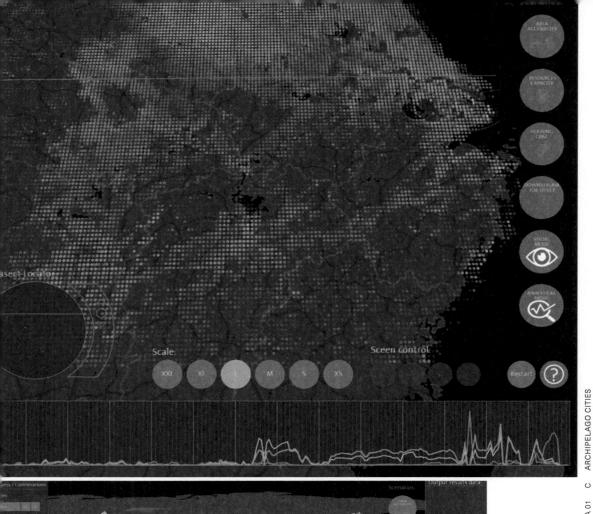

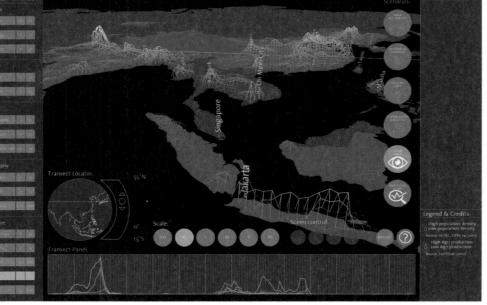

187

Fig. 3   (a–b) Documentation of population densities and crop yields in mixed urban-rural regions of monsoon Asia; above China; blow Southeast Asia, with Java in the foreground.

regions in countries such as China, India, Bangladesh, Vietnam and Indonesia as a means to better understand the way the larger challenges are configured in the context of specific geographies, cultures of design, planning and city making, and systems of government. We offer three contextual clues, below, to indicate how we plan to tackle the overarching research challenges.

Indonesia

In Indonesia, agricultural land is under severe pressure, with loses of over 110,00 hectares per year between 2002 and 2008. These loses were due to several factors, principally rising urban populations, economic growth, standards of living, and government regional planning policies. In Java, where the large majority of Indonesia's population lives (145 million people of a total 255 million, at a population density of close to 1,000 people per square kilometer), agricultural land is needed for housing and industrial estate developments. While on the other islands (composing over 90 per cent of the national land area) land conversion has been caused by the increasing land need for development of infrastructures designed to encourage significant economic growth. The focused development on other islands, especially in eastern Indonesia, have been aiming at distributing the benefits of economic growth outside Java. Currently the national government invests most of state development budget in eastern Indonesia to achieve this goal set out in the national medium-term development plan (2014–2019).

These macro-pressures are compounded by local planning policy and practice. There are weaknesses in land development permit process, for example, that typically involve many informal and opaque exchanges between developers and local government. This usually increases the transaction costs significantly. These additional layers in the transaction process are responses to a number of factors. The first is that formal mechanisms for land permit and development are too convoluted. Second, lack of coordination among government institutions involved in the process of land development permit. Third, the low motivation of local government officer to resist corruption. These factors compound local government failure because of its inability to successfully enforce the land development and spatial planning policies and regulations then consequently increasing conversion of agricultural land become non-agricultural land use.

Bangladesh

Home to the largest delta in the world, Bangladesh supports an extremely dense and productive rural landscape. The major rivers that structure the landscape, principally the Ganges and Brahmaputra, bring rich silt from the Himalayas to the sea, sustaining a population density of 1,100 persons per square kilometer. With two-thirds of the population living in rural areas, Bangladesh remains a predominantly rural society. Yet the high rural population densities challenge conventional assumptions on the urban-rural divide. At the same time, the population continues to rely heavily on the environment for provisioning services. Dry foliage, rice husks, wood, jute stalks, and cow dung are collected by the households for cooking fuel, while wind and water are crucial forms of energy for sail driven transport in a country crisscrossed by rivers. Bangladeshis remain among the lowest energy consumers globally; two-thirds of the country's energy continues to be provided by non-commoditized biomass.

Ecosystems management is complicated in mixed urban-rural regions. Mechanisms that apply to more uniformly urban or rural areas have not been effective, and new approaches are required. Industrial, agricultural, commercial, and household uses all compete for the same ecosystem services, putting tremendous pressure on the environment and particularly the livelihoods of the poor, given their high dependence on the environment for provisioning services. As such, peri-urban areas with multiple and often competing land uses require more management than traditionally agriculture-based communities but are typically under-funded and under-resourced compared to urban areas. This research seeks to understand the variety of actors, technologies and mechanisms that could improve ecosystem management within urban-rural communities in Bangladesh.

China

By the end of 2010, the physical extent of cities in China totaled 39,758 square kilometers. Only 18 percent of this total existed prior to 1980. A full 82 percent was constructed during China's economic boom in the period 1980. This startling figure indicates the speed and intensity of urbanisation that China underwent. By 2010, 44 percent of China was urbanised according to China Statistics Bureau figures. Significantly, rapid urbanisation in China also saw the emergence of mixed urban-rural regions, where manufacturing, commercial and housing properties mixed with rural settlements and cultivated land. This produced ambiguity around the old categories 'urban' and 'rural'.

These developments are an outcome of both global processes of industrialisation and urbanisation, and national and regional policy frameworks. Two such national policy frameworks are useful to describe.

The first is the system of distinct land ownership regulations for urban and rural land. Unlike urban land, rural land in China cannot be exchanged in the non-farming land market. Under these conditions, individual city residents or companies have little access to the rural land, and the rural population cannot benefit directly from the increase in land values resulting from the expansion of neighbouring cities. The government, however, is self-authorised to appropriate rural land, change its land-use status, and resell it at a profit to commercial developers. In many urban-rural areas, this has led to accelerated land appropriation and conversion of high quality agricultural land.

The second policy framework concerns the centralised nature of the government planning system. The governing bodies in China are designed to be politically centralised and administratively all-encompassing. For example, even the members of the administrative committee of a tiny town are appointed by the leading officers of a nearby county or city, rather than by the local residents. In this political system, town committee members are not accountable to the residents of the town they serve, but to their city-based leaders who would typically have more influence on their careers as administrators. In urban-rural areas, this led to the construction of many 'image projects' at strategic locations close to the main avenues and expressways, with good infrastructure and residential buildings. Such projects are often implemented quickly and expensively to fulfill a key performance indicator of the governors in charge. Such practices can lead to a relative lack of investment in areas of the countryside that are not so visible or prominent.

In recent years, government planning authority has increased in urban-rural regions, and this has led to dramatic environmental, social and economic changes. One such region where this kind of transformation is taking place is the Chengdu Plain, some 2,000 kilometers inland from China's Eastern seaboard. Regions such as these make for useful case studies to examine contemporary development strategies, the major stakeholders and their roles, in order to better understand the logic of urban-rural transformation in China. This can serve as a basis for developing refined approaches—economically, socially and infrastructurally—to more resilient urbanisation pathways.

Conclusion

Urban-rural regions in monsoon Asia are visually, morphologically, and functionally distinct from even the most dispersed of western cities (see Jones and Douglass 2008). While they may, at first glance, have a visual resonance with North American suburbs and edge cities, or even take the form of the European *zwischenstadt*, Asia's urban-rural systems are shaped by distinctive ecological, economic and demographic factors. We think this hypothesis has important consequences for developing viable urbanisation pathways in Asia. Decentralised settlement patterns in Europe and especially North America, driven by suburban sprawl, often activated by the construction of centralised systems such as railways or freeways, are regarded with suspicion by many planners, academics and sustainability advocates alike. Such patterns are routinely considered to be threatening the functional diversity of cities, environmental sustainability and, by encroaching on fertile agricultural land, a resilient approach to food production (see Shlomo, Sheppard, and Civco 2005; World Bank 2013; Seto et al. 2014 for contextual discussion on urban extents). Asia's urban-rural regions may not necessarily suffer the same fate. It may be that they contain the seeds of a sustainable form of future city with complex adaptive systems, evolving through incremental growth. This pattern aligns with Shane and McGrath's (2012, 654) vision for a 'metacity', and what Herbert Girardet, in his (2008) book *Cities People Planet*, calls one of the significant emerging urban models of the early twenty-first century.

Bibliography

Branzi, Andrea, D Donegani, A Petrillo, and C Raimondo (1995). 'Symbiotic metropolis: Agronica', in *The Solid Side,* eds. Ezio Manzini and Marco Susani. Netherlands: V+K Publishing / Philips: 101–20.

Casinader, Rex A (1992). *Desakota in Kerala: Space and Political Economy in Southwest India.* PhD Thesis, University of British Columbia.

China Statistics Bureau (2011). 中国城市统计年鉴 [*China City Statistical Yearbook*]. Beijing: China Statistics Press.

DST [Desakota Study Team] (2008). *Re-imagining the Rural-Urban Continuum: Understanding the Role Ecosystem Services Play in the Livelihoods of the Poor in Desakota Regions undergoing rapid change.* Kathmandu: Institute for Social and Environmental Transition-Nepal.

Duany, Andrés, Elizabeth Plater-Zyberk and Jeff Speck (2000). *Suburban Nation: The Rise of Sprawl and the Decline of the American Dream.* New York: North Point Press.

Friedmann, John (1996). 'Modular cities: Beyond the rural-urban divide', *Environment and Urbanisation* 8(1): 129–31.

Friedmann, John (2005). *China's Urban Transition.* Minneapolis: University of Minnesota Press.

Friedmann, John and Mike Douglass (1978). 'Agropolitan development: Toward a new strategy for regional planning in Asia', in *Growth Pole Strategy and Regional Development Policy,* eds. F Lo and K Salih, 163–92. London: Pergamon Press.

Garreau, Joel (1991). *Edge City: Life on the New Frontier.* New York: Anchor Books.

Geertz, Clifford (1963). *Agricultural Involution: The Processes of Ecological Change in Indonesia.* Berkeley: University of California Press.

Girardet, Herbert (2008). *Cities People Planet: Urban Development and Climate Change.* London: Wiley.

Hilberseimer, Ludwig (1949). *The New Regional Pattern: Industries and Gardens, Workshops and Farms.* Chicago: Paul Theobald.

Jones, Gavin and Mike Douglass, eds. (2008). *The Rise of Mega-Urban Regions in Pacific Asia: Urban Dynamics in a Global Era.* Singapore: National Singapore University Press.

Kurokawa, Kisho (1960). 'Agricultural city', in *Metabolism in Architecture.* London: Studio Vista.

Power, Marcus & James D Sidaway (2004). 'The degeneration of tropical geography', *Annals of the Association of American Geographers* 94 (3): 585–601.

McGee, Terrence G (1991). 'The emergence of *desakota* regions in Asia', in *The Extended Metropolis: Settlement Transition in Asia,* eds. Ginsberg, Koppel and McGee, 3–26. Honolulu: University of Hawaii Press.

McGee, Terry (1991). 'The emergence of *desakota* regions in Asia', in *The Extended Metropolis: Settlement Transition in Asia,* eds. Ginsberg, Koppel and McGee.

McGee, Terry G (2009). 'The spatiality of urbanisation: The policy challenges of mega-urban and *desakota* regions of Southeast Asia', UNU-IAS Working Paper no. 161.

McGee, Terry G, George C S Lin, Mark Wang, Andrew Marton, Jiaping Wu (2007). *China's Urban Space: Development Under Market Socialism.* London: Routledge.

Mostafavi, Mohsen (2010). *Ecological Urbanism.* Lars Müller Publishers.

Seto K C, S Dhakal, A Bigio, H Blanco, G C Delgado, D Dewar, L Huang, A Inaba, A Kansal, S Lwasa, J E McMahon, D B Müller, J Murakami, H Nagendra, and A Ramaswami (2014). 'Human settlements, infrastructure and spatial planning', in *Climate Change 2014: Mitigation of Climate Change. Contribution of Working Group III to the Fifth Assessment Report of the Intergovernmental Panel on Climate Change,* eds. O Edenhofer, R Pichs-Madruga, Y Sokona, E Farahani, S Kadner, K Seyboth, A Adler, I Baum, S Brunner, P Eickemeier, B Kriemann, J Savolainen, S Schlömer, C von Stechow, T Zwickel and J C Minx. Cambridge and New York: Cambridge University Press.

Shi Yulong T X (1998). 'Desakota' model and its effects on the model of China's urban economic organisation', *Urban Studies 5.*

Angel, Shlomo, Stephen C Sheppard, and Daniel L Civco (2005). *The Dynamics of Urban Expansion.* Washington DC: World Bank.

Sieverts, Thomas (2003). *Cities Without Cities: An Interpretation of the Zwischenstadt.* London: Spon.

Soja, Edward (2000). *Postmetropolis: Critical Studies of Cities and Regions.* London: Blackwells Publishers.

Sudjic, Deyan and Philip Sayer (1992). *The 100 Mile City.* Orlando: Harcourt Brace.

Sui, Danile, Z and Hui Zeng (2001). 'Modeling the dynamics of landscape structure in Asia's emerging *desakota* regions: A case study in Shenzhen', *Landscape and Urban Planning* 53(1): 37–52.

UN Department of Economic and Social Affairs, Population Division (2010). *World Urbanisation Prospects, the 2009 Revision.* New York: United Nations.

UN Habitat (2010). *State of the World Cities 2010/2011: Bridging the Urban Divide.*

Vidler, Anthony (2000). 'Photourbanism: Planning the city from above and from below', in *A Companion to the City,* eds. Gary Bridge and Sophie Watson, 35–45.

Waldheim, Charles (2010). 'Notes towards a history of agrarian urbanism', in *On Farming,* eds. Mason White, Maya Przybylsk, 18–24. Barcelona: Actar.

Webster, Douglas (1995). 'Mega-urbanization in ASEAN: New phenomenon or transition phase to "Los Angeles world city"', in *The Mega-Urban Regions of Southeast Asia,* eds. Terry G McGee and Ira M Robinson, 27–41. Vancouver: University of British Columbia Press.

World Bank (2013). *Urbanisation Beyond Municipal Boundaries: Nurturing Metropolitan Economies and Connecting Peri-Urban Areas in India.* Washington DC: World Bank.

Wright, Frank Lloyd (1932). *The Disappearing City.* New York: William Farquhar Payson.

Wright, Frank Lloyd (1945). *When Democracy Builds.* Chicago: Chicago University Press.

Wright, Frank Lloyd (1958). *The Living City.* New York: Horizon Press.

Wu, Fulong (2006). *Globalization and the Chinese City.* London: Routledge.

Xie, Yichun, Michael Batty and Kang Zhao (2007). 'Simulating emergent urban form using agent-based modeling: Desakota in the

Suzhou-Wuxian region in China', *Annals of the Association of American Geographers* 97(3): 477–95.

Zhao, Simon X B and L Zhang (2007). 'Foreign Direct Investment and the formation of global city-regions in China', *Regional Studies* 41(7): 979–94.

Dirk E. Hebel, Nikita Aigner, Dustin Fleck, Felix Heisel, Alireza Javadian, Simon Lee, Philipp Mueller, Aurel von Richthofen, Karsten Schlesier, Marta H. Wisniewska

Shifting Paradigms: From Excavation to Cultivation

The Status Quo

As urban populations grow, so does demand for materials and resources to support them. In the era before urbanisation, when urban populations grew at relatively slow rates, such demands seemed proportionate and could be met by supplies in local and regional hinterlands. Now, the resource demands that come with urbanisation outstrip local hinterlands, and can only be satisfied by ever-widening resource catchments and ever-lengthening supply lines. This phenomenon has generated material flows that are transcontinental and planetary in scale and reach, and has brought profound consequences for the sense of ownership and identity of future cities.

The idea of a modern city became in recent years a faceless replica of pre-defined images and with it came a monopolised palette of materials. Steel, glass, and concrete seem to be the only choices architects can think of. No matter where one starts to investigate, in a new African metropolis, in booming Asian hubs or even in Zürich: glass towers without a sense of belonging are mushrooming and reflect away in their mirror facades any rootage or connection to the specificity of a common place.

'The ties that used to bind the city together—whether they were social, through coherent building, or economic, through trade in the souk, or religious, through the coexistent presence—were all lost in the misguided and visionless modernisation of the built environment' (Al-Sabouni 2016). These words were spoken by Marwa Al-Sabouni, a young Syrian architect who blames a ruthless and unreflected architectural practice and wrongly understood modern urbanisation to be partially responsible for the civil war in Syria.

Of all the materials used in contemporary building, sand is one of the most ubiquitous. Sand is used as an aggregate in concrete mixes, the most common building material world-wide. However, supplies have become scarce. In Southeast Asia, whole islands are disappearing due to landslides caused by the mining of sand from ocean floors. Countries like Morocco in North-Africa are losing their beaches due to illegal sand scraping practices. Urban planners in Florida have recognised the threat and have been thinking about alternatives to sand, and have even piloted the use of recycled glass as a sand replacement to maintain their image of their city as a beach tourist destination.

Constructing future cities will inevitably require a mentality shift to the question of where our material resources come from, and if the mining mentality should shift towards a cultivating approach. Future cities cannot be constructed according to a universal one-size-fits all logic that underpin cities of the recent past. Such logic relies on linear thinking in which materials are produced, used, and discarded. Seen from this perspective, the project for urban sustainability must overcome such linear and universal approaches. Rather, the project of sustainability requires a decentralised and circular approach that both acknowledges the global dimension and is sensitive to the ecological, social, cultural, and economic capacities of particular places in order to thrive and endure.

As a response to this challenging situation the Future Cities Laboratory research team of Alternative Building Materials has been concentrating its work on developing alternative construction materials. Based in Singapore and Zürich, it studies application strategies in specific settings, taking into account the availability of raw materials, human resource capacities, and skills. The 'alternative' aspect of this focus emerges from an exploration of innovative and entrepreneurial thinking. This approach has informed and continues to inform newly established laboratories in Asia, Africa and Europe. It is

Shifting Paradigms:
From Excavation to Cultivation

the declared aim of the group to widen the pallet of available construction materials and develop ways of thinking materiality as part of a circular economy.

The research is motivated by a set of challenging questions. Can a grass replace structural elements conventionally made out of steel or timber? Can building materials made out of mycelium structures or hardened by bacteria be a widespread alternative building technology? Could a city conceived along these lines offer neighbourhoods that are as dense as high-rise forms? And could a conscious choice of materials create a new feeling of belonging? Could waste be a future resource for the building sector?

A Paradigm Shift

The research undertaken at FCL suggests that the twenty-first century will face a radical paradigm shift in how designers and builders produce materials for the construction of human habitat. While the period of the first industrial revolution in the eighteenth and nineteenth century has resulted in a conversion from regenerative (agrarian) to non-regenerative material sources (mines), our time might experience the reverse.

Society will see 'a shift towards cultivating, breeding, raising, farming, or growing future resources ... hand in hand with a reorientation of biological production' (Hebel and Heisel 2017). There are various approaches to this work. Resources can be cultivated within the conventional soil-based agricultural framework, or micro-organisms that so far have not been considered useful for the energy or building industry could be bred in soil-less farms. A third approach is the industrialisation of natural and bio-chemical processes to rebuild bio-materials synthetically within a controlled environment. All three approaches are important. The last two, in particular, have the capacity to contribute elegantly to the current trend of incorporating small-scale industrial and agricultural production units within urban environments.

When considering the use of natural and organic raw materials within the current norms of digitally controlled, prefabricated, mass produced products, the imperfections of *living* materials become a key aspect in the process of material development. The underlying effort, alongside a continuous interest in advancing material properties, is the standardisation of natural processes in order to guarantee predictable and controllable properties in every material lot.

The work also concentrates on organisms, which are often seen as unwanted or labelled repulsive. For example, while the pharmaceutical industry uses bacteria with undisputed success to produce some of our most powerful medications such as antibiotics, architecture and construction has not activated nor exploited their capacities. The same is true for other organisms, such as mushroom mycelium.

Another group of materials have been known for centuries as reliable and accepted resources for construction, yet have never advanced to the level of an industrialised product—they have been, as it were, locked in a box called *vernacular*. Bamboo as a construction material is the perfect example of this curious phenomenon of being hidden in plain sight. The potential of bamboo lies not in applications of the raw material, but in its extremely strong fibre. The approach of extracting and reconfiguring bamboo fibres is suited for prompting the industry to develop new production methods and products.

The cultivation of building materials requires a resilient and ethical economical model. Especially when addressing the first option, of producing soil-dependent cultivated materials, there are significant side-effects in an uncontrolled and profit-driven agricultural model. A cautionary tale can be seen in the palm oil industry; whereby natural forests are burned in order to gain more area under crops. A positive side effect is the changing profiles of building experts.

By definition, the work is multidisciplinary: biologists, bioengineers, ecologists, chemists and material scientists collaborate with architects and civil engineers to create a broader understanding of how to approach complex tasks. Supplemented by economists, this multidisciplinary work promises to sharpen our view on alternative urban models, whereby production is an integral part of a future urban society, requiring new types of spaces and infrastructures.

Bamboo Composite Materials

Steel-reinforced concrete is the most common building material in the world, with developing countries using close to 90 per cent of cement and 80 per cent of steel consumed by the construction sector globally. However, very few developing countries have

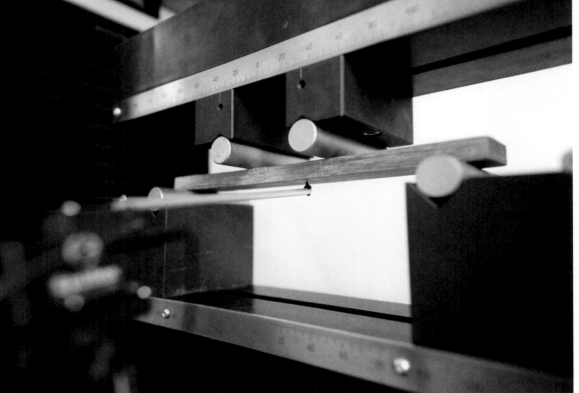

Fig. 1   Advanced Fiber Composite Laboratory in Singapore.
Fig. 2   Bending test of newly developed bamboo composite materials at the Future Cities Laboratory in Singapore.

Fig. 3   The Waste Vault at the Idea City Festival NYC in 2015—a temporary structure built out of discarded drink cartons.

Fig. 4   The colour and composition of the material reflects the character of the waste material in use, such as these discarded drinking cartons.

the ability or resources to produce their own steel or cement, forcing them into an exploitative import-relationship with the developed world. But there is an alternative: bamboo. Bamboo grows in the tropical zone of our planet and its distribution coincides with developing regions. The plant belongs to the botanical family of grasses and is extremely resistant to tensile stresses. In fact, bamboo is one of nature's most versatile products.

Bamboo is also a highly renewable and eco-friendly material. It grows much faster than wood and is relatively easy to obtain in large quantities. It is also known for its capacity to capture carbon and could therefore play an important role in reducing carbon emissions worldwide. The great social, economic, and material benefits of bamboo are currently not reflected in the demand for the material, despite its abundant availability.

Research aims to exploit bamboo's untapped potential by exploring new types of composite bamboo materials. Investigations have focused on the tensile strength of bamboo and explored possibilities of extracting and transforming fibres into a manageable industrial product: a viable building material with the ability to rival steel and timber on residential and commercial scales. This composite bamboo material could be produced and applied in any of the familiar shapes and forms common in traditional construction, but could also be tailored for specific applications that best take advantage of the material's tensile strength, such as newly developed reinforcement spanning systems for ceiling and roof structures.

Waste Materials

Waste is a result of human action and inter-action, bringing raw natural materials from one state of being into another through applying various forms of skills and energy. They assert that waste was seen for centuries as something specific which neither belonged to the family of natural resources nor to the one of finished products. 'Waste was a by-product, unable to be categorised in our dialectic understanding of raw vs. configured' (Hebel, Wisniewska and Heisel 2014).

Waste, however, could also be understood as an integral part of what we define as a resource. We could thereby acknowledge its capacity to figure as the required substance or matter from which we could construct or configure a new product. At the same time, the product could be seen as the supply source for other artefacts after its first life span. This metabolic thinking understands our built environment as an interim stage of material storage, or in the words of Mitchell Joachim: 'The future city makes no distinction between waste and supply' (Joachim 2013).

Urban Mining is a rather young phenomenon, embracing the process of reclaiming compounds and elements from otherwise wasted or at least undesired products or buildings, which contain high levels of valuable materials. In their text 'Mine the City', Ilka and Andreas Ruby describe the contemporary shifting awareness that raw materials are not to be found anymore in a *natural* realm, but more and more in the *cultural* domain of buildings (Ruby and Ruby 2010).

> The material resources of construction are becoming increasingly exhausted at the place of their natural origins, while inversely accumulating within buildings. For example, today there is more copper to be found in buildings than in earth. As mines become increasingly empty, our buildings become mines in themselves.

In the Rubys' view, the city is to be seen as a container of buildings and mines at the same time, much needed for its own reproduction.

Thomas E. Graedel of the Yale School of Forestry and Environmental Science combines his analysis of Urban Mining with the question of how much energy can be saved by recycling wasted materials found in landfills or buildings. For him, buildings do not only store the materials to be recycled, but also a large amount of energy, which could be reactivated. He argues that the reuse of aluminium, which could be recycled from buildings, needs only five per cent of the originally used energy for its production (Graedel 2014).

> Aluminium is extensively employed in buildings, but it does not remain permanently in place. Buildings are remodelled periodically, and even deconstructed, thereby freeing the aluminium for recycling. Therefore, it is not inaccurate to regard this aluminium as 'urban ore' and cities as 'urban mines'.

Shifting Paradigms:
From Excavation to Cultivation

Shifting Paradigms:
From Excavation to Cultivation

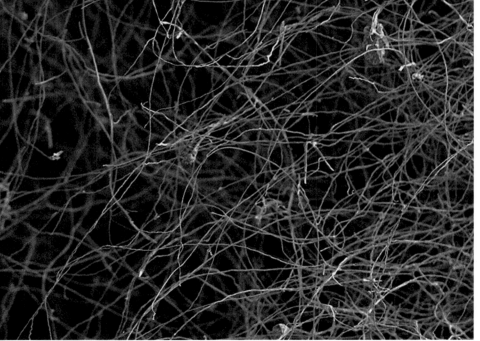

Fig. 5   Sample of alternative sand materials from recycled building waste.
Fig. 6   Different rubble materials form a variety of samples.
Fig. 7   Mycelium bricks can even grow together to form a homogeneous structure.
Fig. 8   A close-up image of mycelium growth.

Urban Mining demonstrates a potential and possibility of how waste products can be resourced at the end of their first lifespan, when entering a second or third lifespan, by being transformed, reshaped, remodelled, or reconfigured. This does, however, open up the question of whether the consideration of the waste state of a product should become the starting point of its design.

In a resource scarce city-state like Singapore, this quest is highly relevant, if not crucial. The research on alternative building materials made out of waste at ETH Zürich and its Future Cities Laboratory in Singapore is currently concentrating on new approaches, products and construction techniques in order to understand, quantify and activate one of the biggest potential resources available to the building industry.

Alternative Sand Materials and Bacteria

Sand is the most used raw material for production of goods of our planet. Sand is mostly composed of quartz, a mineral form of silicon dioxide. It is one of the most abundant materials on the earth surface and also one of the strongest. Over the turn of millions of years, mountains gradually eroded into gravel, sand and dust. Rainfall carries these particles through existing watercourses to the sea

Sand is used in concrete, glass, computers, detergents and even toothpaste. It took millennia to become into being through erosion and sedimentation, and man is mining it at rivers and ocean coasts in a so-far unknown speed. Sand is the megastar of the industrial and digital era—our culture is literally built upon this resource. It is, however, a finite resource.

And not all sand is equal; the construction industry requires grain sizes and rough shapes that are only found in river beds, lakes and the oceans. These properties make it valuable to various industries, but once it is enclosed into concrete as an aggregate, sand cannot be retrieved. Desert sand on the other hand is presently unsuitable to the construction industry. Gradual wind erosion polishes the sand particles into round and even forms and therefore reduces their friction capacity; desert sand is simply too fine and spherical in shape to act as a high-friction aggregate in the concrete matrix.

This is why only aquatic sand is used for industrial purposes so far. According to John Milliman,

mankind sources twice as much sand as all of our rivers worldwide are actually carrying (Milliman and Syvitski 1992). According to the Swiss TV channel SFR (Eco Spezial 2014), the global market for sand is estimated at the gigantic number of fifteen billion tons per year with a value of 70 billion USD.

The United Nations program UNEP mentions a figure of 30 billion tons (Rakacewicz and UNEP/GRID-Arendal 2005) and the actual figures might be even higher.

Fifty per cent of the sand that once reached the sea is being sourced today from our rivers. Switzerland covers nearly 90 per cent of its sediment needs of 40 million tons per year domestically in approximately 250 gravel and sand pits due to its geoposition at a source of the erosion process in the Alps. While Switzerland documents its mining meticulously, other nations and interest groups act ruthless, often illegally and unsustainably.

Ways to activate alternatives to sand as a new resource for the building industry are currently being researched in the Future Cities Laboratory in Singapore and at the TU Delft in the Netherlands. Recycled building materials and construction waste with high mineral content such as glass, ceramics, concrete, and more can be transformed into modern, durable and competitive construction materials. This research is investigating the best methods of producing these.

Little is known so far about the use of bacteria to our advantage when designing construction materials. But they could function as adhesives and bind aggregates into compact and resilient substances. Here, a wide field of research is emerging, with an incredible potential for the future. Biochemical processes could in fact replace oil and gas as the main resources for the chemical industry.

Mycelium Materials

A cutting-edge approach in the building sector might be summarised with a bold statement 'Grow your own house'. To form construction elements through a process of layering particles over time is a concept that is being investigated through experiments with microelements. Previously misunderstood as hazardous waste, microelements have recently been rediscovered as a rich resource with the potential to redefine the categorisation of renewable building materials; the important distinction being microelements' unique self-growing capabilities. Research is underway to develop methods of implementation within the construction sector. The advantages of such products are significant.

As the mycelium follow a metabolic cycle, they may be composted after their original use. In their second phase of life, they become a fertile matrix for following generations. Under the correct conditions, the material may be grown locally, reducing both the energy and time required for transportation. Finally, as they are organic matter, they act to reverse carbon emissions through the absorption of carbon.

A controlled environment is required to produce the mycelium material. Initially the space must be dark, moist and provided with the right organic nourishments. A change in environmental conditions can deactivate the growth process at any chosen point in time, such as altering the humidity levels or exposing the material to a different light or temperature. Due to their spongy rhizomatic and fibrous nature, the mycelium produces a material with high-performance structural and insulative qualities, considered very desirable by the building industry. At the laboratories of MycoWorks (under the supervision of Phil Ross) in San Francisco and the Future Cities Laboratory Singapore, it is believed that such organically grown substances have the potential to become a very real alternative to established materials within the building industry.

Bibliography

Al-Sabouni, Marwa (2016). 'The battle for home', TED-Talk. Available from <https://www.ted.com/talks/marwa_al_sabouni_how_syria_s_architecture_laid_the_foundation_for_brutal_war?language=en#t-390043> Accessed on 2 October 2016.

ECO Spezial: Sand—ein Milliardengeschäft (2014). TV documentary, SFR.

Graedel, Thomas (2014). 'Urban mining', Recycling Embodied Energy. Available from <http://greenbuilding.world-aluminium.org/facts/urban-mining> Accessed on 22 January 2014.

Hebel, Dirk and Felix Heisel (2017). Cultivated Building Materials. Basel and Berlin: Birkhäuser.

Hebel, Dirk, Marta Wisniewska and Felix Heisel (2014). Building from Waste. Basel and Berlin: Birkhäuser.

Milliman, John D and James P M Syvitski (1992). 'Geomorphic/tectonic control of sediment discharge to the ocean: The importance of small mountainous rivers', The Journal of Geology: 525–44.

Mitchell, Joachim (2013). 'Turning waste into building blocks of the future city', BBC Online News, May 2013. Available from <http://www.bbc.com/future/story/20130524-creating-our-cities-from-waste> Accessed on 2 June 2014.

Rakacewicz, Philippe and UNEP/GRID-Arendal (2005). 'Raw material consumption, global trends and US share', GRID-Arendal Webpage. Available from <http://www.grida.no/graphicslib/detail/raw-material-consumption-global-trends-and-us-share_10b3> Accessed on 22 January 2014.

Ruby, Ilka and Andreas Ruby (eds.) (2010). 'Mine the city', in Re-Inventing Construction. Berlin: Ruby Press.

Shifting Paradigms:
From Excavation to Cultivation

Philip Ursprung, Alex Lehnerer

Tourism and Cultural Heritage: A Case Study on the Explorer Franz Junghuhn

One of the main challenges that researchers face when reflecting on urbanisation is the issue of concepts and the means of representation. They are addressing immensely complex phenomena with only a handful of concepts and a rather narrow spectrum of means of representation. For instance, the built environment and the urban are terms that are commonly used as synonyms. The book *The Endless City* (2007) is exemplary for the ongoing trend to focus on the city. The cover of the book features the narrative of the growth of urbanisation, a narrative that we hear on every occasion—'Ten per cent of the world's population lived in cities in 1900, 50 per cent is living in cities in 2007, and 75 per cent will be living in cities in 2050' (Burdett and Sudjic 2007).[1] In the not so distant future, apparently, almost all of our planet's inhabitants will live in cities. The grand narrative of the urban has replaced the grand narrative of progress that dominated twentieth century thought. Simultaneously, nature is stepping back into our line of vision. With its negative connotation, that can be traced back to industrialization, nature takes the form of climate change and natural catastrophes such as floods or desertification. With its positive connotation, nature takes the form of a rapidly growing demand for the beauty of landscapes, for places of retreat, and for domesticated areas for retreat and recuperation.

The question, however, is still open as to *what* is to be understood as urban or nature. I would argue that neither the urban nor nature is appropriate anymore as an analytical term within the architectural discourse. Each has lost its grip as an instrument of

analysis, so to speak. One reason is that politics, real-estate and tourism industries—one of the largest segments of today's economy—have seized these terms and instrumentalised them for their own purposes. Politics, the real-estate and tourism industries refine, if you like, the raw products of the urban into a 'city'—in other words into a controlled and museum-like context that promises entertainment and offers optimum conditions for consumption. The same raw material of the urban can also be marked as suburb, agglomeration, or *informal housing* in order to be prepared and made available for refinement or gentrification.

In parallel, the raw material of nature is domesticated as 'landscape', made ready for 'preservation' and for consumption—as exemplified by the holiday island, the resort, or the nature reserve. Or it is marked as soiled, damaged and contaminated and as such is then primed for reclamation and development. Since the 1970s the most influential example of assigning meaning in this way—and naturally also of increasing value—is UNESCO's award of the World Cultural Heritage status to a site, be it urban or natural, material or immaterial.

Both the real estate and tourism industries tend to present the urban and the rural as divided, as a duality. The reason for this, I would argue, lies in the fact that the border between these zones, the site of exposure of one to the other, is particularly valuable. A house in the countryside or a sea view flat is sought after and expensive. A nature reserve, a holiday resort and a recreational island are increased in value if they are easily accessed, i.e. the nearer they are located to a metropolis or an international airport. A wide-open view to potential expansion, in other words to the resource itself, be it the open sea, untouched nature, or a skyline, raises a property's value. The more of such borders a city can offer, the more attractive it is in real-estate terms. Accordingly, our appetite for new borders is becoming insatiable; for borders with a view of the other, independent of whether it is a natural or an industrial landscape, as in the case of the New York High Line, where, transformed into a park, the disused raised railway line has become a magnet for investment. Another example is Singapore's Gardens by the Bay where reclaimed land opened up new tourist attractions.

1 To quote the cover of *The Endless City: Urban Age Project*, which echoes both in rhetoric and design OMA's book *S, M, L, XL* first published in 1995.

The challenge for architecture in this context is to bring into play new concepts and means of representation. Instead of merely reacting to the terms coined by politics and industry, it should produce its own concepts and images—ideally such concepts and images that will create their own impact on politics and industries. Of course, architects and planners are not independent; they are obliged to await commissions, in effect usually having no choice but to follow the requirements and guidelines set out by policies and industry players, hunting down valuable boundary zones so as to optimize these with astute planning and spatial articulation. But nevertheless they can offer alternatives to the dualistic and teleological way of looking at things that is useful in the realm of politics and industry—this attitude of 'the city's here, nature's over there' or 'that's how it was, and that's how it will be'. What roles can architecture and planning play within these dynamics? On the other hand, it is architecture—and only architecture—that can create atmospheres and images that were previously beyond our grasp. Architecture has the ability to liberate itself from practical constraints and from the dependency of commissions. It can get back to the role as the creator of alternatives, of utopias and of experiments, to change our perspectives—as well as that of politics and industry—and to show things in a radically new light.

The research project *Tourism and Cultural Heritage: A Case Study on the Explorer Franz Junghuhn* aims to find new concepts and means of representation that can help to revise and refine the current research on urbanisation. It follows the premise that the designation of sites and their past as attractive destinations for travel should not be left solely to the tourism industry but that it can be made fruitful for the theory and practice of architecture and urban design. The aim is not to criticise the structures of tourism as such nor to demonise the figure of the modern tourist or the effects of mass tourism. Tourism studies worldwide are already offering plenty of analytical data on these issues. The aim of our project is more fundamental; it is to make use of issues that have motivated architects in the eighteenth and nineteenth centuries but are somewhat left aside today, such as the search of frontiers, the adventure of travel and the fascination of the unknown.

As a frame of reference for tourism, we use Dean MacCannell's *The Tourist: A New Theory of the Leisure Class* (MacCannell 1976). MacCannell's hypothesis is that the tourist is synonymous to the modern, middle-class subject; in his words, '"The tourist" is one of the best models available for modern man in general'. The book that has become a classic in sociology not only offers a useful set of concepts that relate to the history and theory of the tourist, but also deals with the role of the researcher and his relation to the tourism industry and therefore can be readily applied to our current project. For instance, his concept of the tourist as a subject that perceives its own conditions from a distance is a fruitful explanation to why tourism has been so successful for more than a century. In his words:

> The act of sightseeing is uniquely well-suited among leisure alternatives to draw the tourist into a relationship with the modern social society. As a worker, the individual's relationship to his society is partial and limited, secured by a fragile 'work ethic', and restricted to a single position among millions in the division of labor. As a tourist, the individual may step out into the universal drama of modernity. As a tourist, the individual may attempt to grasp the division of labor as a phenomenon *sui generis* and become a moral witness of its masterpieces of virtue and viciousness (MacCannell 1976).

Another important reference for the project is Mieke Bal's book *Travelling Concepts in the Humanities, A Rough Guide* (Bal 2002). Her definition of the concept as 'miniature theories' can readily be transferred to our own research on urbanism and architecture:

> Concepts are the tools of intersubjectivity: they facilitate discussion on the basis of a common language. Generally, they are considered abstract representations of an object. But, like all representations, they are neither simple nor adequate in themselves. They distort, unfix and inflect the object. To say something of an image, metaphor, story or what have you —that is, to use concepts to label something—is not a very useful act. Nor can the language of equation— 'is'—hide the interpretative choices being made. In fact, concepts are, or rather do, much more. If well thought through, they offer miniature theories, and in that guise, help in the analysis of objects, situations, states and other theories (Bal 2002).

A third book that we use as a reference is Anna Lowenhaupt Tsing's *Friction: An Ethnography*

Tourism and Cultural Heritage: A Case Study
on the Explorer Franz Junghuhn

Fig. 1   Image taken from the '17 Volcanoes: Figures in the Landscape of Java' exhibition in ETH Zürich, 2016.

Fig. 2   Image taken from the '17 Volcanoes: Figures in the Landscape of Java' exhibition in ETH Zürich, 2016.

of *Global Connection* (Tsing 2004). Tsing discusses the transformations happening on the Indonesian island of Kalimantan since the 1970s, the interrelations of politics, economy, ecology, the local changes (in language and mentality) and the global financial connections. She discusses the interest of the Indonesian middle-class youth in nature and the territory. But it is not only because of the geographical proximity to the area of Java that we chose for our research project that makes the book so useful, it is also the form that she chooses, interweaving the scholarly accumulation of data and diagrams with a journalistic narrative and an activist attitude that critically addresses the issues at stake, which has inspired our own project.

Unlike much of the existing literature on tourism and urbanisation that emphasises urban patterns and structures in relationship with heritages sites or resorts, our project deals with a very fundamental aspect of tourism, namely the objects of touristic experience. Tourists travel not only to stay at a beach resort or to visit individual monuments, but they also wish to find out about the heritage of the place in general and about entire areas of historical importance. We will investigate the transformation of historical and natural phenomena into objects of touristic interest. Besides the demand for leisure and entertainment, the experience of cultural and environmental history is key attraction for tourism. And furthermore, they are not exclusively attracted by landmarks in city centres, but also by the surrounding environment, the hinterland and the backstage scenery as well. A crucial factor for this experience of universality is the connection between sites, the itinerary, or trail, which allows visitors to experience and discover a variety of sites as something coherent.

Such connections can be established by means of famous individuals. The fact that Napoleon Bonaparte or Albert Einstein had spent a night in a provincial town provides added meaning (and added value) to the site and inspires tourists to make a detour to that spot. They can be established by historical paths—for instance the Silk Road, or the pilgrim routes, Route 66 or the Via Appia. Connections can be provided by natural phenomena, for instance in the guise of geological parks. In most cases, however, these phenomena are separate from each other, divided into segments of, say, leisure tourism, cultural tourism, ecotourism, and more.

In order to combine these various issues, we are focusing on one of the most important explorers of the nineteenth century, the German Franz Wilhelm Junghuhn (1809–1864). Born in central Germany and trained as a doctor in Berlin, his dream had always been to be an explorer like his model, the famous Prussian explorer and writer Alexander von Humboldt. In 1835, in his early twenties, Junghuhn sailed to the island of Java in the service of the Dutch occupation army. He served in Java as a military doctor, but soon started to explore the landscape foddered by his interest in vegetation and geology. The Dutch army decided that he would be more useful if he could relay to them information about natural resources and therefore sponsored his expedition and research. This led him to explore almost the entire island of Java as well as Sumatra and Bali.

Junghuhn was particularly amazed by the island's many volcanoes and climbed over 40 of them, measured their heights, their geological composition, drew the craters, reconstructed earlier eruptions by examining the debris, interviewed locals about the history of the volcanoes and collected written sources from earlier expeditions. He sent his sketches to Germany where a successful series of plates and descriptions was published in 1845.

After more than a decade in the hot and humid climate of Java, Junghuhn fell seriously ill. His employers granted him a trip back to Europe to recover in the cooler climate of Germany and the Netherlands. He travelled back to Europe in the revolution year of 1848 and remained there for seven years. During his stay in Leiden, he wrote a monumental three-volume book on Java with particular emphasis on the volcanoes and published his masterpiece, which is the first accurate map of the island of Java that was used until the turn of the late nineteenth century. Unlike the earlier maps, it was not conceived from without or from the coastline, but from within, from the perspectives of the volcanoes, so to speak.

Junghuhn's legacy in the realm of cartography, botany, geology, volcanology and writing can only be compared to the status of Thomas Stamford Raffles, Alfred Russel Wallace or Alexander von Humboldt (Wulf 2015). In fact, he was often called the 'Humboldt of Java' and was highly respected as a leading scholar of his age. Unlike his famous peers, however, Junghuhn remains largely unknown today. A figure such as Raffles has considerable appeal for tourism up to the present day, be it as a name for hotels and restaurants or simply the fact that he had been present at a certain place. The monument for

Tourism and Cultural Heritage: A Case Study on the Explorer Franz Junghuhn

Fig. 3   Image taken from the '17 Volcanoes: Figures in the Landscape of Java' exhibition in ETH Zürich, 2016. Foreground: a miniature of the so-called Chicken Church made of volcanic stone from Mount Merapi by Zenvin Artstone, Magelang, 2016. Background: a photograph of Merapi plateau by Bas Princen, 2016.

his wife, in Bogor Botanic Garden near Jakarta, for instance, is a central landmark in this area, which is highly attractive for local and international tourism.

The 'Humboldt-Forum' in Berlin, currently under construction in the semblance of the reconstructed Baroque castle, will house a cluster of museums and use the name of the famous explorer—and his brother Wilhelm von Humboldt—in order to attract tourism. Junghuhn, on the other hand, is only known to a handful of specialists. Besides the literature that was published in the decades following his death, we can solely refer to a biography by Renate Sternagel and to a book published on the occasion of an exhibition on his 200th birthday at the Goethe Institut in Bandung, Indonesia (Schmidt 1909; Junghuhn-Commission 1910; Sternagel 2011; Goethe-Institut-Jakarta 2009, 2010). His archive is conserved partially in Leiden, Holland, whereas fragments of his collections remain in Bandung.

The aim of the research project is to use him as an exemplary figure to help decipher the relationship between tourism, travel and research, and about the way sites have been transformed into 'sights' or tourist attractions. Junghuhn himself is not so much the main subject of investigation; instead, it is the way he had experienced the environment and the way we could draw on such experiences today. We consider him less as an object of our studies than a lens through with we can focus on various issues.

The project consists of a series of week-long expeditions from Singapore to Java. Our core team of seven is accompanied by experts such as artists, a volcanologist and a literary historian. Instead of organising a conference in an institutional framework and discussing *about* travel, the groups are organised as a kind of mobile academic *in situ* conference. The figure of the researcher, the explorer and the tourist blurs. We follow the traces of Junghuhn and visit the

Fig. 4   An image of Franz Wilhelm Junghuhn from *Topographischer und Naturwissenschaftlicher Atlas zur Reise durch Java*, Magdeburg, Bansch, 1845.

different areas of Java that he had described in the early nineteenth century. We are led by his lithographs and sketches as well as his descriptions. The artists make photographs and videos, which serve to document the itinerary. Although Junghuhn serves as an imaginary guide, the aim is not merely to depict the past and reconstruct his career, but also to perceive the present situation in a new light, to understand the connections between cultural heritage, landscape, political history, art, and society. Our mission is also to reflect critically the way architects and tourists in general perceive their environment and represent their discoveries.

One of Junghuhn's main interests was the volcanoes of Java. He climbed almost all of them and described them in his monumental study on Java (Junghuhn 1857). Following Junghuhn's footsteps, we move the volcanoes centre stage in our own project. We gave ourselves the goal of visiting seventeen of his favourite volcanoes. As giant figures in the landscape, these volcanoes are deeply rooted in the cultural lives of the Javanese. The volcanoes make up the land and continuously transform it. Their potential destructiveness, for instance Mount Merapi that had last erupted in 2010, is overwhelming. Yet, they shape the land and feed the people by producing fertile grounds for one of the world's most densely populated islands.

Around 140 million people live in Java, an island about the size of Cuba.

Volcanoes cannot be considered landscapes. They are objects with distinct qualities — personalities—and are even able to communicate. Adjat Sudradjat, the doyen of Javanese volcanology, told us that he is particularly interested in Mount Merapi because it 'communicates.' They remain silent for a while, and suddenly start to speak again. By visiting Junghuhn's favourite volcanoes, we converse with each of them as well. The closer we get to them, the clearer we perceive their singularity. They help us to define the island of Java not by its exterior coastline, but from within. The volcanoes form territorial markers that allow us to interweave historical and contemporary narratives of Indonesia.

As politically, economically and culturally charged objects that act and behave in periodic cycles, these volcanoes are neither urban nor rural, neither alive nor dead, neither past nor present, neither good nor bad. Their ambiguous existence makes them particularly interesting for architectural scrutiny.

The volcanoes serve as connecting points where our own journey meets with the journeys made by Junghuhn. They also serve as entry points to the topics of tourism and cultural heritage. As all of them are located in protected areas, they are appealing for

Tourism and Cultural Heritage: A Case Study on the Explorer Franz Junghuhn

a small, but increasingly growing group of mostly young Indonesian tourists who wish to escape the noise and traffic of their daily environment in order to camp outdoors and climb a volcano. Each is different; some serve as sites for religious cults, such as Mount Bromo. Others are visited for their healing waters, such as Mount Guntur. And again others such as Mount Merapi played a role in the political life where eruptions were traditionally interpreted as messages, for instance, toward a Sultan to step down from his position. Difficult to access and to climb, with only rudimentary infrastructure of homestays and simple restaurants, they are not (yet) destinations for international mass tourism. But they allow the inhabitants and visitors of the densely populated and intensely cultivated area of Java to step out of the daily routine and encounter something unheard of that eludes control. We do not know how the economic boom will affect these sites and if they will face the same development that has transformed many coastal areas of Southeast Asia. But we want to encounter them now, in a crucial moment of indecision and to be able to tell their stories.

Bibliography

Bal, Mieke (2002).*Travelling Concepts in the Humanities: A Rough Guide.* Toronto: University of Toronto Press.

Burdett, Ricky and Deyan Sudjic (eds.) (2007). *The Endless City: Urban Age Project.* London: Phaidon.

Goethe Institut Jakarta (ed.) (2009). *Forschen, Vermessen Streiten: Eine Ausstellung Zum 200. Geburtstag Des Java-Erforschers Franz Wilhelm Junghuhn (1809–1864),* Exhibition Catalogue. Jakarta: Goethe Institute Jakarta.

Goethe Institut Jakarta (2010). *Forschen, Vermessen, Streiten, Franz Wilhelm Junghuhn (1809–1864).* Berlin: Regiospectra Verlag.

Junghuhn-Commission (ed.) (1910). *Gedenkboek Franz Junghuhn.* s-Gravenhage: Martinus Nijhoff.

Junghuhn, Franz (1857). *Java, seine Gestalt, Pflanzendecke und innere Bauart.* Leipzig: Arnoldische Buchhandlung.

Mac Cannell, Dean (1976). *The Tourist: A New Theory of the Leisure Class.* Berkeley: University of California Press.

Schmidt, Max C P (1909). *Franz Junghuhn, 1809–1909, Biographische Beiträge Zur 100. Wiederkehr Seines Geburtstages.* Leipzig: Verlag der Dürr'schen Buchhandlung.

Sternagel, Renate (2011). *Der Humboldt von Java: Leben und Werk des Naturforschers Franz Wilhelm Junghun (1809–1864).* Halle (Saale): Mitteldeutscher Verlag.

Tsing, Anna Lowenhaupt (2004). *Friction: An Ethnography of Global Connection.* Princeton: Princeton University Press.

Wulf, Andrea (2015). *The Invention of Nature: The Adventures of Alexander von Humboldt, the Lost Hero of Science.* New York: Alfred A Knopf.

Tourism and Cultural Heritage: A Case Study on the Explorer Franz Junghuhn

Dhaka

Dhaka confounds urban norms. It supports over 40,000 people per square kilometre, 400,000 rickshaws, and zero metro lines or motorways. It produces 4,000 tons of waste per day, processed by many more thousands of waste pickers working with limited mechanical equipment. It is one of the most vulnerable cities to sea level rise, yet remains a focus of aspiration for millions. It is the world's most densely populated megacity, with one of the most fragile infrastructure. As such Dhaka solicits divergent assessments: a city over-reaching its limits; a disorganised assemblage incubating extreme disaster; a site in need of urgent development; or a provocation for an alternative future?

Carlos Cazalis is a Mexican born documentary photographer. He was the winner of 2009 Communication Arts Photography Annual, World Press Photo Award. He has travelled and photographed megacities around the world, including Lagos, Sao Paulo, Cairo and Dhaka.

Alexander Erath

leads the Engaging Mobility group at the Future Cities Laboratory (FCL). The multi-disciplinary team is applying innovative survey methods and Virtual Reality application to better understand, design and evaluate active mobility solutions. Previous projects conducted at FCL in Singapore include the implementation of the large-scale, agent-based transport simulation model MATSim Singapore and 'Measuring Walkability' to quantify what people value when walking in Singapore's dense city centre and tropical climate. He is also the founder of Erveco, a company dedicated to transitioning innovative urban transport planning approaches from research into planning practice. He holds MSc and PhD degrees from ETH Zürich.

Alex Lehnerer

an architect and urban designer, currently holds an Assistant Professor at ETH Zürich in Switzerland. Prior to that, he was based in Chicago, where he was a Professor at the University of Illinois, School of Architecture. He received his PhD from ETH Zürich and his MArch from the University of California in Los Angeles (UCLA). Together with his partner Savvas Ciriacidis, he leads the Zürich based architecture practice CIRIACIDISLEHNERER.

Alireza Javadian

is currently a Doctoral Researcher at the Chair of Architecture and Construction at the ETH Zürich in Switzerland and FCL in Singapore. Alireza Javadian holds a MSc in Civil Engineering from NTU Singapore as well as a MSc in Civil Engineering from NUS Singapore. In 2012 he additionally graduated with a Master of Business Administration from ARU Oxford, UK. In his doctorate, he focuses on alternative composite fibre materials as reinforcement systems in concrete applications. He is researching the mechanical and physical properties of the material. His work includes establishing new norms and regulations for the production and testing of the material.

Anna Gasco

is a Senior Researcher and Project Coordinator at FCL for 'The Grand Projet', a research on mixed-used urban mega-projects. Chartered Part III architect in the UK and an urban designer, she also acts as a consultant for both private and public clients. Prior to joining FCL, Anna worked in practices for over seven years on visionary projects at multiple scales. A native Italian born in Congo, she holds a PhD degree in Architecture and Urbanism from ETH Zürich, a Master degree in Urban Design from the Bartlett UCL London and a Diploma in Architecture from St. Luc Brussels.

Arno Schlueter

holds a degree in architecture from the Technical University of Karlsruhe and a PhD in building systems from ETH Zürich. In 2014 he was appointed Professor of Architecture and Building Systems (A/S) at the Institute of Technology in Architecture (ITA), ETH Zürich. Since 2013 he is also a Principal Investigator at the Singapore-ETH Future Cities Lab (FCL). In his research, he and his team focus on building systems and their synergetic integration into architecture and urban design.

Aurel von Richthofen

is a Senior Researcher and Leader of the Education Research Programme in FCL in Singapore. Prior to Singapore, he spent four years teaching and researching as an Assistant Professor at the German University of Technology in Oman. He was the co-investigator on a research project on sustainable urbanisation patterns in Oman. Before that, he was had been teaching in Germany and at the Ohio State University in Columbus Ohio, USA. At FCL, he held the position of Project Coordinator of the research module 'Alternative Construction Materials' until 2016.

Bernhard Klein

is a Project Coordinator of the 'Big Data-Informed Urban Design' project and Co-Principal Investigator of the 'Cooler Calmer Singapore' impact project at FCL. Bernhard Klein holds a diploma degree in Computer Science from the Technical University of Munich and a doctoral degree in Economic and Social Sciences from the University of Vienna. He has lead several European projects in Smart Cities and Citizen Science. His research interests focus on modelling and simulations, big data frameworks, artificial intelligence and cognitive computing.

Bige Tunçer

is an Associate Professor at the Architecture and Sustainable Design Pillar of Singapore University of Technology and Design (SUTD). At SUTD, she founded the Informed Design research group. The group's research focuses on data collection, information and knowledge modelling and visualization, for informed architectural and urban design. She received her PhD in Architecture (design informatics) from TU Delft, her MSc in Architecture (computational design) from Carnegie Mellon University, and her BArch from Middle East Technical University. She was an assistant professor at TU Delft, a visiting professor at the Chair of Information Architecture at ETH Zürich, and a visiting scholar at MIT.

Caleb Ming
is a Singaporean photographer whose works examine aspects of modern living and its ironies. Ming's works explores the lives of people in our consumerist society. Like his subject matters, the images Ming creates are presented like objects of desire. Through documentary style photography, Ming weaves together stories with the themes. Ming earned his BA in Graphic Communication from Loughborough University of Art and Design.

Carlos Cazalis
is a Mexican-born documentary photographer. He was recently awarded a grant by the National Mexican Council for Culture and Arts (Fomento y Co-Inversion CONACUTLA) in 2011 and won the 2009 World Press Photo Award, First Place Contemporary Issues, Stories. He has documented megacities all around the world including Lagos, Dhaka, Mexico City and Sao Paolo. His recent exhibitions include *Haiti: Year Zero* at the Centro de la Cultura Digital, Mexico in 2015; Syngenta Photography Award Exhibition *Waste-Scarcity* in London in 2015; *Confronting Informality* at The Urban Meta – TU Delft in Delft in 2014 and Syngenta Photography Award Exhibition *Rural-Urban* in London in 2013.

Chan Ghee Koh
graduated with First Class Honours in 1979 from the then University of Singapore. Subsequently, he went on a NUS overseas scholarship to further his graduate study at the University of California, Berkeley, where he obtained his MS and PhD in 1983 and 1986, respectively. He became an Associate Professor at NUS in July 1998 and a Professor in January 2004. He is currently the Director of the Faculty's Centre for Hazards Research. Koh's research interest has primarily been in structural dynamics, with applications on vibration isolation and control, system identification, nonlinear dynamic analysis, and experimental dynamics.

Ting Chen
is trained as an architect and holds a PhD degree from ETH Zürich. To pursue a career in academia, she worked as junior researcher for the chair for the history of urban design in ETH Zürich, focusing on the historical study of designed urban elements. In 2011, she joined FCL in the module Urban Design Strategies and Resources, on the topic of Urban Breeding Grounds, examining the transformation of diverse downtown neighbourhoods in Shenzhen and Singapore. She is currently working as a Coordinator and Postdoctoral researcher in the 'Urban-Rural System' project.

Chen Zhong
is a Lecturer in Spatial Analysis at King's College London. Her research interests include spatial data mining, spatiotemporal visualization, complex network analysis, and the use of such analytical techniques for urban and transport planning. Prior to joining King's, Chen worked as a Research Associate at the Centre for Advanced Spatial Analysis (CASA), UCL. She obtained her PhD from FCL, ETH Zürich (2014), and BEng (2008) and MEng (2010) in GIS from the Wuhan University.

Christian Schmid
is the Professor of Sociology at the Department of Architecture at ETH Zürich. He has authored, co-authored, and co-edited numerous publications on theories of the urban and of space, Henri Lefebvre, territorial urban development, and comparative analysis of urbanization. He co-authored the book *Switzerland: An Urban Portrait* (with Diener, Herzog, Meili and de Meuron), a pioneering analysis of extended urbanization. He currently works with Neil Brenner on the theorization and investigation of emergent formations of planetary urbanization, and leads a comparative research on urbanization processes in Tokyo, Hong Kong/Shenzhen/Dongguan, Kolkata, Istanbul, Lagos, Paris, Mexico City and Los Angeles, at FCL.

Christoph Hoelscher
is a Full Professor of Cognitive Science in the D-GESS at ETH Zürich since 2013, with an emphasis on Applied Cognitive Science. He holds a PhD

218

in Psychology from University of Freiburg, served as honorary senior research fellow at UCL, Bartlett School of Architecture, and is a visiting Professor at Northumbria University, Newcastle. He has several years of industry experience in Human-Computer Interaction and usability consulting. The core mission of his research group is to unravel the complex interaction of humans and their physical, technical and social environment with an emphasis on cognitive processes and task-oriented behaviour.

Daniel Richards
is the Project Coordinator for the 'Ecosystem Services in Urban Landscapes' project at FCL. He studied Biology at the University of Exeter, before moving to the University of Sheffield for a PhD in floodplain habitat restoration. He worked as a Research Fellow at the National University of Singapore before joining FCL. Daniel's research looks at ecosystem services, which are the benefits that people get from nature. His publications cover the quantification and comparison of ecosystem services in freshwater wetlands, mangroves, and urban areas, as well as more general studies into conservation issues.

Devisari Tunas
is the Research Scenario Leader for 'Archipelago Cities' at FCL, Singapore. Her research interests focus on urban socio-spatial segregation, urban development patterns in the developing South, and the dynamics of multidisciplinary research collaborations. She holds a PhD degree in Urbanism from TU Delft (The Netherlands) and a Master in Social and Cultural Anthropology from Katholieke Universiteit Leuven (Belgium). She was the founder of Papiroz Publishing House and Chairwoman of Megacities Foundation in the Netherlands.

Didier Vernay
is the Project Coordinator of the 'Cyber Civil Infrastructure' research project at FCL. He obtained his PhD in 2015 from the Swiss Federal Institute of Technology in Lausanne (EPFL). During his PhD, he developed a probability-based framework that uses measurements to improve simulation predictions of wind around buildings at unmeasured locations. He obtained his Master of Science (2011) in Civil Engineering at the Swiss Federal Institute of Technology in Lausanne (EPFL) with a specialization in structural engineering. His research interests include sensors for identification of parametric structural and environmental models, uncertainty analysis, machine learning, smart cities, environmental sustainability, etc.

Dietmar Leyk
is the Research Scenario Leader for 'High-Density Mixed-Use Cities' at the FCL and Co-Principal Investigator of the research project 'The Future of Cities: New Urban Typologies' at the Singapore University of Technology and Design (SUTD). His research interests are focussed on the high-density city and its architecture, large-scale urban projects and knowledge spaces. Dietmar Leyk is Founding Director of Leyk Wollenberg Architects based in Berlin, accomplishing international projects in all scales. He received numerous prizes in international competitions and for his realised work. Dietmar Leyk is a registered architect in Germany. He is also an Appointed Architect by the Association of German Architects (BDA).

Dirk E. Hebel
is the Assistant Professor of Architecture and Construction at the ETH Zürich in Switzerland and FCL in Singapore. Prior to that, he was the founding Scientific Director of the Ethiopian Institute of Architecture, Building Construction and City Development in Addis Ababa, Ethiopia. Between 2002 and 2009 he taught at the ETH Zürich, at Princeton University and Syracuse University, USA and the American University of Sharjah, UAE. His research interest focuses on alternative resources for the construction sector and their application in specific contextual settings, taking into account the availability of materials, human resource capacities, and skills.

Dustin Fleck
is a Researcher in the Chair of Architecture and Construction at the ETH Zürich in Switzerland and FCL in Singapore. He undertakes his practical semester as part of his Bachelor in Climate Engineering at University of Applied Science, Stuttgart. In his studies he deals with the technical areas of building physics and energy supply technology as well as architectural design and construction and their interactions as part of functional building. Dustin's research deals with the development and growth methods of mycelium materials in regard to their mechanical and physical properties.

Felix Heisel
is the Research Coordinator at the Chair of Architecture and Construction at the ETH Zürich in Switzerland and FCL in Singapore. Preceding this position, he was the Coordinator for the third year architecture program at the Ethiopian Institute of Architecture, Building Construction and City Development in Addis Ababa, Ethiopia. From 2010 till 2011, he worked as an academic research assistant at the studio Wiel Arets at the University of the Arts in Berlin. His research interest focuses on alternative resources in specific contextual settings, taking into account the availability of materials, human resource capacities, and skills within closed-loop application cycles.

Gabriel Happle
is a PhD Researcher for the 'Multi-Scale Energy Systems' project (MuSES) at FCL. His research interests focus on building and urban energy demand modelling, using novel methods to generate realistic spatio-temporal patterns of energy consumption in mixed-use scenarios. He holds a Master of Science in Energy Science and Technology and a Bachelor of Science in Environmental Engineering, both from ETH Zürich.

Gerhard Schmitt
is the Lead Principal Investigator of the 'Responsive Cities' Scenario at FCL, where he is responsible for the 'Cognitive Design Computing and Citizen Design Science' research within the 'Big Data-Informed Urban Design' Project. He is Professor for Information Architecture at ETH Zürich, founding Director of the Singapore-ETH Centre, and ETH Zürich Senior Vice President for ETH Global. Gerhard Schmitt initiated the ETH World virtual campus in 2000 and the ETH Science City Campus in 2004 for which he received in 2010 the European Culture of Science Award.

Heiko Aydt
is the Research Scenario Leader for 'Responsive Cities' at FCL. His research investigates how cities can constructively respond to challenges and disturbances in order to improve liveability in cities. He is also the Project Leader for 'Cooling Singapore' which aims at developing a roadmap for mitigation of the urban heat island effect in Singapore. He holds a PhD degree in Computer Science from Nanyang Technological University (NTU) in Singapore, a MSc degree from the Royal Institute of Technology (KTH) in Stockholm, and a Dipl. Ing. (FH) in Information Technology from Esslingen University of Applied Sciences.

Hsieh Shanshan
is a Researcher for the 'Multi-Scale Energy Systems' project (MuSES) at FCL. She is also a doctoral student at EPFL, Switzerland. Her research interests focus on energy potentials, distributed energy integration and the integration capability of energy networks in the tropical context. Her work includes energy supply system design, modelling as well as contributing to the development of the open-source energy analysis tool, City Energy Analyst (CEA). She holds a bachelor degree in Chemical Engineering and a master degree in the Energy Science and Technology program at ETH Zürich.

Ian F.C. Smith
is the Principal Investigator for the project 'Cyber Civil Infrastructure' in at FCL and Professor at the Swiss Federal Institute of Technology (EPFL) in Lausanne, Switzerland. He received his PhD from Cambridge University, UK in 1982. His research interests are on the intersections of computer science with civil structures and urban systems. In 2004, he was elected to the Swiss Academy of Engineering Sciences and in 2005, he received the Computing in Civil Engineering Award from the American Society of Civil Engineers. Since 2011, he is also an Adjunct Professor at Carnegie Mellon University, USA.

Jennifer Lee
is a researcher in the Urban-Rural Systems project at FCL. She has a Master in Urban Planning from the Harvard Graduate School of Design and has worked as an urban planner in Newark, NJ, USA and an urban consultant. She is interested in the complex relationship between cities, underserved communities, and the environment.

Jimeno A. Fonseca
holds a degree in Architectural Engineering from Politecnico di Milano and a Ph.D. in building systems from ETH Zürich. In 2015, he co-created the City Energy Analyst (CEA), a tool for the analysis of building energy systems at the urban scale. Since 2016 he is Senior Researcher and Project Coordinator of

the 'Multi-Scale Energy Systems' project (MuSES) at FCL. His research focuses on the analysis of building systems in neighbourhoods and districts.

John Zacharias
is Chair Professor at the College of Architecture and Landscape, Peking University since 2012, an appointee in the Chinese Government's Thousand Talents Programme. He was previously Professor at Concordia University where he directed the was the director of the Urban Studies Programme, and also chaired the Department of Geography, Planning and Environment. His work is on behaviour-environment relations across a variety of scales in urban settings, especially with regard to transport, public space, central urban areas and local communities.

Karsten Schlesier
is an Affiliated Researcher to the Chair of Architecture and Construction at the ETH Zürich in Switzerland and FCL. Currently he holds the position of Associate Professor of Architecture and Structural Design at the German University of Technology in Oman. He graduated in Civil Engineering from the Karlsruhe Institute of Technology. Between 2003 and 2008 he taught at the KTI before joining the Ethiopian Institute of Architecture, Building Construction and City Development in Addis Ababa.

Kees Christiaanse
is the Programme Coordinator at FCL, Zürich. He is the project leader of 'The Grand Projet', a research that focuses on large urban projects in Europe and Asia, and the co-principal investigator of the Urban-Rural Systems. Christiaanse studied architecture and urban planning at TU Delft, was a partner at the Office for Metropolitan Architecture (OMA) and the founder of KCAP Architects & Planners which has offices in Rotterdam, Zürich and Shanghai. Since 2003, he is the chair of the Urban Planning Institute at ETH Zürich and prior to this, he held a professorship for architecture and urban planning at the Technical University of Berlin.

Maria Papadopoulou
is the former Research Manager at FCL. She completed her PhD at FCL, affiliated at the NUS School of Design and Environment. Maria graduated first in her class in Mechanical Engineering, specializing in Energy and Environment (UOWM, Greece).

She received an award and scholarship from the States Scholarship Foundation (IKY), Greece, and a Swiss Confederation research scholarship in Sustainable Urban Development, EPFL, Switzerland. At FCL, she helped in the ramping up of FCL-phase 2, coordinating projects linked to publications, monitoring, reporting and networking, and contributed reviews for policy developments and debates in future cities.

Markus Schlaepfer
is a Principal Investigator at FCL, where he leads the 'Urban Complexity' research. He is also a Visiting Researcher at the Santa Fe Institute (USA) and a Research Affiliate at MIT's Senseable City Lab (USA). He received his PhD in 2010 from ETH Zürich (Switzerland) at the Department of Mechanical and Process Engineering, and conducted postdoctoral fellowships at both the Santa Fe Institute and at MIT. He grounds his research on 'big urban data' and applies methods from complexity science to quantify the dynamics of cities.

Marta H. Wisniewska
is currently a Researcher at the Chair of Architecture and Construction at the ETH Zürich in Switzerland and FCL. Prior to her engagement at ETH Zürich, she was working as a lecturer and first year architectural Program Coordinator at the Ethiopian Institute of Architecture, Building Construction and City Development in Addis Ababa. Her research interest focuses on the resource waste and its activation for the building industry.

Michael van Eggermond
is a Senior Researcher at FCL. He supervises the 'Engaging Mobility' team's research into active mobility. The team investigates the potential of virtual reality to inform travel surveys, as well as the potential for cycling in high-density tropical Singapore. His main research interests lay on the intersection of urban planning and transport modelling: how can a cities' diversity, density and accessibility be measured and what are the outcomes of these measures on travel related decisions. He holds a MSc and BSc from TU Delft and is co-founder of Erveco. Prior to joining FCL, he used data visualization and simulation to support healthcare providers' strategic and operational planning.

Milica Topalovic

is an architect and urbanist, researching urban territories and urbanization processes. She is an Assistant Professor of Architecture and Territorial Planning at ETH Zürich. From 2011 to 2015 she studied the relationship between the city state and its hinterlands at FCL. She graduated with distinction from the Faculty of Architecture in Belgrade, received her Master degree from the Dutch Berlage Institute, and was Head of Research at the ETH Studio Basel. She is the author of *Belgrade: Formal/Informal*, *Constructed Land—Singapore 1924–2012*, and is currently also conducting a research project on the European countryside.

Miya Irawati

is a PhD researcher at the 'Urban-Rural System' module in FCL with focus on the Greater Jakarta region. Miya holds a MSc in Construction and Real Estate Management from the HTW Berlin and Helsinki Metropolia joint programme, and a BArch from Trisakti University in Jakarta. She was a Lecturer, Managing Director and Researcher at the Urban Laboratory of Tarumanagara University, Jakarta. Focusing on urban development and housing provision in the developing world, local economic development, and community empowerment, she has conducted various research projects ranging from policies to pilot initiatives in Indonesia.

Naomi Hanakata

is a Senior Researcher and Project Coordinator at FCL. She is trained as an architect and urban planner at ETH Zürich and the University of Tokyo, Japan. Her doctoral research was in the field of urban geography around the question of contemporary urbanization processes with a focus on the Tokyo Metropolitan Region. She has worked on various scales as an architect, planner and consultant in Zürich, Tokyo, New York and Singapore. Naomi also holds a degree in cultural studies and further specialised in sustainable business development strategies at LSE and comprehensive planning strategies with the research project 'Thinking Urban Futures'.

Nikita Aigner

is a Postdoctoral Researcher in the Chair of Architecture and Construction at the ETH Zürich in Switzerland and FCL. Previously, he obtained his BSc and MSc in wood technology at the University for Natural Resources (BOKU), Vienna with his Master Thesis on the mechanical properties and reinforcement of bacterial cellulose aerogels in 2011. Between 2012 and 2015 he obtained a PhD at ETH Zürich working on the development of a nanoscale model of the cell wall of wood. His current research interest is the development of bamboo composite materials, with an emphasis on the optimization of the composite binder toward a fully renewable resource based solution.

Peter Buš

is a Postdoctoral Researcher at the Chair of Information Architecture at the ETH in Zürich. Trained as an architect in the field of computational design modelling, he focuses on generative models and advanced urban simulations. Peter's long-term research is based on an investigation of emergent phenomena within urban environments where he concentrates on more complex relations which forms the urban entirety. Prior to obtaining his PhD degree in Architecture and Urbanism from the CTU in Prague (Czech Republic), he gained experience as a practising architect and as a researcher at FCL.

Peter Edwards

is the Director of the Singapore-ETH Centre and the principal investigator of the 'Ecosystem Services in Urban Landscapes' project under FCL. He has been professor of Plant Ecology at ETH Zürich —the Swiss Federal Institute of Technology in Zürich since 1993, where he has also served as Chairman of the Department of Environmental Systems Science. Peter Edwards is the author of around 300 refereed scientific papers and books covering a wide range of environmental topics including ecosystem processes, insect-plant interactions, environmental management, and biodiversity. His recent research has focused particularly on large-scale processes in terrestrial ecosystems.

Philip Ursprung

is the Professor of the History of Art and Architecture at ETH Zürich. He earned his PhD in Art History at Freie Universität Berlin and his Habilitation at ETH Zürich after studying art history, history, and German literature in Geneva, Vienna and Berlin, and taught at the Hochschule der Künste Berlin (today University of the Arts Berlin), the GSAPP of Columbia University, the Barcelona Institute of Architecture and the University of Zürich. Since 2015 he is the Principal Investigator of the research project 'Tourism and Urbanization' at FCL.

Philipp Mueller
is a Researcher in the Chair of Architecture and Construction at the ETH Zürich in Switzerland and FCL. Before receiving his MSc in Civil Engineering from the Technical University of Berlin in 2014, he trained as a carpenter and worked for four years in the field. At FCL, he focuses on applications and structural reliability of alternative composite construction materials. He is researching mechanical and physical properties of bamboo composite and mycelium composite materials.

Pieter Fourie
is a Senior Researcher at FCL Engaging Mobility and a fellow of the World Economic Forum's Global Future Council on Mobility. He leads the work in agent-based transport simulation development, intending to drive these models using big data sources like transit smart card and cellular phone data. His interests include distributed simulation, improving simulation performance, and data anonymization techniques. Pieter also has a background in motion graphics and television production and regularly produces content for the 'Engaging Mobility' team.

Reinhard Koenig
is a Co-Principal Investigator at FCL, where he co-leads the 'Cognitive Design Computing' research. He is also a Junior Professor for Computational Architecture at Bauhaus-University Weimar and a Senior Researcher at the Austrian Institute of Technology. His current research interests are the applicability of multi-criteria optimization techniques for design problems and the development of big data analysis methods for urban planning.

Remo Burkhard
was instrumental in building up the ETH Singapore SEC Ltd and it's two programmes—FCL and the Future Resilient Systems Lab—to a leading research centre with around 180 researchers. Since its inception, he is heading this centre as its Managing Director. Before SEC, he had co-founded and led the niche knowledge visualization firm Vasp Datatecture GmbH with 20 consultants and designers, where he worked on over a hundred innovative projects for leading organisations including banks, insurance companies and non-profit organisations. His research niche is 'Knowledge Visualization'. He has written over 50 scientific publications and organized large scientific conferences in this field.

Richard Hassell
is the co-founder of WOHA architects. He was born in 1966 and graduated from the University of Western Australia in 1989. He was awarded a Master of Architecture degree from the RMIT University, Melbourne in 2002. He is a board member of Singapore's Urban Redevelopment Authority's (URA) Design Advisory Committee and served as member on the Housing and Development Board (HDB) Architectural Design Panel. He has served as a board member of the Building and Construction Authority of Singapore, as well as committees for the URA and the Design Singapore Council. He is currently an Adjunct Professor at the University of Western Australia.

Shi Zhongming
is a PhD Researcher for the 'Multi-Scale Energy Systems' project (MuSES) at FCL. His research interests focus on energy-driven and generative urban design for high-density mixed-use cities at a neighbourhood scale. He holds Master of Science in Urban Design from Georgia Institute of Technology, Master of Architecture from Tongji University (China), and Bachelor of Architecture from Dalian University of Technology (China). He used to work for the Sino-US Ecological Urban Design Joint Laboratory based both in Shanghai and Atlanta.

Simon Lee
is a Researcher in the Chair of Architecture and Construction at the ETH Zürich in Switzerland and FCL. He received his BSc and MSc in Mechanical Engineering from Technical University Munich (TUM) in 2012 and 2014 respectively. Simon Lee's research at FCL focuses on the optimization and advancement of Bamboo Fibre Composites. His work aims to apply carbon composite processing standards as well as analytical methods to bamboo fibre composite materials.

Simon Schubiger
is teaching computer graphics and game design at the University of Applied Sciences North western Switzerland and was the former head of

software development at Esri R&D centre in Zürich, Switzerland. He is the co-founder of the ETH spin-off company Procedural Inc. Previously, he was a lecture at ETH Zürich, worked for Swisscom Innovations, and was an associate researcher at the University of Fribourg. He is a co-developer of the procedural 3D modelling software CityEngine, the Soundium multi-media platform and the NOVA software. His research interests include computer graphics, multimedia performance systems, programming languages, and user interface design.

Stefan Mueller Arisona
is a Professor of Computer Science at FHNW and Senior Research Fellow at ETH Zürich, Switzerland. His main interests are the application of computer graphics, digital media, and human-computer interaction principles to a variety of fields such as architectural and urban modelling, digital art and entertainment, or digital media authoring. Stefan graduated in electrical engineering at ETH Zürich, received his PhD from the University of Zürich, and was Swiss NSF fellow at the University of California, Santa Barbara. As a principal investigator at FCL, he resided in Singapore from 2010–2014.

Stephen Cairns
is the Director of FCL in Singapore, Professor in Architecture at ETH Zürich, and Principal Investigator of the 'Urban-Rural Systems' project at FCL. He completed his PhD at the University of Melbourne where he was also appointed as a lecturer. He took up a Senior Lectureship at the University of Edinburgh, and was appointed Professor of Architecture and Urbanism there in 2009. He is an architect, writer and teacher who is motivated by a curiosity about buildings, cities and society and how design, as a discipline and practice, can catalyse innovative and sustainable relationships between them.

Tanvi Maheshwari
is an architect, urban designer and researcher. Prior to joining FCL, she was developing UrbanCanvas, a visualization and analysis tools for urban planning, real estate, and transportation professionals. She co-founded arch i Platform, a non-profit for sustainable design and architecture in Delhi in 2009, where she led an international multi-disciplinary collaboration, Delhi 2050. She also presented her work at the International Architecture Biennale in Rotterdam

in 2012. She writes regularly for popular media and has authored *Life of an Afghan Hammam*, a book about the restoration and culture of Hammam in an Afghan community.

Thomas Schroepfer
is the Professor and Associate Head of Architecture and Sustainable Design at Singapore University of Technology and Design (SUTD), established in collaboration with MIT. His research focuses on environmental strategies in architecture and urban design. He has published and lectured extensively on his work that has been exhibited at important international venues including at the Venice Biennale. He is the recipient of prestigious recognitions including the International Union of Architects Award and most recently the A' Design Platinum Award. He holds both Doctoral and Master's degrees with Distinctions from Harvard University, where he was also a professor prior to joining SUTD.

Timothy Morton
is Rita Shea Guffey Chair in English at Rice University. He gave the Wellek Lectures in Theory in 2014. He is the author of *Dark Ecology: For a Logic of Future Coexistence* (Columbia, forthcoming), *Nothing: Three Inquiries in Buddhism and Critical Theory* (Chicago, forthcoming), *Hyperobjects: Philosophy and Ecology after the End of the World* (Minnesota, 2013), *Realist Magic: Objects, Ontology, Causality* (Open Humanities, 2013), *The Ecological Thought* (Harvard, 2010), *Ecology without Nature* (Harvard, 2007), seven other books and 120 essays on philosophy, ecology, literature, music, art, design and food. He blogs regularly at http://www.ecologywithoutnature.blogspot.com.

Tyler Thrash
is a Postdoctoral Researcher in the Chair of Cognitive Science at ETH Zürich. He obtained his PhD in psychology from Miami University of Ohio in May 2013. He studies spatial cognition and navigation with an emphasis on simple, perceptual explanations for complex spatial behaviours. His recent projects investigate spatial behaviour in the built environment, the impact of crowds on individuals' spatial decision-making, and the relationship between stress and navigation. Towards this end, he often employs virtual reality technology and mathematical modelling techniques.

Victor Schinazi
is a Senior Lecturer (Oberassistent) at the Chair of Cognitive Science at ETH Zürich. He is also a Co-Principal Investigator of the 'Cognition, Perception and Behaviour in Urban Environments' project at FCL. Victor is an urban planner by training and holds a PhD in Geography (CASA, UCL). Prior to joining ETH, Victor was a Postdoctoral Fellow at the University of Pennsylvania and also served as the Chief Science Officer for Strategic Spatial Solutions, Inc. Victor's research combines behavioural and neuroimaging techniques in order to investigate how spatial information is encoded and used to guide navigation.

Werner Sobek
is an architect and consulting engineer. He is the head of the Institute for Lightweight Structures and Conceptual Design (ILEK) at the University of Stuttgart, Germany. He is further a visiting professor at various, international universities. He is the founder of the Werner Sobek Group, a globally practicing office for architecture, structural and facade engineering, as well as consulting for sustainability and design. Projects of the Werner Sobek Group are characterised by high-quality design and sophisticated concepts to minimise energy consumption and material usage.

Zeng Wei
is an interactive visualisation specialist at the 'Collaborative Interactive Visualization and Analysis Laboratory' (CIVAL) at FCL. His research focuses on visual analytics, information visualization, human-computer interaction and urban data modelling. He received his BE in 2011 and PhD degree in 2015, both from the School of Computer Engineering at Nanyang Technological University. He has published papers in top visualization research conferences and journals, including IEEE Visualization Week, IEEE Transactions on Visualization and Computer Graphics (TVCG), Eurographics Visualization (EuroVis).

Urbanisation Indicators
Pages 12–22
Fig. 1   Reproduced from
Steffen et al. 2015.
Fig. 2   Reproduced from
Steffen et al. 2015.
Fig. 3   Reproduced from
© United Nations,
2014, World Urbanization
Prospects, United
Nations Publishing.
Licence: shop.un.org/
rights-permissions.
Fig. 4   Reproduced from
© United Nations, 2014,
World Urbanization
Prospects, United
Nations Publishing.
Licence: shop.un.org/
rights-permissions.
Fig. 5   Reproduced from
© United Nations Human
Settlements Programme,
2016, World Cities
Report, United Nations
Human Settlements
Programme Publishing.
Licence: shop.un.org/
rights-permissions.
Fig. 6   Reproduced from
© United Nations Human
Settlements Programme,
2016, World Cities
Report, United Nations
Human Settlements
Programme Publishing.
Licence: shop.un.org/
rights-permissions.
Fig. 7   Reproduced from
© Asian Development
Bank, 2012, Key
Indicators for Asia and
the Pacific 2012, Asian
Development Bank
Publishing. Licence:
www.adb.org/
terms-use#copyright.
Fig. 8   Reproduced from
© Asian Development
Bank, 2012, Asian
Development Outlook
2012, Asian Development
Bank Publishing.
Licence: www.adb.org/
terms-use#copyright
Fig. 9   Reproduced from
© OECD/IEA 2016 Key
CO_2 Emissions from
Fuel Combustion,
IEA Publishing. Licence:
www.iea.org/t&c.
Fig. 10 (a–b) Reproduced
from © OECD/IEA 2016
Key CO_2 Emissions
from Fuel Combustion,
IEA Publishing. Licence:
www.iea.org/t&c.

The Grand Projet: Towards
Adaptable and Liveable
Urban Megaprojects
Pages 51–58
Fig. 1   mimizun.com,
broadcastingcable.com,

static.guim.co.uk,
news.qoos.com,
kingcross.co.uk,
baseminibcn.org,
hafencity.com,
skyscraperpage.com,
Grand Projet 2016

Reconciling Urbanisation
with Ecology
Pages 59–66
Fig. 1   Michelle Yingying
Jiang, 2016.
Fig. 2   Serene Ng, 2015.
Labrador Park.
Fig. 3   Michelle Yingying
Jiang, 2016.
Fig. 4   Serene Ng, 2015.
Commonwealth Drive.
Fig. 5   Michelle Yingying
Jiang, 2016. Skyville at
Dawson.

Multi-Scale Energy Systems
for Low-Carbons Cities
Pages 67–73
Fig. 1   Creative
Commons, 2009.
Fig. 2   Bruelisauer et al.
2015.
Fig. 5   Fonseca et al.,
2016a.

Dense and Green Building
Typologies
Pages 74–81
Fig. 1   Patrick
Bingham-Hall, 2013.
Fig. 2   Victor Ramos.
Fig. 3   Robert Hart,
2000.
Fig. 4   MVRDV, 2000.
Fig. 5   Ateliers Jean
Nouvel, 2008.
Fig. 6   Kirsten Bucher, 2015.
Fig. 7   Iwan Baan, 2011.
Fig. 8   Iwan Baan, 2015.

Conversation on Designing
Future Cities with
Measures for a
New Urban Agenda with
Richard Hassell
Pages 82–86
Fig.1   Hassell 2016.

Conversation on
Research and
Technological Innovation
with Werner Sobek
Pages 87–90
Fig. 1   Zooey Braun.

Challenges for Responsive
Cities
Pages 96–102
Fig. 1   Carlina Teteris,
2013.

Big Data-Informed Urban
Design
Pages 103–113
Fig. 1   Lauener and
Berger 2015.

Fig. 2   Reinhard Koenig
2016.
Fig. 3   Schläpfer et
al. 2016
Fig. 4   Martinez-
Cesena 2015.
Fig. 5   (a–c) ETHZ 2016
Retrieved from http://
www.ia.arch.ethz.ch/
modeler.html
Fig. 6   (a–d) Ludovica
Tomarchio 2016.

Cyber Civil Infrastructure
Pages 114–121
Fig. 1   Adapted from
World Economic Forum,
Strategic Infrastructure,
Technical Report,
April 2014.
Fig. 3   Simplified from
Pasquier et al. 2016.
Fig. 4   EPFL-IMAC, 2009.

New Ways to Understand
Mobility in Cities
Pages 122–132
Fig. 1   Carlina Teteris.
Fig. 2   Carlina Teteris.
Fig. 3   Artem Chakirov,
2014.
Fig. 4   Tanvi Maheshwari,
2014.
Fig. 5   (a–b) Michael Joos,
2016.
Fig. 6   Alex Erath, 2015.
Fig. 7   (a–b) Alex Erath,
2014.
Fig. 8   Pieter Fourie,
2015.

Theoretical and
Methodological
Challenges for Cognitive
Research in the Built
Environment
Pages 133–140
Fig. 1   Reproduced from
Ruth Conroy Dalton.
Fig. 2   Becker-Asano and
colleagues (2014).
Fig. 3   Ye Yu.
Fig. 4   Reproduced from
Ye Yu.

Advanced Tools and
Workflows for Urban
Designers
Pages 141–148
Fig. 1   CIVAL 2016.
Fig. 2   CIVAL 2016.
Fig. 3   CIVAL 2016.
Fig. 4   CIVAL 2016.
Fig. 5   CIVAL 2016.
Fig. 6   CIVAL 2016.
Fig. 7   (a–c) CIVAL 2016.
Fig. 8   CIVAL 2016.

Archipelago Cities:
Planning Beyond Urban
Boundaries
Pages 162–169
Fig. 1   Devisari Tunas
2016.

Fig. 2   Lincoln Lewis
2015.

Palm Oil: Territories of
Extended Urbanisation
Pages 170–182
Fig. 1   Luigi Ghirri,
Modena, from the series
Atlante, 1973
Fig. 2   Assistant Profes-
sorship of Architecture
and Territorial Planning,
ETH Zürich and ETH
Future Cities Laboratory
Singapore: Hinterland.
Singapore Beyond the
Border. Research: ETH
Architecture of Territory
2011–2015. Map research,
design and mapping:
Karoline Kostka 2015.
Fig. 3   Assistant
Professorship of
Architecture and
Territorial Planning, ETH
Zürich and ETH Future
Cities Laboratory
Singapore: Hinterland.
Singapore Beyond the
Border. Research:
ETH Architecture of
Territory 2011–2015.
Plan drawing: Ani
Katariina Virhevaara,
2015.
Fig. 4   Bas Princen, 2015.
Fig. 5   Bas Princen, 2015.
Fig. 6   (a–c) Bas Princen,
2013.

Urban-Rural Systems in
Monsoon Asia
Pages 183–190
Fig. 1   Stephen Cairns,
2009.
Fig. 2   Stephen Cairns,
2010.
Fig. 3   (a–b) Urban-Rural
Systems, 2017.

Shifting Paradigms: From
excavation to cultivation
Pages 191–199
Fig. 1   Carlina Teteris.
Fig. 2   Carlina Teteris.
Fig. 3   Albert Vecerka/
Esto.
Fig. 4   Albert Vecerka/
Esto.
Fig. 5   Carlina Teteris.
Fig. 6   Carlina Teteris.
Fig. 7   Mycoworks.
Fig. 8   Mycoworks.

Tourism and Cultural
Heritage: A Case Study
on the Explorer
Franz Junghuhn
Pages 200–206
Fig. 1   Martin
Stollenwerk, 2016.
Fig. 2   Martin
Stollenwerk, 2016.

Fig. 3   Martin
Stollenwerk, 2016.
Fig. 4   Franz Wilhelm
Junghuhn, from
Topographischer und
Naturwissenschaftlicher
Atlas zur Reise durch
Java, Magdeburg,
Bansch, 1845. Image
Credit: gta exhibitions.

Austrian Institute of Technology
Bauhaus University Weimar
Centre for Liveable Cities, Singapore
École Polytechnique Fédérale de Lausanne
EiABC Addis Ababa
ETH Global
ETH Zürich
HolcimLafarge
Housing Development Board
ILEK Stuttgart
Land Transport Authority
Mycotech
Mycoworks
Nanyang Technological University
National Research Foundation
National University of Singapore
Rehau
Singapore University of Technology
    and Design
Smiling Gecko
Swiss Federal Laboratories for Materials
    Science and Technology EMPA Dübendorf
Swiss Federal Laboratories for Materials
    Science and Technology EMPA St. Gallen
Universitas Indonesia
Universitas Tarumanagara
Urban Redevelopment Authority
Werber Sobek Group

Adrianne Joergensen
Adrienne Grêt-Regamey
Alexander Lehnerer
Andrew Whittle
Armin Linke
Bas Princen
Benny Raphael
Berit Seidel
Branko Glisic
Christophe Girot
Clive Oppenheimer
Daniel Dahlmeier
Dirk Helbing
Donald Kossmann
Elgar Fleisch
Elisabeth Bronfen
James Brownjohn
Jane M Jacobs
Lei Ya Wong
Mallika Naguran
Marco Proverbio
Martin Kunz
Matthias Roth
Matthias Troyer
Numa Bertola
Pablo Acebillo
Paolo Burlando
Patrick Janssen
Paul Tange
Peter Bishop
Peter Rowe
Peter Sloot
Robert Wijaya
Rudi Stouffs
Sai Pai
Sebastian Linsin
Siang Huat Goh
Simon Schubiger
Simone Fatichi
Sonal Nitin Tavkar
Stefan Müller Arisona
Stefanie Rubner
Tan Puay Yok
Thomas Gross
Thomas Schulthess
Wenjun Cao
Ying Zhou
Ze Zhou Wang

Future Cities Laboratory
Indicia 01

Editors
Stephen Cairns, Devisari Tunas

Design
SJG / Joost Grootens,
Dimitri Jeannottat, Chen Jhen

Copyediting
Gaia Consult

Printing
NPN Drukkers

© 2017 Lars Müller Publishers
and the authors

Future Cities Laboratory
ETH Zürich /
Singapore – ETH Centre
www.fcl.ethz.ch

Lars Müller Publishers
Zürich, Switzerland
www.lars-mueller-publishers.com

Distributed in Southeast Asia, China, and Taiwan
by National University of Singapore Press.

ISBN 978-3-03778-545-4

Printed in the Netherlands